January 1972

From three Californians
to our world travelling sister
Happy Birthday
John, & Gladys

THE CALIFORNIA SYNDROME

BOOKS BY NEIL MORGAN

With Leo Smollar, M. D.
KNOW YOUR DOCTOR

WESTWARD TILT

With the Editors of Time-Life Books
THE PACIFIC STATES

THE CALIFORNIA SYNDROME

THE CALIFORNIA SYNDROME

BY NEIL MORGAN

Prentice-Hall, Inc., Englewood Cliffs, N. J.

• For Judith, who cares •

FOREWORD

Almost any reader of *The California Syndrome* might conclude that Neil Morgan enjoys a passionate love affair with this State. But a careful reading will show that Mr. Morgan's feelings extend far beyond a love affair. I am confident this book will not be eagerly embraced by the California Chamber of Commerce. Mr. Morgan looks at California through an objective, often critical eye.

As a 33-year resident of this State and as a public official, I have been exposed to considerable literature about California but I have never encountered a more definitive effort to grasp its dimensions.

Any native Californian reading this volume must feel remiss that a relative newcomer like Neil Morgan should be the one to have so solidly explored, and delighted in, the exquisite variety of pleasures and disciplines afforded by the State.

Any non-Californian, I believe, can only be impressed with this encompassing chronicle of America's most populous state.

This is not a "quickie," superficial account of a unique geographic or governmental body. I believe it far more readable than John Gunther. I am even more impressed with the hard evidence upon which Mr. Morgan buttresses his observations. The historical material is balanced and solid.

It is more than brilliant reporting. Indeed this is an exciting exercise in scholarship.

Mr. Morgan is duly apprehensive of the peril of a continuing quantum jump in California's future population. He muses about the fact that one of every sixteen families in California has a swimming pool; there may be some correlation between such an abundance of back-yard water and the fact that California's thirst for bourbon (which leads the nation) is three times that of Illinois, which is the next state in consumption of that beverage.

On one hand, Mr. Morgan reminds us that Los Angeles had one of the first viable mass transit systems (now, alas, dissipated in a morass of concrete); with the other he draws a vignette of a pathetic funeral procession trying to maintain some dignity as it moves along a high-speed freeway in Hollywood.

Mr. Morgan's stories of the Sierras and the John Muir Trail recalled to me the excitement I shared for many summers "packing in" with my father. And his discussion of California agriculture reminded me of days on my uncle's ranch in the San Joaquin Valley before the era of agri-business.

As a lawyer, I can testify to the validity of Mr. Morgan's observations on the "impermanence" among Californians. This is tantamount in many areas to almost total alienation, particularly in the area of family formation and dissolution. We do need revision in our divorce laws.

As a Regent, I have never seen a more succinct description of the nine proud universities which make up the University of California. But I would have to disagree with the author's contention that "to oppose education in California is like damning tobacco in the Carolinas." In November of 1968, I headed the drive for a ballot proposition designed to provide more urgently needed medical and dental schools. This was defeated by the California electorate and, in recent local school board elections, the percentage of defeats has taken a quantum jump of almost 3 to 1.

As a trustee of several private institutions of higher education, I regret that Mr. Morgan devoted virtually no space to our magnificent private colleges and universities which do, after all, produce one-fourth of our graduates at the liberal arts level.

I think the reader will be particularly impressed with the narrative on the California Mother Lode country. This territory, of course, has been covered before. But not so well described in other literature is the exciting opening of the lower California desert.

As a politician, I would perhaps tend to be somewhat critical of the section entitled, "The Incorrigible Electorate." But then this effort does not hold itself out to be a volume on California politics and Mr. Morgan refers, in a complimentary fashion, to the only book which I believe traces California's political history in a rational manner, Gladwin Hill's *The Dancing Bear*.

This book could not have come at a better time. This year, 1969, California celebrates the 200th Anniversary of its founding. The Spanish era is deftly picked up in a remarkable "mini-history" describing in great detail not only the familiar story of Father Serra, but California's passage into statehood through five flags.

And most importantly, along with his fellow Californians, Neil Morgan in this volume looks to the future. He has well defined the fact that California is a microcosm of the United States and whatever index you use—the result of presidential elections or the mix of urban problems—the success or failure of this state will be the success or failure of the nation.

In short, it is true as Richard Armour has put it in the concluding lines of his poem, "I Loved You, California":

> *So leap with joy, be blithe and gay,*
> *Or weep my friends with sorrow.*
> *What California is today,*
> *The rest will be tomorrow.*

Washington, D.C.   ROBERT H. FINCH

• Contents •

. 1 .

PUTTY CULTURE

> What's the use kicken? I got non coming. When
> I came west I got the cream let the come latlys have
> the skim milk.
>
> —CHARLES M. RUSSELL, THE WESTERN ARTIST, IN A LETTER TO A
> FRIEND IN 1926.

Chilled by the Japanese current and streaked by breezes
from the northwest, the sea pounds in against the ocher sandstone
cliffs of California at La Jolla. The land twists back to form an
inlet, a tranquil blue coverlet for a violent underwater aberration: a submarine canyon which man has not yet explored. If
the Pacific were pushed from over its walls, the canyon would
reveal itself to be almost as sheer and dramatic as Grand Canyon.

An oceanographer's pier leads resolutely out from shore toward the brink of the canyon, and here on the restless edge of America, where man's westering urge must waver, scientists are mapping underwater lands. The hazards they face are quite as real as those of the old Western frontier.

In these waters they are not alone. Sea lions honk and splash. Aboard purse seiners named for Portuguese women, fishermen spread their nets in the night. Cork buoys mark the locations of lobster traps along the shallow bottom ledges. Divers in black rubber suits, with air tanks strapped to their backs, go spearfishing, or measuring underwater currents, or photographing marine life. As the breezes stiffen in the afternoon, tiny striped sails become splotches of red and yellow and green on the surface of the sea, skimming over the water and back in to shore at a beach club that is a fortress of what Southern Californians regard as entrenched society. On the slopes around the club and up a mountainside above the village there are pleasantly sprawling homes, some of them bearing the flavor of the Spaniards who were here first, and others casual with more modern flowing lines in redwood and glass. Just beyond the club is a public beach, a favorite of surfers; its grassy park is lined with tall proud palms. On toward the north is the pier and the Scripps Institution of Oceanography, whose research vessels ply all the oceans of the earth. Above, on the flat brown mesas of this parched shoreland, grows another campus of the vast University of California. It is no play school. It carries its quota of Nobel laureates, of skeptical philosophers who cry out challenges to California and the world, and pyramiding thousands of students who already have had to prove themselves to be somebody in order to get here. Nearby in a concrete castle on the edge of the cliff, Jonas Salk leads a select team in cloistered pure research—within scientific realms more familiar to Californians these days than those other frontiers which until recently were associated with Western America. Beside the Salk laboratories is a soaring field where gliders are towed off the edge of a two-hundred foot cliff to catch updrafts from the sea below. Two or three thousand feet higher, jets fly back and forth on the southern leg of a commuters' route between California cities that has become the busiest airway in the world.

This arc of sea and cliff and sky, frenetic with work and play, is the view from the window of my study in a cottage that passes in this part of the world for very old. It dates back to 1907, and in Southern California that is antique. It is built over a labyrinth of water caves; sometimes in the night the thrashing of the surf far below sets off tremors in my walls. The cottage perches in a grove of venerable eucalyptus, cypress, palm and pepper trees. Because the coastline here turns back on itself, this is one of those strange rare sites along the Pacific coast of America with an eastward ocean view. When I am awake early enough I see the sun rise out of the ocean to the east and for a moment everything seems out of kilter; that is the way it was on the coast of North Carolina when I was a boy. But then the sun brightens the sky and it becomes a California scene: the burnt tile roofs of the club across the bay, the graceful thin silhouette of the oceanographers' pier, the rambling frame structures in the eucalyptus groves through which the new university hacks its way, and the cool gray ramparts of the Salk laboratories.

That trick of geography along these cliffs makes it seem that in my study I sit offshore, away from California, looking back at it across the water as though from an island. Sometimes the illusion is constructive, imparting clarity through some sense of physical detachment. There are moments when I actually believe I understand California. For about twenty years it has been my business to try, at least, and in those years there have been many times that I felt certain of only one thing: that to satiate the world's curiosity about this golden coast, an unprecedented mass of ill-informed, shallow and contradictory interpretation has been spewed out. California has been hailed variously as the archetype of the future or the regurgitation of the past. Raymond Chandler wrote of Los Angeles as "a tired old whore," but the critic Clifton Fadiman, while living in that city, wrote of it as in the "vanguard of American social development." It was easy for both men to advance convincing arguments. From the start, California has been shrouded in controversy and misinformation. This is a land

so new, so large and so varied that it may provide evidence of
almost anything, and so those who would play the role of booster
or those who would show it to be a monster can seem to draw
proof from within its seemingly limitless scope. Perhaps there is
no other part of the world about which so much pap has been
written.

A very basic problem for its interpreters has been that California does not hold still to be profiled. The years since World
War II have represented a few lifetimes of change. Anyone who
has watched intently has seen an accelerated evolution that is
typical of the whole short history of California, except that now
it is more intense. So it is everywhere in the world, yet somehow
in California everything seems *more so*. The intensity of the
environment is matched by the intensities of its people. This is a
unique terrain, this desert beside the sea, this thousand-mile empire that ranges from the dusty borders of Mexico to the fir forests
of the Oregon border, from the searing stillness of Death Valley
to the eternal winter of Mount Whitney. Those who have made
this land their home, pouring West in the largest migration of
world history, are an unusual people, measurably different in a
number of wholly unarguable ways from those who have stayed
behind, and different in other ways that are less precise and
therefore subject to misinterpretation. These are the restless people
who have pulled up roots and made the move, driven less often
by poverty or oppression than by the eternal hope for better. The
new-found prosperity and mobility of the American are the
cornerstones of their move, whether they are the jobless Negro
escaping a ghetto of East or South for one in the West, or the
academician sensing some nebulous air of independence in a less
structured California faculty. California has become the bell-
wether of American innovation as it has been settled by the
people from every state who are seeking change, through movement if in no other way.

The Californian is driven, restless, mobile, probing, innovative, and dedicated to the Western mystique. He has created a
putty culture—yeasty, swollen, penetrable, unshaped, elastic, impermanent, but with a tendency to adhere at least for a time to

anything solid. It is all that Californians can do to keep this
culture from surging out of control while the slow struggle goes
on to give it form and to add hardening agents.

It has always been marvelously simple to be disenchanted with
California. There *is* something different about California, and so
the state has always been a target of curiosity and derision. Californians are an unusually motivated people in a unique region,
and as a result their behavior is variant. There are times when
it seems useless to think that California will point the way to
anything noble in the American future. Yet California still belongs
to a world almost everyone has sometimes hoped for and often
despaired of finding. The California of today is still as *relatively*
bright with prospect as ever.

We have found ourselves in so many incongruous roles in so
short a history, we Californians, that we answer these days to
almost any name. Once we were the western frontier; now we are
the near shore of the Pacific basin. This is lotus land, but our
technological centers are the threshold to space. It is the center
of the great outdoor leisure boom, and it is the most urban state
of America. Here in California have gathered belligerent indi-
vidualists, and a number who have slid past that point. We have
been the promoters' valhalla, a sanctum for fleecers. We have
shown America the first dandy working models for campus anarchy, for race rioting, for hippie heaven. No teenybopper is genuine without the California label. We have gone from an economy
of gold to wheat to cattle to cotton to fruit to film-making to
manufacturing to space and now God-knows-what-else over on
the other side of that freeway.

Call California an empire, a nation of its own, and its economy
would rank sixth among world powers. In gross product, California is exceeded only by that of the United States, the Soviet
Union, West Germany, Japan and France. Its per-capita income
exceeds that of any country, including the United States. In
manufacturing, California vies with Japan for fifth place in the
Free World. The total value of its import-export trade outranks
a hundred nations; it is more populous than 111 nations, and
larger in area than 92. It has more telephones than any nation
except the United States, and it ranks only behind the U.S.,

France and the United Kingdom in number of motor vehicles. The agricultural domain of California, with a four-billion-dollar annual production, provides another barrage of superlatives.

California's greatest resource, however, may be youth. The world must increasingly equate California with youth. Already the percentage of Californians over 65 years of age is below the national level, and the trend to youth in the state will be more dramatic during the years ahead. Demographic charts for the years between 1965 and 1986 project a 99 percent national increase in the segment of population between the ages of 25 and 34; in California, that percentage is almost half again as great. In the age bracket of 35 to 44 during the same years, California is expected to show an increase almost twice as great as the national average. The preponderance of the young in California adds irresistible force to the momentum of innovation and change that has characterized the state since the Forty-Niners came for gold.

It is in the realm of change that California has shocked the world. In politics, it has been California's pioneering in the mergers of show business and politics, a phenomenon that has been in the wind since television covered its first presidential conventions in 1952. In California the trend was pushed along by the early successes of political management firms, another California innovation that seems to be spreading around the nation as rapidly as the ranch house. California was a breeding ground of the organized protest movement of the Sixties. In earlier days, a break-in meant two weeks in New Haven. The producers of today's social upheavals may not think they can always be heard above the babble of California, but they recognize it as a swell spot for a try-out. Something new and bizarre seems always in the wind, and we will come up with it in a day or two. You don't need to give us time. We don't use it. This is tomorrow already in California and keep moving along there, baby, your seat is up front.

In California you are not certain about today, only about tomorrow. Tomorrow is worse and better but mostly bigger. More crowded and a little less like the California that all of us help to destroy by becoming part of it. These days a California writer is a pariah among his neighbors if he writes pleasantly of his own region: "Tell them all about the high taxes and the smog and the crowded freeways and parks and beaches. Maybe they'll keep away." The name of a leading conservation quarterly is *Cry California*. Books with titles like *The Destruction of California* and *How to Kill a Golden State* are in vogue. When Ronald Reagan boosted inheritance taxes sharply soon after he became governor, a new tritism was born: "California is a wonderful place to live, but I wouldn't want to die there."

California seems to ride some juggernaut into tomorrow, and to many, tomorrow does not seem a pleasant place to be. Yet wispy hopes and visions have hung on the California horizon ever since it was wrested away from the Indians. Each generation has borne prophets who herald the coming of an exalted state that will fulfill the dream as Walt Whitman expressed it:

> *The   new   society   at   last,   proportionate   to*
> *Nature. . .*
> *Clearing the ground for broad humanity, the true*
> *America, heir of the past so grand,*
> *To build a grander future.*

Underlying the mounting self-criticism in California—of crowding, of urban blight, of the destruction of resources or the shallowness of purpose—is the persistent hope for the better. Euphoria is traditional. Californians are so accustomed to bigness that we seem quite ready—almost eager—to claim the biggest problems. We add hastily that in our flexible, adaptable society we will be the first to come up with solutions. The record does not always support our optimism, but the California mystique has become clearer. Some of it can be documented. Much of it refutes the characteristics of extremism and eccentricity that have come to be associated with California. The attitudes toward California that have gained credence outside the state have often been the extreme ones, for that is what the world seems to want to believe about California. There has always been a powerful influence of moderation in California that is not so easily sensed as its more blatant traits, and surely not so inflammatory. It is a moderation that has inevitably put down the quacks and sorcerers, the exploiters and messiahs, for they are parasites on the juggernaut; they are pushed off.

The truth is that the Spanish caballeros of early California were a fairly somnolent bunch of cattle men, that Hangtown wasn't all *that* sinful in 1853, that a lot of buildings survived the San Francisco earthquake, that Senator Hiram Johnson's earnest reforms as governor opened the door for most of the political idiocy of the past fifty years in California, that Aimee Semple McPherson died in 1945 from an overdose of sedatives, that Hollywood is a dull place, that you can still drive forty miles in California without seeing another human being, that Southern California is not likely in this century to become a single megalopolis from Santa Barbara to the Mexican border, and that grandsons and granddaughters of the Okies whom John Steinbeck depicted in *The Grapes of Wrath* are now driving sports cars around California university campuses.

Even the labels of California bigotry and extremism are open to challenge. No one has yet demonstrated that Californians in the mass exhibit these symptoms to a greater degree than other Americans; after all, Earl Warren was the only three-time governor in California history. The California electorate usually behaves in the self-serving, play-it-safe fashion of an upper-middle class provincial, a *nouveau riche* whose first thought is to protect his wealth and fend off regulation, to maintain the status quo. The winning candidate is usually the nice guy who has managed to seize the defensive. The California electorate stands indicted less for what it *is* than for what it *is not*. That is about the way it is in most of America.

We know a few specifics about Californians, and they do not all fit the popular image. Californians are more prosperous, longer-schooled, and much more mobile than the American norm. They have high rates both of leisure and production, relatively little interest in formal churchgoing, and only mild interest in social status or tradition. They are at or near the top in suicide, divorce and crime. They buy more household appliances, frozen foods and foreign cars, and their families are smaller. They drink more rum, wine and vodka but less gin, blended whiskey and Scotch.

(The sale of bourbon in California is indeed remarkable: 12,596,-000 gallons in 1967, almost three times as much as in Illinois, the state with the second greatest thirst for bourbon.) The level of permissiveness is high. In an era of sexual emancipation, California is at the forefront. Racial violence came early to California cities, and reaction set in early. The Californian is paying record high taxes, and about half goes to education.

Can the people of a single state actually be so different from other Americans? History suggests that they can be. The Forty-Niners were typically young, male, single, and from the Eastern seaboard. More than half of all Californians in 1850 were in their twenties. Historians make much of tracing a line from them toward the present. "Selective forces were at work," wrote J. S. Hittell, an historian of early California. "The immigrants were by and large well educated. They had essentially the same traits as other Americans of the period, but the traits were more striking, because the immigrants made up—not a cross-section, but a *selection* of the American people." The contemporary historian Earl Pomeroy adds: "In their imprudence, their enthusiasm, their success, the Forty-Niners justified improbability and anticipated the shape and tenor of the [West] coast in the century to come." In the opinion of the historian John Caughey, California is the only place "where a rush for gold was made to serve as the base for an ever-widening superstructure of attainment."

It is a common phenomenon of migration that selective human characteristics are accentuated by numbers. The pyramid rises. Migrants attract more migrants. California quickly established its reputation as an unorthodox land that was open to suasion—a place where a man could swing whatever he had to swing. If you exclude the migrant workers and the continuing Negro move west, Californians are by and large people who have left a relatively good life in search of a better life. They are Americans exercising self-option without outer pressures. Persecution and famine do not figure in the California migration.

To the sociologist, California is a selective migration to a region of opportunity and *laissez-faire*, resulting in an open, unstratified society made up of communities of strangers. The sociologist's aptest word for the California condition is *anomie*, a state in which the human being finds himself uprooted, drifting, and unfocused. The economist sees California as an exploitation of a region of extraordinary natural resources by a people of aggressive, inventive nature who are not afraid to try to live by their wits. In either view, the two interacting factors are present: the *place* and the *people*. In California, both place and people have distinguishing characteristics that have imparted distinctive traits to the society that tries to emerge.

But without the distinctiveness of the *place*, California would not work. Part of the lure is that nebulous attraction of the far western shore of the continent; the urge to wester is not yet dead. Climate is usually exaggerated as a factor, but it is nevertheless strong; it provides diverse settings for year-round outdoor leisure and it is less likely to impede the movement of Californians with the harshness of hot or cold. The California sun coaxes out buds on orange trees, and tourists on Highway 66. The benign climates of California do not seem to figure prominently in our daily lives until we are away and miss them. It has fascinated me how many migrants to California move "back home" after a year or two, and then return to California permanently after another winter in their former home. "I'd forgotten what it was like back there," they will tell you.

More important are the extravagant resources of California. To the visitor, California may mean Disneyland or San Francisco or Yosemite. Berkeley and Cal Tech and Stanford are one world to the scientist and educator, while to the real estate subdivider, Santa Clara and Orange Counties are Mecca. All these involve man-made resources. But the oil man knows the offshore deposits that have made Long Beach rich, or the rolling brown hills where the Great Central Valley begins its climb westward over the coastal mountains, dotted with derricks and villages of rocker pumps. The cattleman finds his California far up the Central Valley and on the grazing ranges of the lower Sierra or in the noxious feed pens of Imperial Valley. The inventory of California's agricultural production is the richest of any state, so varied and immense that it runs a gamut from artichokes to zucchini, from cotton to grapes. From California wineries come four of every five bottles of wine consumed in the United States. More than two hundred farm products are grown on eight million acres of farmland, most of it irrigated by the most complex system of water movement ever devised. California has more than four hundred different varieties of soil and, it sometimes seems, almost as many contrasting climates. In such factories of the field, as elsewhere, the innovative nature of the Californian seems admirably paired with the challenge of his setting. Without water, he could not farm: he has brought water overland in aqueducts that range almost the entire length of the state. Farming has been mechanized to a degree unknown elsewhere, with nut trees shaken by pneumatic pickers and lettuce heads harvested by rubber hands.

Rich natural resources have been bolstered as a factor in California growth by the vagaries of history and by the federal dollar. Industrialists have learned to overcome their relative remoteness. With about one-fourth of the federal aerospace budget going into California, there is an economically hazardous reliance on Washington funding. But such spending has at least undergone a transition from the era when the West was regarded in almost colonial status; today federal money goes into California not only because of its natural resources but because of its brains and skills. Business and industry are distinguished by innovation, high risk, heavy federal involvement and not a little luck. California has usually seemed to be in the right place at the right time.

The California economy is in fact quite ebullient much of the time, and the Californian is obsessed with material success, perhaps in part because of his nature and in part to prove to himself and to those "back home" that he was right in breaking old roots. To most people material success is the simplest evidence that some good new life has been achieved. The Californian's obsession is nothing new in American history. But there are fewer restraining influences in the putty culture of California, and any obsession grows at an alarming rate.

California is still so young, so belligerent, and has so much to learn, that one may shudder at the thought that the state is a window on the future or that California's today may be America's tomorrow. Its rapid growth and vigor are not goals but symptoms. In dedication and direction, California flounders like America, and with its flair for overstatement, its lack of purpose can be monolithic. Yet Californians have seemed capable of almost anything. These unusual people in this extraordinary place come equipped with vitality and with dreams. In California it is not yet too late.

. 2 .

THE ENVIRONMENT FIGHTS BACK

I met a Californian who would
Talk California—a state so blessed,
He said, in climate, none had ever died there
A natural death.

—ROBERT FROST, *New Hampshire*

During the Depression of the 1930's a zealous newcomer
to Southern California founded the Heaven-on-Earth Club in San
Diego. He issued million-dollar bonds redeemable in California
sunshine and papered the nation with bogus bills conveying the
boosters' enthusiastic plea to "come and bring all your folks."

Not long afterward, on the campus of the Scripps Institution
of Oceanography at La Jolla, the Hell-on-Earth Club was born.

Among it founders was the oceanographer Roger Revelle. As he recalls it, members of the Hell-on-Earth Club held these to be truths:

Californians live in constant dread of earthquakes. The Pacific surf is too cold to swim in and its tides too treacherous. Mornings along the coast are always murky; inland, it is either hot or cold. The dry brown hills are ugly and a dire fire hazard. There is scarcely enough water to sustain life, but when it rains, it floods. Smog encroaches over all the area and is a threat to human life. Streams and lakes and rivers are polluted and will someday poison Californians.

"Our little club," Revelle said not long ago, "has been notably unsuccessful." We sat beside his swimming pool in the golden sunshine of an August morning in La Jolla. On the beach below, swimmers and surfers bobbed in the waves.

"Even back before World War II we were nostalgic for the old days in California," he said. "We wanted everybody who'd got here after we had to go away. We should have had the guts to say, 'Go away, period. No matter when you came.' "

The tenets of the Hell-on-Earth Club, laid down some thirty years ago in half-jest, read much like some bill of particulars filed against society today by ardent conservationists who believe the Golden State is being raped. Five hundred acres of California go under the blade each day for subdivision or freeway. Open space disappears. The senses are assaulted by ugliness and pollution. It is not that much different from what has happened to other parts of America, but California somehow has more to lose. It is California, after all, and not Pennsylvania or Mississippi; we are all conditioned to expect more of California. Yet it is being despoiled at a time when Americans are more conscious than ever before of their need for beauty, and when society is able to do more, if it will, to stop the assault. It is an urgent matter. Because millions pour into the state at a rate of migration heretofore unknown, the face of California changes with breathtaking rapidity and on a grandiose scale.

California is an uncommon environment. The juxtaposition of mountain and sea is an unfamiliar one to most Americans. In one sweep the eye takes in scorched desert and snowy mountain. Land and sea, along most of the twelve hundred miles of California coastline, are so spectacular that they are not easily overlooked. Inland are the mountains and deserts, commanding and awesome, where man intrudes still at the peril of his life.

Just as this environment has seemed outsized, so have the settlers who have molded nature to their own use: to transport water and power for hundreds of miles across deserts, spending billions of dollars in the world's most massive irrigation projects, damming rivers and boring tunnels through mountains, creating lakes and otherwise subverting the original intent of nature to their own uses.

Nature has fought back in ways that ecologists have come to predict, and in other ways that are so individual to California that they seem to be nature's perverse reaction to the particular recklessness with which it is being attacked. A century ago when America was agog at the novelty of Southern California, the journalist Charles Nordhoff wrote that this was "the first tropical land which our race has mastered and made itself at home in." It was an overstatement.

Although climate was and still is one of the strongest attractions of California, there are unsettling obstacles to any life of tropical ease. To cite a moment of uncommon harassment, one can go back to the occasion when E. H. Harriman, as president of the Southern Pacific Railroad, sat in his office at San Francisco and received the news that the Colorado River had gone wild and was pouring into the Imperial Valley, threatening to destroy his tracks and stations as well as the farms and towns of twelve thousand people. As he was told of the crisis, he was staring out at a city that had just been devastated by the earthquake and fire of April 18, 1906.

"There is something disturbing about this corner of America," J. B. Priestley once wrote, "a sinister suggestion of transience. California will be a silent desert again. It is all as impermanent and brittle as a reel of film." That kind of observation seems archaic and ludicrous today, less a prediction than a spoof. Yet neither is California the lotus land that Nordhoff described. The truth, as it so often does, lies between. Californians live under an uneasy truce with the elements. As in so many other ways, Californians are subject to extremes in the outbursts of nature.

The image of California is of a bland land, golden and mild. Such adjectives can be aptly applied only to the relatively small coastal strip of Southern California and its inland foothills. Even here the usually placid climate is subject to violent disruption. It was the late Monty Woolley who insisted that only in Southern California could one freeze to death under a rose bush in bloom. Better documented than Woolley's are the reports of the ravages of hot dry Santa Ana winds, the mud slides that carry houses away in the rainy winters, and the raging brush and forest fires that raze whole neighborhoods and towns in the dry summers.

California extends along the Pacific through nearly ten degrees of latitude, the equivalent along the Atlantic seaboard of the distance from Cape Cod to Savannah. Its diverse climates are the result both of this vast north-to-south range and also the stepladders of its elevations. Only one characteristic is common to almost all of the state: the absence of summer rains. In most areas of the earth summer is the time of maximum rainfall. But in California rain is associated with cool weather. In Southern California January is the rainiest month. Lloyd's of London offers insurance against rain cancellations of outdoor events; its premiums become negligible during the summer months.

The rate of rainfall declines along the California coast from north to south, ranging from an all time high of 190 inches at Honeydew to an average of about nine inches a year at San Diego. The coastal mountains and the Sierra Nevada sap inbound sea winds of their moisture and create the deserts to the east where precipitation fades to an inch or two; Bagdad, a weather station in the Mojave Desert, has gone for as long as two years without showing a trace of rainfall. Areas with eight inches or less of annual rainfall are usually classified as desert.

Within this sprawling state there are climates and landforms, soils and vegetation of prodigal diversity. Coastal temperatures are moderate; but inland they move quickly to extremes. A reading of 130 degrees is not uncommon in Death Valley, and in the peaks of the Sierra Nevada the thermometer plunges as low as minus 45 degrees. The state's complexity of geologic history, ranging from pre-Cambrian to the contemporary Cenozoic, affords a natural laboratory for study of the earth sciences. It takes no more than a casual stroll along a park path to find the earth's story for a million years or more delineated in the colorations and the configurations of erosion on bare cliff walls or canyons. More than five hundred distinct soil series have been identified within California, representing most of the world's soil groups.

The ecology of California suggests that of an island. Cut off by desert on one side and the sea at the other, distinctive bird life such as the giant California condor has developed. Many mammals exist here with unique characteristics. In Webster's *New International Dictionary*, Third Edition, the word California sprawls over three columns of definitions, most often in identifying unique flora and fauna to which California has given its name. The list begins with California barberry and California bayberry and goes on through California dandelion, California halibut, California orange, California tree poppy. It ends with the radioactive element discovered at Berkeley and named Californium. There are species of plant and animal life that exist only in the alpine climates of California mountain peaks, in its deep dark redwood forests or on its offshore islands.

Despite the stampede to California, less than one-fifth of its area is yet urbanized or cultivated. Grazing occupies almost one-third of the land area, and forestry is the economic basis of another one-fifth. In the north and along the Sierra Nevada, the state retains the largest areas of ancient virgin forest in the United States, about ten million acres. Despite more than a century of logging, a substantial number of these virgin stands are under the nominal protection of various federal and state agencies and many of them seem certain to be preserved.

The climates of California's cities are the most talked-about of California's many climates. None is more fabled than that of San Francisco, where crisp winds whip over the hills and restless clouds, reflecting the bay, help to give the city its aura of piercing light. For such moments the city is best loved, and for those afternoons when fluffy banks of fog move in through the Golden Gate and flirt with the city's bridges and its skyline, surging through the narrows and banking up against the foothills. If you are a California commuter, you stride a little faster and gaze a little more intently when you are walking through San Francisco streets. Here summer is delayed often until September; in July and August, San Francisco is likely to be the coolest major city in the United States.

"Although weather talk is common to all mankind," Harold Gilliam wrote, "it achieves here a particular flavor and intensity unknown elsewhere . . . Commuters into San Francisco compare notes on their respective communities, and no one is greatly surprised if Berkeley has fog while Alameda is in bright sun, or Mill Valley has rain while Palo Alto is dry and clear."

Los Angeles is warmer and drier than northern California. The city has no monopoly on air pollution, but the haze that lies over the basin of the metropolis in varying density most days of the year is heavy with the hydrocarbons of its freeways, held down over the city by the temperature inversion common to the region. On days when the sea breezes sweep briskly across the vast basin and the inversion is absent, the ring of mountains and the offshore islands stand out boldly and the sun is brilliant. These are the good moments in Los Angeles, and when they come on a night after a winter rain has washed the city clean, even the sprawl of Los Angeles can seem to be a sparkling tub of jewels. More often the air is tinged with a faint ugly yellowness and visibility is vague. The smell is slightly acrid and the city and everything around it seems in need of a bath. The temperature is mild and the season is indeterminant. It is as though Los Angeles had been a child invited to choose a climate and, hesitating, had been handed a mass of fluffy cotton candy to last the year round. It is usually harmless but unexciting.

In San Diego the sun dominates everything. It is the driest of the coastal cities. Its air is the clearest and its thermometer the shortest. The climate of coastal California is similar to that of Mediterranean areas, especially northwest Africa, but climatologists set apart the San Diego coast as unique. The ridge of high-pressure air over the North Pacific known as the Hawaiian High holds back weather from San Diego to a greater extent than any other part of the California coast. Morning clouds and sea breezes keep temperatures moderate. The absence of frost provides a year-round growing season in which tropical trees like lemon and avocados thrive. The civic obsession can be detected in the naming of streets. Community developers are running out of sunny names. In 1968 a metropolitan San Diego street guide gave thirty-five listings for Sunset and twelve for Sunrise. There were multiple listings for Sun, Sunshine, Sunswept, Sun Valley, Sunburst, Suncrest, Sunview, Sunray, Sunglow, Sunline, Sundale, Sun Dial, Sundown, Sunridge and Sunrich—and a suffocating number of suffixes to go with Sunny.

When ecologists talk of California as an island, it is easy to recall that the state took its name from the queen of a mythical island of gold described by the Spanish novelist Ordoñez de Montalvo. The world has always seemed anxious to attribute supernatural phenomena to this land. The excessive enthusiasm of early California settlers and writers has become part of the California myth.

To some who came a century or more ago, California was an exotic new land. To others, it seemed to combine the best of ancestral lands. One early traveler wrote of Santa Barbara County as a melange of European beauty, its mountains "Swiss, its valleys Scottish, its bay that of Naples." Climate became an obsession, both for its pleasantness and for its benevolence toward growing things. The lists of human ailments subject to cure by the California climate soared toward a ridiculous infinite, until even the Southern California Medical Society appointed a committee to cite and publish them.

Above all the exotic quality of California excited the American fancy, and in curiously related ways it does so today. Kate Douglas Wiggin wrote of "how intense everything is in Southern California! The fruit is immense, the cañons so deep, the trees so big, the hills so high, the rain so wet, and the drought so dry!" New Californians are astonished by the lack of seasons, the size of fruit, and by rivers that flow beneath the ground. Quirks of geography delight them, like discovering that Reno, Nevada, lies west of Los Angeles. Usually they talk only among themselves of the nagging sand fleas, their fear of drought and earthquake, their yearnings for the changing seasons, or the persistent apprehension that in so mild a climate they may be enervated and reduced finally to tropical indolence.

The world goes on pondering the novelty of the California scene. Designers of bathing suits and automobiles seize on California place names to stimulate product sales. Climate and the way of life are somehow involved with everything from the production of artichokes to surfboards. A recent television documentary attempted to establish that because of climate the California girl is larger in body but perhaps smaller in soul. There is still a lingering belief among some that the climate is not conducive to intellectual pursuit or hard work. But now the exaggerations about California do not involve globe-sized tomatoes or the healing climate so much as they do the image of California as a playground.

The playground has its horrors. There are moments when its blandishments seem only a trap to lure millions to a land that was not meant to be lived in.

California newspapers tally box scores on every local rain shower, and precipitation of even one one-hundredth of an inch can be found listed under the heading, "Current Storm." Extreme weather in other parts of America becomes front-page news. No matter how they may try to moderate their reactions, Californians gloat over their escape from the winter storms or summer heat that they accepted as a matter of course in places they once lived.

But the game is played in both directions. When California is struck by earthquake, fire or flood, the unfortunate news is warmly received by millions who have heard all they care to hear about the glories of life in the Golden State. No deviation from the placid norm of the coastal California environment is more fearsome, nor more avidly heralded outside the state, than the rumbles that surge up periodically from deep within the earth. Professing visions of impending quakes, fundamentalist sects stage periodical exoduses from California.

"California," wrote the geologist C. L. Camp, "occupies a badly fractured and unstable segment of the thin earth crust, along a coast rising from the sea." The state is part of the "ring of fire" that has helped to create and then to plague the Pacific Basin —a related group of faults that forms a loop from New Zealand through the Philippines to the southeast coast of China, Japan, across the Bering Sea to Alaska and down the west coasts of both Americas. Throughout the loop there is periodic volcanic activity. When slippage takes place along the fault lines, there are earthquakes. About four out of five of the earth's quakes occur in this seismic belt.

Among the thousands of minor shocks that occur each year in California, an average of five hundred are strong enough to be felt by at least some people. Most of these go relatively unnoticed and appreciable damage is caused only rarely. There have been three quakes of major scope—with a magnitude rated at about eight or higher on the Richter scale. The scale is gradated in vast detail as to its effect, but it can be oversimplified in this way: It takes a Richter-Five or higher to become a conversation piece among Californians; everything above a Richter-Six can strike at the heart with a unique terror.

The first of the three big quakes, on January 9, 1857, centered in sparsely populated Tejon Pass, north of Los Angeles in the Tehachapi Mountains. The reports of its effect indicate that it was probably as strong as the later San Francisco earthquake. There was only one fatality, but buildings swayed in Los Angeles.

On March 26, 1872, the second of the "monster quakes" came in the Owens Valley east of Mount Whitney. It was the strongest in the recorded history of California. In the Owens River, which was later diverted into the Los Angeles water system, fish were thrown out onto dry banks by the shock and for several hours the river went dry along part of its course. Aftershocks continued for three days, totaling about one thousand. But this was a sparsely settled area too, and only about sixty deaths were attributed to the disaster. Today a picket fence surrounds the mass grave where victims were buried. Between the towns of Lone Pine and Independence the up-and-down displacement of the earth along the fault exceeded twenty feet; ridges of earth with abrupt twenty-foot walls can be found near Lone Pine. On the horizon is the sheer eastern escarpment of the Sierra Nevada, which itself was formed in somewhat the same way by submergence of great blocks of earth.

The earthquake that has become known simply as the San Francisco earthquake struck at 5:12 on Wednesday morning, April 18, 1906. Jesse Cook, who later became police commissioner, recalled the noise coming on from the distance, "deep and terrible." Then, as he looked up Washington Street, the earthquake moved toward him: "The whole street was undulating. It was as if waves of the ocean were coming toward me and billowing as they came." It was, another San Franciscan wrote, like a "terrier shaking a rat." For the first forty seconds there was mounting intensity. Then there was a sudden horrible calm that lasted ten seconds before the rumbling approached again; it was all over in another twenty-five seconds. Streets dropped three and four feet. Buildings collapsed. Street car tracks were twisted and bowed. Water lines were wrenched apart and in the streets there was the ominous hiss of escaping gas from broken lines. In the produce district, where the day's work was already at full pitch, dead horses and their splintered wagons lay beside their dead drivers amid heaps of fallen brick and mortar. Soon the fires began, raging on for three days and two nights until dynamite cleared a vacant path to halt it by removing its tinder. Most of 490 blocks of the city had been ravaged, burning the heart of San Francisco and the homes of a quarter of a million people.

In terms of death and property loss, the San Francisco earthquake exceeds all other California quakes combined. More than six hundred died in the quake and the ensuing fires and the loss of property was estimated at $400,000,000. Every community along the San Andreas fault for four hundred miles felt its destructiveness. The earth was ripped apart for two hundred miles from San Juan Bautista at the south to the mouth of Alder Creek on the Mendocino coast. In Sonoma County a large redwood growing astride the fault was split neatly down its middle. A road that crossed the San Andreas fault in Marin County was offset twenty-one feet when the land on the west side of the fault moved north by that distance and the land on the east remained stationary.

This San Andreas fault is the principal one among hundreds in California. It is a crack beneath the earth's crust probably twenty to thirty miles deep and extending for 650 miles through Southern and central California and along the northern California coast. At the surface its course can be detected only by the eye trained in geologic aberration; there is no open, bottomless gulley. Geologists compare the action of the fault to that of two immense blocks of stone being rubbed together. All of California to the west of the San Andreas moves north at a rate of about two inches a year, building up stress in the subterranean rock. When the rock ruptures to relieve that stress, there is an earthquake.

The San Andreas is venerable. There has been a total slippage along its west side of about three hundred miles, indicating it has been in motion for 65,000,000 years. Its work is seen in the shape of valleys and mountain ridges. It leaves strange mementos. In an orange grove near the Mexican border, rows of trees were moved abruptly ten feet out of line by a 1940 quake. Evidence of the slower, more gradual earth movement of the fault can be found at the Almaden winery near Hollister. One winery building lies astride an active branch of the fault zone that is tearing the building apart at the rate of half an inch each year; workmen patch the cracks in the floor and brace sagging walls. The winery superintendent, John Ohrwall, moved near this site as a child with his parents after they had watched their San Francisco house dynamited to help halt the 1906 fire. Determined to escape further earthquake danger, Ohrwall's father built a house two miles south of the present winery. But the San Andreas fault was less understood in those days; Ohrwall's new house was astride the San Andreas fault, and the jostling went on for the rest of his life.

Seismographers are almost unanimous in predicting that another massive earthquake is building up, and many of them believe it will center in Southern California. There is no escaping the hazard anywhere within the state. Every community is within striking range of one or more faults. The longer the interval between major quakes, the more severe they tend to be.

The danger is increased by the massive build-up of California population. An earthquake in a populous area with the intensity of the San Francisco tremor could be a far greater catastrophe today. Technology has not made the city more able to cope with the disruption caused by such catastrophe. Bridges and freeways are easily destroyed or blocked. Ambulances and fire engines would be less able to maneuver in rubble-filled streets than the horse-drawn vehicles of San Francisco in 1906.

To the horror of seismologists, rows of suburban tract houses have been built astride the fault, particularly in the San Bernardino area east of Los Angeles, and purchased by the unsuspecting. Far lesser quakes than that of San Francisco have created chaos when they have centered at other urban areas. Santa Barbara sustained heavy damage in 1925 and Long Beach in 1933. Both were relatively modest tremors. But there were 120 deaths at Long Beach, attributed largely to construction of buildings inadequately resistant to earth shock. Building codes have since been upgraded. For years the height of new buildings seldom exceeded twenty stories, but by the 1960s, after a period of freedom from destructive quakes, buildings were soaring to forty and fifty stories in both Los Angeles and San Francisco. Civil engineers and architects have convinced most politicians that they know enough about lateral bracing to make such buildings earthquake-resistant. The custom is to avoid the parapets, balconies and cornices that drop off with lethal effect in strong quakes.

But the test has not yet come. Meanwhile, a conspiracy blended of complacency, ignorance and economic judiciousness leaves most Californians unfamiliar with basic safety procedures to guard against injury in earthquake. There has been some effort by chambers of commerce and real estate interests to minimize the fear of earthquake in California. It is common to point out that the automobile is a greater killer than the earthquake. Civic leaders seem generally aloof to the inevitable danger. Scientists are at work on new laser devices that will measure subterranean strains and, they hope, make it possible to predict earthquakes, perhaps days in advance. Just now they are dependent on opinions such as that of Louis C. Pakiser, chief of the U.S. Geological Survey's National Center for Earthquake Research, who says: "Without knowing exactly when, we can say that between now and the year 2000 California and adjoining areas will have many moderate earthquakes, a few severe ones and perhaps one great one."

Engineers do not shrug off California's vulnerability. At several points along the San Andreas and other faults, water engineers are taking unusual precautions as they build a giant water transfer system that will move northern California water south of the Tehachapi range as far as the Mexican border. They are striving to build pipes and canals that will withstand most earthquakes, or that can be repaired promptly if the lines are severed. Where the route of the California Water Project aqueduct crosses fault lines, tunnels and pipelines are abandoned in favor of surface canals. Automatic gates will halt the flow of water if canals are ruptured and reservoirs on the downstream side of the faults will provide emergency water supplies.

It was, after all, the lack of water to quench fire that caused the direst terror at San Francisco in 1906. Water is the most basic force of nature that Californians seek to control. They are seldom diverted from their chosen course of action by the perfidy of nature, but they begin to learn that they cannot ignore the inevitability of its backlash.

Earthquake is not the only contortion of nature in this land. The ecological balance of the desert is fragile. In Southern California it was upset with the coming of the industrious white man, when the dusty chaparral was cleared from a hillside for the first mission farm and its seasonal rivers first dammed and diverted for irrigation.

Through most of the year Southern California treads a middle path between drought and flood. Yet turning over a spadeful of soil at a ceremonial ground-breaking may often require that a laborer be brought in ahead to loosen the hard dry soil with a jackhammer. Irrigation is so customary, even of city parks, that it provides a part of the folklore. Scout troops camping overnight in parks are periodically drenched awake at dawn when they have slept too close to automatic sprinklers. Such sprinklers have become a basic tool of crowd dispersal in riot control.

Because it thrives virtually without water, the most prominent tree of the arid Southern California coastal plain is the eucalyptus, an Australian gum imported first in 1858 because it is extremely resistant to drought. For years there was a eucalyptus boom as speculators sought to exploit the eucalyptus as a wood-producer. Though it has a stately beauty that lends charm to the landscape, the eucalyptus was a dud in commerce. Its lumber tends to shrink, warp and crack. So the tree has found use only in windbreaks and as firewood, a commodity not easily found in the lowlands of Southern California.

The insignificant scrub of the hillsides and mesas, the chaparral, is as vital as are the trees of other areas in holding the soil firm against eroding flood; it is also as vulnerable to a flaming match. Then, with the ebullience that is typical even of nature in California, the hazard is heightened by the hot dry Santa Ana wind.

By early fall, when there has been virtually no rain for five or six months, air masses shift and the wind perversely changes direction. The cool sea breeze is gone and the wind comes now from the desert. Pressed down by barometric depression, it gains heat and force as it moves. Landing patterns at airports are reversed. The atmosphere clears with dramatic suddenness and detail sharpens to provide superb vistas; the smog has blown out to sea.

Southern California becomes an oven. Humidity plummets. Temperatures soar; the beaches are hotter than the desert. Gardens and patios are instantly parched and littered with blowing leaves and debris. Outdoor furniture is overturned. Trees and plants snap because they are being blown in an opposite direction from that in which they have grown. Soon sooty clouds of smoke darken the sky and at night, red hot spots on the horizon mark some forest ridge or suburban community where firefighters wage epic holding actions that may go on for days. The smoke of unseen fires gives the sky a yellow cast. The unaccustomed heat causes shimmers even over the surf.

So the Santa Ana wind has become a lodestone both of climatology and folklore. It is similar in nature to the *foehn* wind that sweeps down over the north crest of the Alps. In Switzerland the fire hazard is so increased by the lowered humidity that certain communities forbid smoking entirely and pharmacies offer anti-foehn preparations to relieve the strange tensions and feelings of apprehension that are common at such times.

Physicists have recently discovered that before and during the foehn, as well as Southern California's Santa Ana, the air carries unusual proportions of positive ions, probably transformed from the more soothing negative ions by the friction of air transit. Positive ions tend to be unsettling, and the Santa Ana puts an already restless people more on edge. Raymond Chandler wrote that during the three or four days for which such winds usually blow, "every booze party ends in a fight. Meek little wives feel the edge of the carving knife and study their husbands' necks. Anything can happen."

When the Santa Ana blew on for two weeks late in 1957, reaching gusts of a hundred miles an hour, the regional malaise grew to intense proportions. Some new epidemic of violence was uncovered with every day's news. As fires raged and oil derricks toppled, traffic fatalities soared. A Pasadena attorney killed his wife, their two sons and then himself; on the next day, a woman at nearby South Gate was murdered and thrown from a speeding car. Crime rates soared in almost every classification.

The most ominous violence of the Santa Ana is fire. In canyons like the fabled ones of Bel Air and Malibu, homeowners unreel their garden hoses, wet down their roofs, and stand guard against the sweep of flame that is so likely to flare down the canyon, crackling and spitting, driving snakes and rabbits before it as firemen shout evacuation orders through their bullhorns and old converted bombers fly in low to drop their loads of borate.

Such a fire in the wealthy residential area of Bel Air in November, 1961, took rank as the fifth costliest fire in national history and the worst in California since the one that followed the San Francisco earthquake. The scene was set with the driest season in modern Los Angeles history; less than a tenth of an inch of rain had fallen in five months.

The Santa Ana had begun to blow three days before the fire broke out on November 6, and the relative humidity had dropped to three percent. Los Angeles Fire Department specialists stood by waiting. Fire was sure to come; the only question was where.

The first report came in about 8:00 A.M. from near the crest of the Santa Monica Mountains in the elite northwest district: it was a little brush fire at that moment, probably set by an abandoned cigarette, but fifty-mile-an-hour winds were blowing. Fire officials moved quickly to set up a command post in the area. Quickly the fire moved out of control, searing down the canyons toward the city. A total of 124 city engine companies went into action along with 23 tanker units and sixteen aircraft. Still the fire jumped from one canyon to another, breaching each line of defense. It jumped freeways as sparks were borne on the wind; flaming tumbleweeds blew through the air and set new fires where they touched down.

By now the evacuation was under way. Four thousand persons left their homes; 2550 fire fighters joined the battle line. At midafternoon the wind began to die and firemen were no longer fighting a runaway juggernaut. They began to contain its spread. Before the last of the hot spots was quelled on the next day, 484 homes had been burned within a twenty-mile perimeter with losses of about twenty-five million dollars. The homes of Burt Lancaster, Zsa Zsa Gabor and Joe E. Brown were reduced to rubble. Miss Gabor reported recovering some of her jewels from the ashes, but Brown lost a lifetime collection of trophies and mementos. Lancaster, like most of the burned-out, rebuilt his home promptly on the same site.

Although loss of life is common in lesser blazes, the Bel Air fire of 1961 took none. Near Descanso in the San Diego foothills a bronze plaque commemorates the death of five prisoners and a correction officer from a nearby honor camp who lost their lives fighting a forest fire in 1956. Property damage is not so great in such rural fires, but the effect is devastating. In 1964 about 229,-000 acres of forest and watershed lands were burned in Southern California, aggravating problems of erosion, imperiling agriculture and recreational facilities through destruction of soil, timber and brush cover.

State and local governments have been moving earnestly to head off recurrence of any fire on the scope of the 1961 Bel Air blaze. Improved communications systems and aerial firefighting equipment give increasing mobility to those who guard the tinderbox of Southern California in the times of the Santa Ana wind. Fire-resistant plants are being newly bred and set out on dry hillsides. But a continuing prospect of disaster is carried with the wind and grows into the nerve core of the people. One may joke that he lives in a community so new that it hasn't even had a fire yet. At the height of a drought, when the land is parched and brown, the Californian shrugs and insists that the golden season is at hand. He is a fatalist. He stays, and if he is burned out he rebuilds. Once a Californian, there is no turning back.

The fires that denude the canyons and mountainsides prepare the land for yet another disaster: the mud slides and flash floods of the sudden rains. In a new residential subdivision at La Jolla several years ago I stood watching one new house after another slide out of sight down a canyon as torrents of rain swept away the fresh earth from beneath them. A carpet-layer approached police who formed a cordon around the scene and shouted: "Lemme through! I've got to lay carpet there today!"

On freshly graded hillsides, the Californian is quick to set out great stands of mesembryanthemum, more commonly called ice plant. It is a hardy succulent that spreads out its sinewy roots to lock sandy soil in place and serve as a brake to erosion. Subdividers and freeway builders gamble that their ice plant will do its job before winter rains attack newly moved banks. There are times that even the ice plant fails; in Hollywood, a woman whose house has been dug firmly into the side of a hill for forty years lost her composure when a storm washed away her whole hillside of ice plant. Beyond that moment, there seems no defense against the rains.

Southern Californians, no matter where they came from, are uniformly incompetent to cope with rain. When it falls, they huddle in office building doorways with shocked expressions. Many of them lack raincoats and umbrellas. Lawn sprinklers in parks and at civic buildings, automated for daily periods of performance, come on in the midst of downpours and provoke nasty letters from taxpayers. People stay off the streets and stare from windows. Many who do go outside seem to have forgotten how to drive cars in rain. Children so young that they do not remember such a phenomenon cry out in astonishment. When the rains come, they are often of torrential proportions.

Nowhere is there a great city more peculiarly vulnerable to flooding than Los Angeles. It is not a conventional type of danger, no gradual buildup of high waters over a great watershed as sometimes occurs in northern California. In Southern California a flood is a lightning-fast disaster that occurs when sudden or prolonged rainfall is of too great a volume for the usually dusty stream bed or the concrete flood channels, empty and dry most of the year, in the Los Angeles basin. The waters rush down out of the mountains, bringing along boulders and brush trees and great quantities of soil. Two of America's most improbable rivers, the San Gabriel and Los Angeles, wind through the basin from the mountains to the ocean. The San Gabriel, only 39 miles long, has been the object of more spending in flood control than rivers many times its length that carry ten or twenty times its volume of water. More than half a billion dollars has been spent in harnessing these two rivers, which are reduced to a trickle or to dust for most of the year. Yet when the floods come there is no mistaking their fury. A flood in Los Angeles in 1934 took thirty lives. In 1938, when eleven inches of rain fell in the mountains within five days, eighty-seven lives were lost and damage was eighty million dollars. Dams and concrete-lined channels have since minimized the hazard of such rainfall, but the force of flooding in this semi-desert remains immense. In March, 1968, a pretty 25-year-old college instructor skidded off the Pasadena Freeway during a rainstorm. Her car tumbled down an embankment and threw her out into the muddy Arroyo Seco flood channel, breaking her leg. Although the swirling waters were only three feet deep, she was battered from side to side of the concrete channel and pushed downstream through the midst of the city; after ten minutes she was lifted from the river channel by helicopter, four miles closer to the sea.

The incongruous forces of drought and flood in Southern California are blended in the folklore of the region, most colorfully in the career of the late Charles Hatfield, who is remembered as Hatfield the Rainmaker. There are men who stubbornly contend that Hatfield himself was responsible for almost washing the city of San Diego into the sea in 1916.

Four years of drought had begun to cause panic among farmers and cattlemen. Behind their dams in the foothills, the San Diego city reservoirs were drying up. City councilmen toyed with a proposal from Hatfield, an amateur meteorologist who had been selling his services as a rainmaker since 1904 from Los Angeles northward through the farm valleys and the wheat fields of the Northwest. Now Hatfield had written San Diego councilmen that he could bring down forty inches of rain over the Morena reservoir, sixty miles east of the city.

Hatfield had impressive scrapbooks. The Lake Hemet Land & Water Company had paid him a fee of four thousand dollars and Hatfield had moved to the site, erecting towers and devices that he called "evaporating tanks," filled with "certain chemicals the character of which must necessarily remain secret." At Lake Hemet eleven inches of rain had come and the water level behind the dam had risen by twenty-two feet. San Diego city councilmen decided they had nothing to lose. Despite protests of one member that it was "all a lot of nonsense," they instructed the city attorney to draw up a contract to pay $10,000 to Hatfield if he fulfilled his promise to fill the reservoir within twelve months. The attorney did as he was told, but his cool legal mind prevailed; the contract was never signed.

Yet Hatfield moved his equipment to Morena Reservoir by wagon and built his tower. He discouraged visitors and refused to discuss his procedures. (Years later, in 1925, David Starr Jordan of Stanford would give Hatfield a scholarly debunking in the pages of *Science* magazine as an opportunist who made a study of weather probabilities and made contracts for rain only in the rainy season. But Hatfield was so entrenched in American folklore that his exploits became the theme of Broadway and Hollywood productions as late as the 1950s.)

At San Diego in 1916 he achieved his most awesome rapport with nature. Off the Pacific coast, a high pressure area usually holds back North Pacific storms from Southern California so that only left-overs of weather reach so far south. Early in January, 1916, that high pressure area began one of its rare moves southward, opening a path for storms to drench all of California. Four separate air masses moved into the resultant low pressure area, creating what meteorologists call a pinwheel of weather fronts. Heavy rain is inevitable with such a configuration.

At Morena, where Hatfield went on mixing his mysterious brew, an unprecedented 12.73 inches of rain fell in four days. He telephoned city hall: "I just wanted to tell you that it is only sprinkling now. So far we have encountered only a couple of showers. Within the next few days I expect to make it rain right . . . just hold your horses until I show you a real rain."

The United States weatherman at San Diego reminded local citizens that the storm was general, but he could not be sure how widespread; wires were down, roads and bridges washed out, and trains delayed. A San Diegan rescued from his home by rowboat urged councilmen to pay off Hatfield and send him home.

The rain eased for five days, then returned in greater fury. Rivers overflowed, the ground was saturated, and the floods began sweeping down out of the Southern California mountains and through the valleys, seeking the sea and carrying everything before them. Not far from where Hatfield still entreated the skies from his tower, Otay Dam gave way and a wall of water swept away trains and farms and houses and carried fifteen people to their death. Mail service to San Diego was now by naval vessel. Marines stood guard to prevent looting.

By the end of the second storm, more than thirty-five inches of rain had been measured at the Morena reservoir. Hatfield had filled the reservoir, and he came down out of the hills to collect his fee. But now he found himself villain, not hero. City councilmen, facing more than three million dollars in law suits over loss of property and life, were counseled not to accept liability by paying Hatfield. Six months later he offered to settle his ten-thousand dollar claim for eighteen hundred dollars. The city agreed if he would assume responsibility for suits against the city. He demurred. The two suits that went to trial resulted in verdicts citing the flood as an "act of God." Hatfield's fee was never paid. But he continued to ply his trade until about the time that construction of Boulder Dam eased some of the fear of drought in Southern California.

Soon after Hatfield died in 1958, at the age of eighty-two, an editorial in the San Diego *Evening Tribune* suggested that the Hatfield spell had not entirely dissipated. "He trained no one in the magic art that some say nearly washed San Diego into the sea," it read. "Whatever special skills and knowledge he may have possessed seem to have departed with him—a sorry fact to report. In a way it is as though Pasteur or Dr. Salk had refused to let humanity know the secrets of their great discoveries."

When heavy rains come now in San Diego, someone is sure to suggest that Hatfield's survivors be paid his fee. They insist that the Hatfield curse remains.

. 3 .

THE RESTLESS EDGE

I don't know whether he's gone to lunch or back to
L.A.

—A SECRETARY AT THE OFFICES OF THE DILLINGHAM
CORPORATION IN HONOLULU.

The captain of the jetliner was an old friend, and after
we had climbed and turned from the runway of San Francisco
International Airport, I walked forward and sat in the jump seat
at his side. It was midnight. Behind us, two stewardesses served
coffee to those passengers who were awake. In the rosy darkness
up forward, the captain and his copilot and engineer communed
with their panels of instruments.

Below us lay California. It was a clear and luminous night.

From 19,500 feet the arteries by which California moves on the ground seemed outlined by towns and cities and linked by the piercing jabs of automobile headlights. Most of these roads were the high-speed, multi-lane divided highways with limited access and no tolls, part of the California freeway network that by 1980 is to reach 12,500 miles in length; already it is the most intricate and expensive highway system in any comparable area of the world.

San Jose slipped away beneath us, and the dark arc of Monterey Bay appeared off our right wing. Directly below was the freeway that links San Francisco with Los Angeles. As we flew south, the lanes of northbound cars were outlined by yellowish white ribbons laid down by headlights; the southbound lanes were a fainter red from the taillights of the cars we overtook. Already, off our left wing, we saw intermittent sparklings of cities that have risen in the Great Central Valley at regular intervals, like those of Biblical Jordan: Modesto, Merced, Madera, Fresno—and, a distant glow on the black horizon, Bakersfield.

We whisked through the air at five hundred miles an hour as a radio-controlled meter in front of us ticked off the air miles, one every seven seconds. The captain slipped his earphones aside and began to talk.

"I bought a new house," he said. "Six kids now. Need more space."

"Still in San Diego?"

"Sure. I rehearsed all afternoon down there with a group I sing with. We're singing at a supermarket opening next weekend. Good extra money."

"Is this your first round trip tonight?"

"Oh, no. I flew up from San Diego to San Francisco, then back to Los Angeles, then back to San Francisco, now down to San Diego; and I'll go back to San Francisco tonight and fly an early run tomorrow. That's about twenty-five hundred miles to a shift, right here in California."

For a while it was quiet at the nose of the big jet. The copilot murmured something into a microphone and apparently received the reply he wanted. He sat back, his body loose and at ease. Off to our right was Paso Robles, the halfway town between

San Francisco and Los Angeles. Then came Santa Maria with the Vandenberg Air Force missile base twinkling between it and the Pacific. The grid of lights ahead on the left, in the flatland of the Great Central Valley, was Bakersfield. Beyond lay the hump of the Tehachapi Mountains that separate north and south in California; from almost twenty thousand feet, the range was an anthill.

The coastal highway at our right, coming up on Santa Barbara, showed gaps of darkness. Traffic seemed to jam the other big north-south arterial at our left, the route through the Great Central Valley.

"Sometimes there on the Grapevine, climbing the Tehachapi," the captain said, "you can even see the red lights where the highway patrol has given chase. That route is busy all night."

Now the southern sky turned milky and there could be no doubt we were coming up on the vast Los Angeles Basin. The big jet trembled in the air currents of the Tehachapi, and then the panorama of Los Angeles came clear. The homes of a million people in San Fernando Valley seemed separated from the rest of the Basin by the flimsiest of dark, serpentine shadows, but these shadows were the Hollywood Hills. From four miles in the sky at night, even Los Angeles is beautiful.

On a panel in front of us, a radar scanner etched the outline of the Pacific Coast for fifty miles; at its western perimeter was Catalina Island. We looked out where the darkness of the sea swallowed up the lights, and followed the outline from radar screen to earth. Our visibility was as flawless as our radar; far over to the side, twinkling lights betrayed Catalina.

The captain's right hand squeezed the throttles and the sound of the jets grew softer. We had started our descent for San Diego, still over the heart of Los Angeles, but only sixteen minutes from touchdown at Lindbergh Field. A straight course between San Francisco and San Diego leads sixteen miles out to sea at that point where the land recedes in a concave arc between Los Angeles and San Diego. Now, for the first time, low clouds hugged the coastline and hid land from sight.

The captain slid his earphones back in position and the three men at the controls of the big jet leaned forward almost in unison. From the compartment behind came the voice of a stewardess, reminding passengers to fasten their safety belts for the landing at San Diego.

I told the captain that I hoped his concert at the supermarket went well. I thanked him for the ride and said goodnight. As he turned to shake my hand he was grinning.

"It's easier up here, isn't it?" he said. "I mean getting around California."

During the year 1966, in the pithy but unsensational little journal called *Cry California*, there was a picture story that appeared to document a novel case: a family who lived on the freeways of Los Angeles in their motor home, one of those outsized vehicles with sleeping area, kitchenette and bathroom. When their first baby had come, the story related, Marilee Farrier had given up her job. Installment payments and bills had mounted, and her husband had taken a second, nighttime job. Still they were in trouble. Rather than sell their motor home, which they enjoyed for weekend holidays, the Farriers had sold their tract home and their car.

A night photograph in the magazine showed their motor home parked in a public lot not far from the Los Angeles Music Center. At 7:00 each morning, Marilee Farrier was quoted as saying, she got up, changed the baby, plugged in the coffee, and began driving out the Hollywood Freeway. Mike Farrier noted proudly that his wife didn't wake him until they passed the Cahuenga off-ramp. They parked for a light breakfast outside the Burbank factory where he worked. Then she drove back over the Golden State and San Bernardino freeways to her mother's home, where she left the baby and went to a half-day job. Later she reversed the route to pick up her child and her husband. He drove back to downtown Los Angeles as she prepared dinner. More photographs showed the Farrier family making a deposit at a drive-in teller's window at their bank, attending a drive-in movie, and pulling into a drive-in restaurant for a dinner out.

With the story, the editor of *Cry California* produced a map of metropolitan Los Angeles freeways, tracing the Farrier family's daily route. It was a jumble of circuitous dots and arrows indicating runs totaling 128 miles.

Farrier was quoted:

"One day is about the same as another: about ten gallons of gas a day. We've begun to feel that the freeways, particularly the Hollywood Freeway, belong to us. It's not the same feeling you get about a house on a lot, but it's definitely a sense of ownership. We don't have any neighbors, of course, but actually we had a few neighbors before that we were happy to leave behind."

When the story appeared, I was one of several newsmen who went to the magazine's editor, William Bronson, in an attempt to locate the Farriers. Bronson told us the story was a hoax, and that he had used friends and borrowed a motor home for the photographs. He has insisted doggedly ever since that it seemed to him to be so patent a farce that he did not think it necessary to label it. But in California the Farriers did not seem outrageous enough to lead readers to doubt them. I still do not entirely accept Bronson's disclaimer. I suspect people like the Farriers are driving about Los Angeles today.

In California the automobile assumes tribal significance. Limitless ingenuity is displayed in adapting it to man's desires. Freeway commuters grow so blase that a Los Angeles mortuary has directed its radio and roadside advertising toward those who daydream or read, shave, study or neck while they drive along at sixty or seventy miles an hour. When traffic slows toward the stop-and-go commuter rush hours, the student can be seen grasping his slide rule or turning to an anatomy chart. Businessmen are dictating into tape recorders. Others are plugged into tutor tapes, learning languages. Women are applying lipstick, brushing their hair, hooking their dresses. The automobile serves as office, bedroom and signboard. In San Francisco, a neighborhood divorcée became the talk of the service stations by gluing her phone number in plastic tape to her car's oil stick. At Laguna Beach, a blonde's Volkswagen bore the legend "Have Pills—Will Go." When freeways and beaches grow too crowded, young people can be found embracing in their cars on the top floors of public garages. Teenagers prize ancient hearses as personal vehicles; they can be equipped to carry surfboards and sleep two. The automobile is even used as a mobile listening post to maintain the sanctity of the home. In San Diego, a photographer answered a newspaper advertisement offering a camera for sale, and discovered that he had telephoned a pay booth outside a drive-in restaurant. "That's right," a voice answered, "you wanted the guy with the camera. He drove up here this morning with a book to read, parked outside the phone booth and answered the phone for about half an hour until he'd made his deal. I asked him if he didn't have a phone at home. 'Sure,' he said, 'but this way I can sell the camera and not have to sit around listening to the damn phone ring all day and night.'"

Since there is now relatively little rapid mass transit in California cities, every man's car is his mobile castle. The number of motor vehicles in the metropolitan Los Angeles area alone is approaching five million; only the states of New York, Pennsylvania and Texas have more cars than Los Angeles. In Southern California there is a car for about every two people; in New York City, there is one for every six. Close to eight million gallons of gasoline are burned each day in the Los Angeles Basin. Throughout California one finds the greatest concentration of motor vehicles in the world, and it shows no sign of diminishing. In 1968 the California Department of Motor Vehicles was seeking a new method of license plate numbering. Under its system using three letters and three digits on each plate, there were only about sixteen million possible combinations, and they were being exhausted. Officials were predicting that twenty-two million cars would be registered in California by 1980. San Francisco is choking with cars, the highest density of automobiles of any city: 7000 per square mile. The San Francisco freeways, blocked from completion because outraged citizens regarded them as eyesores on the lovely San Francisco skyline, now dump their daily burden of cars at the edges of downtown. The city awaits completion of the Bay Area Rapid Transit District, an interurban rail commuter system which has been mired in debt and debacle during its construction. Meanwhile, from off the Bayshore Freeway, the Golden Gate and the Oakland Bay Bridges, motor vehicles are funneled into the city until it seems sure to burst in an exploding aneurysm of steel, rubber and fume.

In Los Angeles, which has desperately accepted all proffered freeways—sightly or not—almost half a million cars roll each day through the central interchange known as The Slot. Only for about four hours each day, at peak commuter rushes, does the intricate freeway system overload enough to bring automobile speeds down below maximum. By the early 1980's the three Southern California counties of Los Angeles, Orange and Ventura alone will be slashed by a network of 1535 miles of freeway costing more than five billion dollars; close to one-half of it is already in existence. It is possible to drive on freeways from San Diego almost five hundred miles northward through Los Angeles and through the Great Central Valley without encountering any traffic signal, stop sign or toll station; for cars with sufficient fuel capacity and drivers of adequate durability, there is no compulsion to pause. It is not a sightseers' route.

So the Californian and his car go on their often bloody way together, plying the freeways, clogging the streets and polluting the air in a frenzy of movement at work and play. The Californian thrives on extreme mobility and has grown to demand it. With this eccentric obsession, he and the equally compulsive autocracy of freeway builders have fed off each other until the Californian's condition of near transiency is granted official sanction by the state in the form of its concrete freeway ribbons that unroll at costs of up to fifteen million dollars a mile. Yet such freeways often devastate the lives of individuals and cities and despoil what had been scenic majesty.

Although the time span from drawing board to completion of a freeway may be eight to ten years, there is an immutable momentum associated with it. The formidable California Division of Highways has been granted powers of eminent domain superior to those of other state agencies. A constitutional provision allots all gasoline taxes and most motor-vehicle fees and taxes to the Division. Federal grants boost its annual budget to about one billion dollars. Highway commissioners are appointed by the governor and are not subject to recall; their decisions are seldom reviewed by the legislature. Wallace Stegner of Stanford has referred to the highway commission as "having nobody to control it, too much money, too much power, and an engineering mentality." Criticism has come also from a former highway commissioner, newspaper publisher Joseph C. Houghteling, who charged that "what actually exists (within the Division of Highways) is a condition wherein the inmates run the asylum, with the Chief Inmate serving also as Chairman of the Board of Visitors." Even as a highway commissioner—or member of the "Board of Visitors"—he approached the professional freeway builders in the same "friendly, powerless relationship one has when negotiating with the Bureau of Internal Revenue." This Division of Highways has virtually the power of God, and considerably more momentum.

The success of San Francisco city supervisors and voters in blocking freeway links within the city has focused attention on the more destructive aspects of massive freeway construction. The twenty-year freeway program approved by the legislature in 1959, to add more than twelve thousand miles of freeway at a cost of more than ten billion dollars, will swallow up or make useless almost half a million acres of California land. By 1980, two percent of the state's area will be committed to the automobile. Freeways involve demolition of homes and businesses and forced relocation. When an interstate freeway was opened, bypassing the village of Jacumba in the Southern California mountains, two of the town's service stations went out of business within an hour. A motel and restaurant had closed two weeks before. The owner of the remaining restaurant in Jacumba dismissed all but two of his staff. In San Diego, an automobile tire dealer found himself dispossessed in three successive locations by new freeways. The Santa Monica Freeway, seventeen miles long, absorbed 4129 parcels of property including banks, churches and factories. Such property is removed from tax rolls, adding to the taxpayers' burden. In 1968 California highway planners made a brave start when they set out to make resettlement of displaced persons an integral part of the seventeen-mile Century Freeway project in the south-central Los Angeles area, which includes Watts. In effect, the Division of Highways became an arm of urban redevelopment for a blighted area.

The element of esthetics now receives some consideration in freeway planning, largely because of effective mobilization of public opinion by citizens' organizations. For some years after the freeway program was initially funded and launched, by legislative passage of the landmark Collier-Burns Act of 1947, engineers designed freeways as nearly as possible on the simplistic basis of following a straight line between two points. Public outrage has since led to less brutish design. In the sweeping curves and dual levels of newer freeways, it is not impossible to sense elements of beauty. Freeway landscaping is now emphasized. Public protests led to alteration of proposed freeways through state redwood parks along the North Coast and along the lofty, wooded ocean cliffs of the Big Sur south of Monterey. The defense of the Big Sur was led by the architect Nathaniel Owings and his artist wife. One outcome was the adoption of the concept of a scenic corridor to remain free of blemishing freeway structures, and zoned to limit roadside construction. Other scenic corridors are now protected within the California Scenic Highway Program, which offers incentives in state funds for road beautification if local residents protect the adjacent property from blight.

The basic issue is the need for a finer balance between the role of freeways as a means of transport and as a disruptive force in the lives of people, in the growth of commerce and cities, and in the conservation of scenic open spaces, coastal beaches and parks. The freeway system is essential to the California way of life. The urban Californian refuses to live in a community that brings his home, his place of work and his shopping facilities within a narrow range. In general he rejects mass transit systems when he has an option, preferring to be independent of route and schedule and free to move at his own convenience. He even tends to boycott factory and office car pools until employers begin to offer incentives like close-in free parking to those who commute in such pools. He prefers to own at least two automobiles so that while he has one at work, his wife may use the other to give her access to community and market and to transport children to and from school and after-school lessons or amusements. Because of the low density growth of all California cities except San Francisco, the pattern of low-level urban sprawl has tended to make the car the only satisfactory method of transport. The car and freeway come to seem more basic even than the telephone. (An acquaintance telephoned me for information one day from a community about twenty miles distant. I excused myself from the telephone and when I came back within a minute or so the line had gone dead. He appeared in my office half an hour later, chiding me for taking so long. "I had to hang up," he said. "After all, that was a long distance call.")

Around the freeways of California there has grown up a contemporary lore that is as often affectionate as bitter. The freeways are, after all, impossible to ignore. Freeway engineers often station television cameras beside freeway entrances and exits to help them study the California drivers' habits, and to predict their errors. Engineers may follow up such filmings by visiting a driver to discuss his reaction to some troublesome on-ramp or off-ramp.

The structural massiveness of the freeways is overwhelming. For a four-level interchange between two interstate highways at San Diego, approximately as much concrete was used as in that city's modern fifty-thousand-seat stadium. The cost of the interchange and its approaches was close to fifteen million dollars, a sum approximating the basic construction costs of the same stadium. Engineers computed that within the interchange and its ramps one could travel for about thirty miles without retracing his route. Such a complex structure must of course approach engineering perfection. During its construction, engineers sent their tanker trucks to haul water from a seawater desalinization plant. The reason was one that chagrined water officials: California Division of Highways specifications for such concrete require water containing less than four hundred parts per million of sodium chloride and sodium sulfate. Ordinary tap water brought by aqueduct from the Colorado River into the city mains of San Diego—and drunk without harm by hundreds of thousands of citizens—could not meet the purity specifications for mixing freeway concrete.

Californians have begun to associate qualities of omnipotence and inevitability with their freeways. The freeway assumes command over those who build and use it. The means become the end. The loss of human individuality to the freeway is never more vivid than when a funeral procession appears. A hearse in the slowest lane, too underpowered for fast freeway traffic, lumbers along at the head of the line. Mourners in the following cars try to keep their ranks intact as tail-gaters speed up behind their cars and lane-changers weave in and out. In San Diego, the annual Toyland Christmas Parade was once canceled because construction of a freeway along its traditional route made the parade impossible. Until recently in Los Angeles, at the junction of the Harbor and Santa Monica freeways, a hotel tried to go on with business although it had become an island isolated in a sea of freeway ramps. The safety factors involved in freeway driving are beyond dispute. More cars move faster with fewer accidents. Yet those that do occur are often spectacular in scope and may involve fifty or more automobiles. One of the most incongruous freeway mishaps came on the Ventura Freeway one afternoon in 1963 when four steers on their way to a Los Angeles slaughterhouse were abruptly dumped, during a sudden stop, from a truck into traffic. They weaved their way among the cars of astonished drivers and disrupted traffic for four hours before police with lassos, using trucks as barriers, corraled the last of the animals. The freeway is off-limits to anything non-vehicular. I remember when Harvey Dinnerstein, a New York artist, came to California to sketch illustrations for a magazine article that I had written. He flew home with a traffic citation as his California souvenir. But he had never been behind the wheel of a car. He was cited early one morning on the Pasadena Freeway, and the ticket spelled out his grievous offense: "Defendant sitting beside freeway making sketches. Signs posted at entrance, 'Motor Vehicles Only.'"

The freeway is an obvious common bond among Californians. In many of the state's sudden cities the freeway and its traffic provide some bizarre sense of community. As drivers look fleetingly back and forth from lane to lane, their neighbors in the cars speeding along beside them may seem for an instant to be their friends. They share shrugs of despair at slow traffic, or expressions of elation when traveling at high speed. In any sense of imminent crisis there is comradeship among strangers, and the freeway provides such a setting. Near Oakland, a commuter blew out a tire during the morning rush and pulled off on a narrow shoulder. A road worker, seeing his plight, moved his yellow cone traffic markers and "Men Working" sign around the commuter's car so that he could change his tire and stay alive. One little monument to traffic togetherness was a Christmas tree that grew until recently in the center island of a busy stretch of coastal road near Oceanside. Just before Christmas in 1958 a truck driver, bearing a load of Christmas trees, had a mechanical breakdown. Other drivers stopped to help. The driver gave each of his samaritans a tree of his own; in a moment of whimsy, they planted a small tree in the center island and watered it from a can. It took root. During the long dry summers for years afterward, truck drivers stopped to water the tree, and highway maintenance men spared it until it was finally lost in a freeway realignment.

The stranger to freeway traffic is especially prone to sympathetic communication from other drivers. A Missouri visitor, unnerved by his first hours in Los Angeles traffic, pulled off a freeway and sat quietly, hoping to regain his composure. A highway patrol officer drove up behind him to investigate. He listened to the Missourian's story and nodded with feeling. "Would you mind," he said, "if I sat down and joined you for a while?"

What the promenade around the central plaza is to Latin cities, the freeway is to the Californian: the parade of his peers, the lemming urge, the common meeting ground. Yet by contrast it is chillingly impersonal, suicidally frenetic, and so vacuous as to make its inhabitants appear as the robots of a city that has become a puppet of technology. Once the newcomer has settled into this stream of movement, he begins to adjust to the marathon distances of Los Angeles and to the absence of a conventional central core of municipal and commercial facilities. Soon he begins to realize that Los Angeles sidewalks are never crowded. This phenomenon underlines the mystique of loneliness so often found in the literature of the region. Aldous Huxley wrote of it in *After Many a Summer Dies the Swan.* So did J. B. Priestley in

Midnight on the Desert. It is equally prominent in the mystery
novels of James M. Cain, Raymond Chandler and Ross Mac-
Donald. In Los Angeles there is nothing within walking distance.
The shortest distance between successive engagements is usually
by car. It is no canard that Beverly Hills police, patrolling slowly
in their prowl cars, have halted for investigation a list of citizens
that would make up a who's who of the entertainment world;
anyone who is out for a walk in many residential neighborhoods
—unless he has a dog on a leash—is suspect as a prowler. From
their two- and three-car garages, Californians drive by freeway
into underground or overground parking garages, enter office
buildings through rear doors or by basement elevator, and then
ascend to office level. Only the white-collar workers will drift
out to the sidewalks at lunch to patronize a neighborhood coffee
shop or a stand-up counter; from the salesman up to the president, lunch means another venture by automobile to a restaurant
or club that may be ten or twenty miles across the city.

What loss to the human psyche is involved in this strange urban
isolation? Some sense of aloofness from society must result from
the insulation of steel and glass. Even the abrasiveness of crowding on the sidewalks and in the subways of New York and London
and Tokyo seems more humane; cruelty and hatred are present
in any crush of people, but the awareness of mankind is inescapable. Seldom but in downtown San Francisco, with its more
conventional urban structure, are California sidewalks thronged.
There the automobile is a liability; walking seems not only possible but exhilarating, and there is a sense of belonging to the
crowd. Such thoughts, however subliminal, are more than incidental when visitors appraise San Francisco as a more civilized
city than Los Angeles. Part of what they sense is that in San
Francisco, human intercourse is conventional and viable. It may
not be more compassionate, but the contact is at least that of
brushing shoulders, hips and arms, not scraping fenders and
denting bumpers.

Critics of Los Angeles usually adopt one of two themes: the
automobile itself caused Los Angeles to grow askew, or the
restless vagrancy of those who migrate to Los Angeles opens them

to dominance by the automobile. So pervasive is the relation between the Southern Californian and his automobile that it is easy to assume that one has shaped the other. But both themes have basic flaws. A now defunct interurban rail system, the Pacific Electric, did more to shape Los Angeles than the automobile. The freeway system supplanted the PE. Without a car it is now virtually impossible to live normally in Los Angeles. In Southern California, mass rapid transit died an earlier death than in other cities, and an extensive road-building program was launched sooner. Lewis Mumford wrote of the automobile as the "sacred cow" of our "curious religion of technology" for which "no sacrifice in daily living, no extravagance of public expenditure, appears too great." No matter how enthusiastically a Southern Californian might agree with Mumford's critical appraisal, he cannot get along without the automobile. The challenge of Los Angeles is to live with movement. Reuben Lovret, a Los Angeles city planner, wrote that "if you have complete dependence on the automobile it can lead to nothing but change. As long as you are oriented toward the automobile, any location is subject to reorganization or redevelopment according to how the driver can exert pressure—for shopping centers or apartment houses. As long as unbridled fluidity exists, there can be no permanent pattern."

The automobile has not always been the device of unbridled fluidity in Los Angeles. The Pacific Electric was formed in 1901 by Henry E. Huntington, whose uncle, Collis P. Huntington, had been the most ruthless but efficient of the Big Four railroad builders. The big red cars of the PE probed from downtown Los Angeles up into the foothills of the Sierra Madre Mountains and westward to the Pacific shore at Santa Monica. Its routes did much to develop Pasadena, Hollywood, Long Beach, Santa Ana, San Bernardino, Redlands and Riverside—cities whose borders now merge into the Los Angeles megalopolis. For Huntington, the rail line was an ideal tool to develop his real estate holdings. The PE offered day-long picnic excursions that ranged from mountain to sea and brought glimpses of forests of oil derricks, groves of orange trees, and fields of sugar beets. Even then, Los Angelenos traveled almost as much for pleasure as in more serious pursuits. In 1910, when Los Angeles was a city of just over 300,000 people, it was already popular to live in a distant community and commute great distances by rail. The pattern of Los Angeles sprawl and the mobility of its residents was established. In 1913, with the motor car still a novelty but the PE a giant among interurban rail systems, an article called "The Red Car of Empire" appeared in *Sunset* Magazine with this florid appraisal:

> Within a radius of thirty-five miles of Los Angeles, there are forty-two incorporated cities and towns with countless country homes between. All these are literally of one body, of the healthiest and most rapidly growing body in America. The arterial system that holds them together is the double trackage of the interurban electric road. The red corpuscles that race to the end of every farthest vein to proclaim and carry the abundant life are the flitting crimson cars.

The tracks of the PE reinforced the patterns of topography and travel that had existed since Indian days. As motor car traffic began to dominate Los Angeles, streets and highways paralleled the PE rails. Many of today's 76 incorporated cities within Los Angeles County were laid out along PE routes. In 1930, with 1200 miles of track, the PE was the longest commuter system in the world, and as late as 1945 its cars carried 109,000,-000 passengers in a year. Then it declined rapidly. It was not entirely that the automobile had grown more popular, but that the PE failed to take advantage of technological improvement.

The PE carried its last passenger in 1963. The paradox was that it helped to form a metropolis that seems no longer suited for mass transit systems, which find a firm economic base today only in urban areas with population densities greater than ten thousand persons per square mile. Almost one-half of all land in the central business district of Los Angeles is devoted to streets, freeways and parking. More than half a million people commute to downtown Los Angeles, five by car to every two by the municipal bus system that remains as the only vestige of mass transit.

There are continuing proposals for new rapid transit, with Los Angeles having spent more than two million dollars for more than two dozen transit studies since 1945. Still there is little prospect for conventional mass transit in Los Angeles. Its history of mobility always unique, Los Angeles seems likely to move early toward some system of automated freeway traffic in which vehicles operate under electronic control. The era of the robot draws near. Freeways will be the veins and arteries of the super city.

The frequently heard claim that Los Angeles has the worst traffic congestion in the world is not valid. More Southern Californians move to more places, more quickly and easily, than do the residents of any comparable area in the world.

California planners turn their worries toward the skies. They compare the crowded California corridor of transport between San Francisco, Los Angeles and San Diego, with the Northeast Corridor between Washington and Boston. In the California corridor there is enough air commuting to make the Los Angeles-San Francisco airlanes the most traveled in the world, with close to four million round trips in a year. In a three-lane air corridor about ten miles wide, two hundred flights move in an average day between Los Angeles and San Francisco, sometimes with planes passing so close that passengers can see each other at the windows. To a still small number of business and professional people, commuting by jet between these cities is as casual and often at least as workable as commuting lesser distances by train between Manhattan and Long Island, Connecticut or Westchester County. The clear California skies make tight air schedules relatively reliable. A San Diego painting contractor spent part of each work day at offices in Los Angeles and San Francisco. J. Floyd Andrews, the president of Pacific Southwest Airlines, often commutes from his San Diego home to participate in a Thursday night bowling league in San Francisco. It is commonplace to see such air passengers as a bronzed blonde teenager in a white tennis dress and blazer, carrying only her racquet and perhaps a trophy. Pilots of commuter jets delight in pointing out to their passengers at dusk the lines of lights marking peak-hour freeway traffic below. The speed of commuter air travel was underlined for a Los Angeles executive who parked his car in haste to catch an early-morning flight to San Francisco. Back in the Los Angeles airport parking lot at the end of the day, he found his car where he had parked it, its key in the ignition, and the motor still idling with half a tank of gas to go.

With soaring traffic, airlane crowding grows as critical as that of the freeways and makes congestion in the new airport communities as serious as in downtown centers. At Los Angeles International Airport, hotels and office buildings cluster around the terminal area. The hotels provide the usual overnight rest stops for international passengers and centralized conference facilities for businessmen who converge from many points by air. The office buildings are a newer concept. For the new breed of mobile, airborne executive commuter, they offer a temporary office facility. Home away from home is an old image; now comes the office away from office.

More than thirty thousand people are employed at Los Angeles International Airport itself. If they and their families lived in the immediate neighborhood, a city of close to a quarter of a million people would result. If they do not live around the airport, as is presently the case, they clog freeways and streets going to and from the airport with their own commuting, making these arterials more sluggish for air passengers going to and from their jets. The situation at San Francisco is only slightly less grim. As megalopolises like these grow, small private airfields often give way to subdivision and shopping center, thus adding to congestion at major airfields. The impending operation of Boeing four hundred passenger jets finds California airports no more adequately prepared for crowd handling than most others in America. The situation is particularly vexing to planners like Clyde P. Barnett, California state director of aeronautics, who recently said: "Here we are, hip deep in our own garbage, throwing rockets at the moon."

Much of the planning for the future of California transport takes place in a small one-story building beside a eucalyptus grove on the edge of San Francisco Bay. Here, in the Richmond Field Station of the University of California, Dr. Harmer Davis heads the Institute of Transportation and Traffic Engineering. "There has been a uniqueness about the California obsession with mobility," Davis said. "Now it seems to be becoming an American obsession."

Like transportation experts everywhere, Davis is surrounded with surveys, studies and proposals, all of them dependent for activation upon both public opinion and the most intricate mix of negotiation and funding by public and private agencies. Like other Californians on the cutting edges of innovation, Davis looks beyond paperwork to the even more complex puzzle of human behavior. He sees the Californian as one who has thrown off traditional inhibitions against frequent movement until he is traveling more both in work and in play than other Americans —although others are moving to close that gap. In California, a land accustomed to constant flux, the science of transport has overtaken that of urban planning. Men like Davis feel they must know immediately whether Americans will live in denser cities like San Francisco or in dispersed, fragmented ones like those of Southern California. But they hold only a single piece of the urban puzzle, and they cannot solve it alone.

"It is almost within our grasp of technology to serve any form of urban arrangement that people want to have," Davis said. "But first we must have some notion of how we want to organize ourselves, how we want to live."

It is a ridiculous image, of course: the American who can go anywhere, anytime, with infinite ease, and so in the end can't decide where he wants to go or why. But to a stranger driving along a Los Angeles freeway on a Sunday afternoon, that image does not seem remote. After all, this is the city where a motorist appeared in municipal court on a charge of driving with a suspended operator's license. The license had been ruled invalid because of the defendant's history of mental illness. So his counsel stepped forward with an impregnable defense: Not guilty on grounds of insanity. In such a society, motion can become the goal rather than the means.

. 4 .

SIERRA NEVADA

Eastward I go only by force; but westward I go free.

—HENRY DAVID THOREAU, *Walking*.

The Sierra Nevada is a majestic mountain range, exceeding even the Rockies in height and length. Like the Andes of South America, these mountains are a link in the chain that parallels the Pacific coast from the Aleutian Islands to Cape Horn. Both in height and area, the Sierra Nevada almost matches the combined Swiss, French and Italian Alps. At its feet, early settlers found gold. In its high valleys and along its glaciated peaks, today's Californians find more; for in an almost spiritual sense, the Sierra Nevada is the symbol of the California homeland.

From the wall that rises near volcanic Lassen Peak at the north, and on southward for 430 miles to the fringes of Los Angeles, this lavish range provides Californians with their eastern horizon. Its waters cool the rich endless fields of the Great Central Valley. Once the sheer eastern escarpment of the Sierra Nevada barricaded the promised land, sealing off California against its early settlers and making it seem unattainable. Now, with the proud helmet-shaped granite peak of Mount Whitney rising over all, the Sierra Nevada tends to unite Californians in some sense of community. In its alpine fastness, one cannot escape the feel of history. Here lies an unyielding, unchanging California in contrast to the one below. Many of those who are most deeply involved with the madness in the cities of California climb here to this retreat in search of perspective, to rest and to seek logic. Etched in granite above the entrance to one of the State Capitol buildings in Sacramento is the poet's line, "Bring me men to match my mountains." The Sierra Nevada stands as symbol of the quest.

The love of mountains is a personal matter. I first learned that love as a boy in the Great Smokies, a range that seems to me both gentle and yielding. The Sierra Nevada is neither; it demands much, it promises much, and it must be won in a fight if it is to be had. Then its charms prove infinite and always new. No man has loved the Sierra Nevada more deeply or more wisely than the naturalist John Muir. "These blessed mountains," Muir wrote of Yosemite, which lies at the heart of the Sierra Nevada, "are so compactly filled with God's beauty, no petty personal hope or experience has room to be."

When my daughter Jill reached her early teens, we read from Muir's books together and planned a holiday in the High Sierra, an alpine land that rises above the timberline, sparkling with more than twelve hundred lakes and scores of rapids and cascades. Scoured by glaciers in the Ice Age, the High Sierra is a region of shaded forests, of clean-swept tumbled granite, sleek and polished, with smooth-walled canyons and ledges leading up to a sky of indefinable brightness. Like most fathers, I had been busy, and so had Jill. Alone on the Sierra trails but for our guide and our mules, I thought, we might find fresh reasons for being friends. We decided to make the circuit of small tent camps that the Yosemite Park & Curry Corporation maintains for the nine or ten weeks each summer that weather permits access.

For 160 miles, from Walker Pass overlooking the Mojave Desert, up to Tioga Pass, the precipitous summer exit to the east from Yosemite, no road crosses the Sierra Nevada. Yosemite is only one of three national parks within these pristine highlands. But for variety and grandeur, Yosemite is unsurpassed. Its boundaries sweep up from the purplish foothills of the Mother Lode country, dotted with scrub oak, on through the ice-carved valleys of the Merced and Tuolumne rivers with their waterfalls and granite domes. The park encompasses groves of sequoias that began to grow a thousand years before Christ. In its upper reaches, where we planned to go, Yosemite is a lonely, unsullied world of stone and tree and torrent.

For unknown centuries Indians had this land to themselves, living on both east and west flanks of the Sierra Nevada. The frontiersman Jedediah Strong Smith led a party over the range and down the east slope into the Great Basin desert in 1827, the first white men to cross the Sierra Nevada. For Smith it was an eight-day ordeal that cost the lives of two horses and a mule. Six years later the trapper Joseph Reddeford Walker made a frigid October crossing, writing in his log of "mile-high cliffs" and powerful waterfalls that were probably those of Yosemite Valley. He described the giant sequoias: trees "sixteen to eighteen fathoms round the trunk." But there was no rush into the Sierra Nevada. Gold had not yet been found in California, and traffic was sparse.

In the fall of 1846, George Donner led a party of settlers from Illinois toward California. Trapped by October snows near the Truckee River—along a route now traversed by the freeway from Reno to Sacramento—Donner and his group ran out of food. Relief parties failed to get through. Weak and soon desperately ill, Donner's group ate bark and leather and finally their own dead. It was not until spring, after 36 had died, that rescuers were able to reach the survivors. Today motorists speed over Donner Pass, seldom pausing to read the plaque erected in memory of the dead.

When gold was discovered at Sutter's Mill in 1848, foothills of the Sierra Nevada bore the brunt of the frenzy. In the Mother Lode, between the Feather River and the San Joaquin, the havoc of the miners' diggings has only lately been softened by the growth of oak and pine and manzanita. The Mother Lode was a land of ruin by 1864, when Mark Twain came on the scene.

Higher in the Sierra Nevada there seemed to be little but scenery, and the first trickle of tourists into Yosemite had just begun. In 1851 a punitive expedition, the Mariposa Battalion, had entered Yosemite Valley in pursuit of Indian marauders; the valley took its name from that of the Indians who were captured and removed to a Fresno reservation. In 1855 a versatile young miner named James Hutchings organized the first party of sightseers to enter Yosemite Valley, and a horse toll-trail was established. The journey remained arduous for many years. A geological survey began in Yosemite in 1863, but in the next year the total number of visitors in the valley was only 147. Among them were venturesome mountain climbers who from the start have been lured to the perpendicular granite walls of Yosemite Valley, and the needle-like peaks of the high country above.

Muir, a richly perceptive Scot, first visited Yosemite in 1868 and returned the next year—taking a job first as a sheepherder and later as a sawmill operator so that he could remain. He roamed the Sierra Nevada in happy solitude, scrawling notes by night with his quill pens and publishing them as paeans to the mountains that he named the "range of light." More than any other man, he brought the attention of the world to the Sierra Nevada and to Yosemite in particular. His writing helped spur the establishment of Yosemite as a national park by Congress in 1890. Muir helped form the Sierra Club, now one of America's most powerful conservation societies, and served as its president until his death in 1914. The memorial he would surely have liked best is the John Muir Trail, a path for hikers and horsemen that winds along close to the crest of the Sierra Nevada for 212 miles from the floor of Yosemite Valley to Mount Whitney at 14,496 feet. For me, there is no more sublime trail in America. It leads through ten passes above ten thousand feet, and along its route can be seen 148 peaks that exceed thirteen thousand feet—including eleven of the thirteen California summits over fourteen thousand feet. About seven thousand hikers make their way to the crest each summer, but few have traversed the length of the trail.

Less demanding trails are abundant, and in California almost anyone may turn up as a mountaineer. Along these trails in summer one finds teachers and doctors and clerks and secretaries. The prodigious membership of the Sierra Club, drawing from every walk of life and growing at the rate of thirty per cent each year, is testimony to the awareness and concern of the Californian with the Sierra Nevada. It is not mere vacation sightseeing. In a state where almost everyone seems to have come from somewhere else, these mountains have become home.

One night Jill and I drove northward through the veinous labyrinth of Los Angeles, and wound over the Tehachapi mountain range that sets Southern California apart. We dropped down on a highway that Californians call the Grapevine and were suddenly into the southern end of the five-hundred-mile-long Great Central Valley. The highways are interminably straight here, bisected at right angles by secondary roads leading off into the flat irrigated farms. This is the heartland of California's agricultural empire, a region of massive corporate farms where the side roads may be known only by number, as devoid of human feeling as the walkway within a foundry.

It was July; in summer, when one can choose, one drives through the Great Central Valley at night. It is not cool even then, but the land has taken respite from the fiery sun that rules it by day. The heat ripples are gone, but in their place is the heavy mugginess that rises from mile after mile of irrigation canals. For night companions along the concrete mats of the freeways there are ponderous trucks, plying the main shipping route between San Francisco and Los Angeles, sometimes hauling out the richness of the valley: cotton and grapes, wine and fruit, nuts and vegetables. Gasoline tank trucks return from refineries to valley towns that never escape the putrid odor of their own oil wells. The Great Central Valley is a gargantuan trough down the center of California, set between the coastal mountains to the west and the Sierra Nevada towering to its east. The valley is ugly and dreary but incredibly rich; it is made so by the water that roars down out of the Sierra Nevada and is captured in the most intricate system of irrigation canals that man has ever built.

There are three main approaches to Yosemite Valley, all of them adapted from horse or carriage trails laid out soon after the first white men entered the valley in 1851. Jill and I began to drive out of the Great Central Valley on a two-lane macadam near the vineyards of Fresno. Through the foothills, with their shadowy scrub oaks, and finally into the forests of fir and spruce and pine, we climbed steadily under a full moon. It was four in the morning when we entered Yosemite Valley. Moonlight coated the granite domes and cliffs with satin and placed halos at the crests of the falls. In spring, the white falls thunder over these cliffs into the valley and then the Merced River flows gently on toward the Pacific. By midsummer, the flow has thinned or stopped completely. But at any season, here in this valley, a mere seven miles long and a mile wide, is one of nature's most compelling variety shows. The valley represents less than one-half of one percent of the total area of Yosemite Park, and yet its enthralling beauty was first responsible for the existence of the park. Almost all Yosemite visitors—now close to two million each year—congregate on this valley floor, a pinhead in size within the great Sierra Nevada, which in many other areas remains very much as it has been since the Ice Age.

It was daybreak, 55 miles later, as we swung in beside Tenaya Lake at 8141 feet, approaching the back country that is the Yosemite portal to the High Sierra. Even in midsummer, it is cold here; steam rose from the soda springs of Tuolumne Meadows. As the eastern sky over the Great Basin began to lighten, we found our base camp, a community of ocher-colored tents arranged irregularly on a rise beside a gentle waterfall. A college student, acting as a kind of desk clerk, helped us into a tent and built a log fire in a tin stove. Here on the same meadow where John Muir had tended herds of sheep and later sat around campfires pleading the cause of conservation with all who would listen, we slept through breakfast.

It is good to spend a quiet day or two growing accustomed to the thin air of the High Sierra. We met Lloyd Hansen, a soft-

spoken mule wrangler and mountain man who was to be our
guide. He introduced Jill to her mule Boots, and me to Bessie.
We took a preliminary outing, through the trees on a narrow path
past a stamped metal marker: JOHN MUIR TRAIL. Far to the south,
leading always along the crest of an upthrust granite wave, this
trail ends at the summit of Mount Whitney which, until Alaska's
Mount McKinley, was the highest peak in the United States.
It is a trail that can be traversed in segments, and there are many
who devote successive vacations to the trail over several years.

Next morning we packed sweaters and a few essentials in two
knapsacks. Muir had made his way alone through these mountains for days with only bread and cheese and some raisins and
nuts, sleeping in hollow logs or on beds of boughs. But Lloyd had
sized us up: he met us beside the trail—our three mules saddled
and an extra one in harness as pack mule—carrying spare provisions and a bottle of sour-mash whiskey. He led the way up a
steep trail through pines past the Cathedral Lakes. Ten miles
away was the newest of the Yosemite high tent camps, Sunrise,
our first day's goal. In moments we were out of sight of anything
that suggested the touch of man. Gray-streaked granite soared
upward and outward to a cobalt sky. Glacial lakes appeared above
us, around bends in trails, like shimmering sapphires. Stately
hemlocks and lodgepole pines rose together in fragrant tilted
groves so still and deeply carpeted that the sudden sharp cries of
birds seemed irreverent.

Nothing I did as a rider seemed to influence Bessie, and I spent
the hours on the trail simply staring. Even at our plodding pace,
the jagged peaks, the smoothly chiseled domes and meadows
passed too soon from sight. There is little traffic on these trails.
But since they are the sole supply lines of the High Sierra, we saw
occasional trains of as many as fifteen mules, each loaded with
food or bed linens or fuels.

"Each wrangler has his favorite egg mule," Lloyd said. "That's
a mule we can trust not to bang up against trees along the trail
or to get excited and have a wreck. We load eggs on egg mules."
Mules, he explained, are agitators; they agitate their riders
through the day by their insensibility to command and their
allegiance to rote. At night, they agitate each other, usually by

biting. But their reputation for dependability on precipitous trails is more than legend; they are nerveless creatures, too phlegmatic to be alarmed by sheer drops or a crumbling path underfoot.

Our trail led at midday down into one of Yosemite's loveliest retreats: Long Meadow, a spongy green valley strewn with boulders, which meanders between the mountains for two miles. When we sprawled in the grass to rest, the field seemed populated by armies of soldiers in crimson and scarlet uniforms; they were little stalks of owl's clover and Indian paint brush. At midafternoon, Lloyd led the way up off the meadow to a ledge with white tents camouflaged beside huge rocks and set at erratic angles for privacy. This was Sunrise Camp.

Like most of the Yosemite high camps, Sunrise accommodates a maximum of forty to fifty visitors, most of whom have reserved space as much as a year ahead. One couple is in charge; four college boys and girls serve meals, wash dishes, deliver firewood to tents, and make beds. Their services are welcome. Even pulling up blankets during the cold nights at 9600 feet can cause hard breathing for one unaccustomed to the altitude.

At dinner we eavesdropped. "I promised my husband I wouldn't drink so much tonight," said a woman at the end of our table. With that she pushed her cup away; but in it was only water. Among purists of the High Sierra trail, a moderate drinker is one who has only an occasional drink of water—and never in the morning; excessive liquid leads to the nuisance of stops along the trails. We discovered there is real cleavage between hikers and riders on these trails. Hikers with heavy packs are less able to look about as they climb, for they may be bent under the weight of knapsack and bedroll. From muleback we had more freedom to stare about us, but it was made clear to us by certain hikers that we were thus deprived of the intimacy of man and mountain. It is a matter for a man and his conscience; despite Bessie's incessant insolences I grew more grateful to her with each mountain we climbed.

One delight of these High Sierra camps is the variety of side trips for which they serve as base. Next morning we rode out to Clouds Rest, a 9926-foot pinnacle just above Half Dome; both are seen from Yosemite Valley far below. Our route led over a promontory on which we found metates used a century or two ago by the Yosemite Indians to grind their corn. We looked down into one of the most unearthly sights of the Sierra Nevada: the Tenaya Cascade, a quarry-like arena of glacier-polished folds of granite about a mile wide. We stood on the stage of an infinite amphitheater. Above this gaping mouth was our goal, Clouds Rest, which looked from here like a thin whitecap of stone. It is the largest area of naked granite in Yosemite. Beyond was Half Dome, that sheerest and most compelling of all Sierra precipices, of which Muir wrote: "A most noble rock, it seems full of thought, clothed with living light, no sense of dead stone about it . . . steadfast in serene strength like a god." Outside these mountains, Muir's prose reads with a certain flamboyance of phrase that was typical of his day; yet once within the High Sierra, one thumbs through Muir to recall his reactions and there is no sense of excess; his raptures pall in relation to the wonder seen so close at hand.

We rode on through wooded meadows where the trail was lost in high grass and masses of tiger lilies. A fat eight-point mule deer stood beside the trail and stared at us without alarm. A mountainside rippled green with aspen as evenly spaced as in an orchard, but growing bushlike, none more than six or seven feet high. Around one bend, we came upon a massive landslide of glacial rock and earth—stolid evidence for perhaps twenty thousand years of the violence that shaped Yosemite. One rock, almost a perfect cube of twenty feet, was split two ways from top to bottom into quarters so evenly matched that Jill climbed up and paced them off for size. The cuts were as neat as if made by a sculptor. "It looks," Jill said, "as though somebody dropped it too hard and it cracked." Another stone, about five feet high, was as gracefully balanced as a statue and seemed poised to leap; the outline of lichen on its face suggested a warrior in armor. Nearby lay a perfect staircase in stone.

Much of this artistry in granite throughout the Sierra Nevada is due to the glaciers that flowed over these peaks and down these canyons. Before the Ice Age the Sierra Nevada was a land of rolling hills and broad valleys. Then a slow upheaval tilted a four-hundred-mile block to the west and turned its sluggish rivers into torrents rushing seaward. The rivers began to carve out the canyons; Yosemite itself was V-shaped at first. Then came the Ice Age, and accumulated glaciers began their carving and polishing, carrying along their abrasive baggage of grinding stones as they flowed, eating away the walls, and smoothing the valleys into U-shapes, and helping to round off the peaks into onion-shaped domes. Moraines such as the one along which we rode on our way to Clouds Rest are deposits of rock left stranded by the death of a glacier. Such glaciers moved from a few inches to several feet a day, tongue-shaped masses of ice that grew over the centuries to depths of thousands of feet. In the Sierra Nevada the glaciers advanced and receded three times and then the Ice Age was ended, leaving these mountains very much as they are today.

John Muir was the first to understand how the glaciers had shaped Yosemite Valley. He was in his early thirties, almost unknown, when he began to argue his glacial theory. Yosemite was newly discovered and a source of intense curiosity across America and Europe. Muir was derided by a respected Harvard scientist, Josiah Dwight Whitney, who had been appointed California state geologist. Whitney insisted that glaciers had taken no role in shaping Yosemite, but that the valley floor had dropped in some prehistoric cataclysm. "The bottom," Muir replied, "never fell out of anything God made." Journalists of the era fanned the flames of dispute. Whitney was soon scoffing at Muir as "a mere sheep-herder," "that shepherd," and "an ignoramus." Whitney was among the finest geologists of the nation; Muir was shy and lacking in technical training. In 1870 Muir began three summers of exhausting research in Yosemite, following watercourses back through rugged canyons to their sources, seeking the scratches and glacial boulders and the strange glacial scoops known as cirques. By 1873 he had piled up incontrovertible evidence of the glacial origins of Yosemite Valley. He published his findings in a series of "Sierra Studies." Slowly, geologists came over to Muir's side. By 1901, a U.S. Geological Survey referred to Yosemite as "quite an ordinary product of glacial erosion." Muir was vindicated before his death in 1914; the mountain man had prevailed over the scientists in their own field.

For Jill and me, the trail up to Clouds Rest led along the sheer edge of the glacial moraine called Tenaya Cascade and I felt I might be safer if I walked.

"Stay on Bessie," Lloyd ordered. "I don't know about you, but she'll never step off."

I had forgotten the surging excitement of the final climb to a mountaintop. Atop Clouds Rest, breathing hard, standing wide-legged against the wind, we saw nothing below us for a mile. All around in every direction was Yosemite and the High Sierra. Antlike, a car reflected the sun from a valley road more than six thousand feet below. To our east were the glacial peaks of the highest country, just before the inland flank of the Sierra Nevada drops off to the desert.

We rode hard until almost dusk to get back to our camp. Loving these mountains does not make their physical challenges any less grueling for the visitor. But any moment of satisfaction with one's stamina is likely to be lessened by the example of some hiker who overcomes any challenge. As I struggled to stay awake through dinner, a slight woman and her three young sons told of their hike that day. They had left camp at daybreak, outdistanced us on foot, and made the steep final ascent by cable-hold to the top of Half Dome.

The next day was Sunday and I awoke with the sun. At a breakfast of coffee and doughnuts just made in the camp kitchen, we heard that one of the best-liked ministers ever to serve the tiny Yosemite parish—and its charming century-old chapel in the valley—had requested another pastorate despite his deep love for the region.

"He couldn't take any more of it," an old Yosemite guide said. "Rangers and the rest of the valley residents kept telling him they'd come to church more often except they felt closer to God in the great outdoors. Up here, it's tricky to argue that point."

A bear had prowled the area during the night. The camp was at capacity; the two college boys who served meals were sleeping on cots in the pantry. The bear, which during breakfast seemed to grow as high as the pantry door in the retelling, had awakened them as it prowled for food; the boys had slammed the door closed and gone back to sleep. After breakfast we walked out on a granite ledge to see a bronze marker honoring Mary Curry Tresidder, whose parents brought her into Yosemite in the 1890's as a child, when they launched the company that was predecessor to the current park lessees. As a young woman she packed alone into this high country for an entire summer. Sunrise Camp is dedicated to her; it was a favorite campsite for her and her late husband. With me as we rode I carried a thirteen-page typed list of flowers she had identified along these same trails.

Past the plaque, the long grassy meadow drew me irresistibly. It was the front lawn to a farther mountain range. I walked out on its cushion and in minutes the camp was out of sight. I sat on a boulder, feeling small and at peace. A small gray figure—rakish and dapper—faced me from a hole in the ground less than five feet away. The head was motionless. A dozen other gray heads popped up from other burrows and stared. I was soon surrounded. It was my first visit with the picket pin, the ground squirrel of the high meadows, named for his stolid, fence-like stance. I held still for five or six minutes, but it was not good enough. I was not part of the Sierra landscape. One picket pin jerked his head down out of view. Then they all were gone. In a moment, the meadow and I were alone again. Jill and Lloyd, already saddled up on their mules, found me and we were off along the trail to Merced Lake. During ten miles of riding we dropped from 9400 to 7150 feet. I found myself resenting this partial descent, although it was to be temporary. Below eight thousand feet I began to feel out of the high country. Mosquitos and swarms of gnats—absent at the higher levels—began to appear, and a poisonous diamondback rattled insistently beside the trail. Lloyd killed it with a rock and snipped off an eleven-rattle tail. It jangled ominously in Jill's pocket for the rest of the day.

We followed Echo Creek down to its junction with the granite chasm through which the Merced River descends to its dramatic and familiar leaps at Nevada and Vernal falls, within easy walking distance of the Yosemite Valley floor. But we met the river at a point about thirteen miles up from the valley, where it forms a blue oval lake in a stone nest surrounded by lodgepole and Jeffrey pine and aspen. Merced Lake Camp, oldest of the high camps in Yosemite, is a pine-shaded quadrangle of sleeping tents with a larger tent for meals. We found five couples there who visit this camp each summer and fear that their paradise will be overrun. They entreated me to report, if I had anything to write, that the fishing is bad, the mosquitos vicious and the food uninspired.

After dinner Jill and I walked upstream beside the river and paused outside a log house where smoke curled from a chimney. A sparsely built young ranger in uniform appeared at the door, obviously startled to see us, but quick to invite us inside. He was the district man for the National Park Service, whose patrol includes much of this high country. Inside, in the one main room used for living, eating and sleeping—to minimize the time needed for splitting firewood—his wife was clearing their dinner. The life he described in talking of his work seemed not without kinship to the life Muir led in Yosemite a century earlier. His hospitality was warm and genuine; here in the high forests, where people are scarce, the relative rareness of contact with another human being adds value to the experience. There is a lesson here, but it is one of despair, for human scarcity is a disappearing phenomenon.

Next morning I placed a long-distance call over the camp telephone—a crank device labeled Merced Lake 2. Nothing violates the wilderness along these trails except the single strand of telephone wire, lashed to pine and fir and hemlock, which provides each camp with communications. The system is as casual as it appears. After I had hung up, I was called back by the ring of an operator at some distant switchboard. She had neglected to time the call from Merced Lake 2, and she asked me to estimate how long I had talked. In an age when automated equipment is monitoring both itself and its inventors, her challenge seemed charming. I gave a generous estimate. "You couldn't have talked that long, sir," she said. "I cut back in before that." We reached an impasse of agreeableness.

On this day's ride, Bessie gasped and sweated. Our trail rose steeply above the timberline to Vogelsang Camp at 10,300 feet. It is the highest of the Yosemite camps, sometimes blocked by snow until August. We rode to the broken, tilted crest of

Vogelsang Peak on ever-tightening switchbacks. We were above everything but tumbled granite in its mad disarray, gleaming little live glaciers and their blue lakes, scrubby alpine willows and bushy pine. Tiny flowers burst bravely from gravelly crevices that gave them life: tough-stemmed white daisies and phlox, and Lilliputian versions of the ever-present Indian paint brush. At this altitude plant life grows ever smaller and then disappears altogether.

On the shores of Fletcher Lake we found the tents of Vogelsang—a setting at once open and overpoweringly lofty. A creek rushes along beside the tents, and the flower-laden shores of the lake can be encircled on foot in several minutes. Soon there comes the soothing joy of finding that even on a mountaintop with scale so massive, there is order in minutiae; like their larger cousins, each alpine buttercup has five perfect petals. But here each was no larger than a teardrop.

At this altitude in the Sierra Nevada, above all, there is dazzling brightness. John Muir wrote of the "white beams of the morning streaming through the passes, the noonday radiance on the crystal rocks, the flush of the alpenglow, and the irised spray of countless waterfalls." Conceivably there is some subtle relationship between this visual brilliance and the popularity of Vogelsang with physicists and mathematicians. Those who seek out the highest camps seem distinguished by high intelligence and individuality, and even the meekest little ladies are likely to be naturalists or professors' wives or librarians. It is a setting that seems aloof from earth, a place for those not easily disoriented or undone, those who can stand up to nature at its most awesome and think their own thoughts.

Yet here, as almost everywhere in our world, one cannot escape the experts. A bushy white-haired man saw me poring over a Department of Interior map of Yosemite which I carried in my saddlebag. It was a 1948 edition.

"See, dear," he said loudly to his wife, "they're still using our old map."

He was a university cartographer. He took the map and began to point out several errors. They were too minute to concern me. Jill, perhaps detecting a familiar trapped look in my eyes, feigned childish impatience and insisted that I join her in an after-dinner walk beside the lake. We found several of the hardier breed of High Sierra campers settling for the night—some in sleeping bags beside campfires, others with small tents under clumps of scrub willow. A stocky city man in jeans stood tugging, shouldering and entreating a burro to follow him; finally he drove a stake on the spot and tied the burro to it. The trade-name patch on his stiff new blue jeans read Wrangler. The label was not convincing.

"I think it's good," Jill said gently, "that we have Lloyd along with us to bully our mules." She gave the impression that she liked me, but was not blind to my incompetence.

On high slopes like Vogelsang, twilight moves in with the setting of the sun but then is forced into retreat as the alpenglow envelops the peaks and swoops into the valleys with its soft roseate light. Nature, after all, is master of the psychedelic. A phenomenon known only to the highest peaks, the alpenglow is a result of the refraction of light rays from the west, caused by the cooling of the air after the land has passed into shadow. Its hues are most often among the pinks and roses; this night at Vogelsang, the spectrum exploded. For four or five minutes we stood beside the lake at the foot of a tiny glacier and the very air seemed to take on a rapidly changing sequence of color. Vogelsang was a great cathedral, and we stood bathed in the brilliance of its stained glass windows. Even the fishermen stood distracted beside the lake that night, holding their trout rods, not so much in hope of a catch as in reluctance to break off contact with nature.

On the steps behind the stone-walled kitchen, one of the two small permanent structures at Vogelsang, Jill and I met the students who staffed the camp. We sat down to help with the evening project: filling Coleman lanterns with white gas and pumping up the pressure. They had just returned from a successful flashlight search among the boulders with a tired hiker who had flung down his pack as he arrived at dark, come in for dinner, and then forgot where he had left his pack. A transistor radio played as we worked, and we heard our first news in days. I was sorry.

Stars flooded the sky recklessly as if sprayed upward from an aerosol can by a naughty child. Above the camp, the snow slopes sparkled in the light of a full moon that seemed almost too shy to compete with the stars and with the glaciers of Vogelsang.

Next day the trail led downhill. We saw familiar peaks and slopes, landmarks that rose above the base camp at Tuolumne Meadows. We had made the circle. The Sierra wilderness no longer seemed ours alone. On the trail were fresh contingents of outgoing hikers and a mule train. This one was led by a man whom Lloyd called Dirty Murphy. He seemed of a different breed from others we had seen: seedier, uncommunicative, more a caricature of Old West television wranglers. Lloyd explained that this mule train carried supplies for the Park Service rangers, and this wrangler was a federal civil service man. Unlike Lloyd and his colleagues, who work for the park concessionaire, Dirty Murphy had no contact with Yosemite visitors; he was his own man, his surliness fortified by the employment safeguards of the United States Government so long as he drove his mule train with skill. The park company wranglers do not fraternize with civil service wranglers, and civil service wranglers fraternize with no one. They are the hermits of the Sierra Nevada.

Tuolumne Meadows finally appeared around a bend in the trail. We were not ready yet to mingle with what seemed by now to be a crowd. We stopped beside the waterfall and ate the box lunch we had brought from Vogelsang. Then we rode our mules on into the corral. I tossed our packs into our car. Jill hung back, sprawling on a bale of hay to watch a wrangler's methodical attempts to saddle a wild colt. She pleaded to delay our drive down out of the mountains, and I walked alone into the edge of the forest and back along the John Muir Trail. A scholarly man, Muir had been changed forever by Yosemite. He had taken menial jobs rather than leave these mountains. "I should like to live here always," he wrote. "It is so calm and withdrawn, while open to the universe in full communion with everything good. . . . These beautiful days must enrich all my life."

Jill's goodbyes at Tuolumne, with Lloyd and Bessie and Boots, were agonizingly drawn out, and her eyes were moist when we walked toward our car. Lloyd flashed me a father's smile.

"It's the Sierra," he said. "Once they get home, they're the same as ever."

He was wrong, of course.

. 5 .

VAGRANT SOCIETY

The land was ours before we were the land's.

—ROBERT FROST

I was free for lunch during a day of appointments in Los Angeles and so I telephoned a man whom I regard as an old friend—as such relationships go within the loose pattern of social vagrancy that is found in California—although I had not seen him for more than a year. We agreed to meet at a Sunset Boulevard restaurant. It seemed the ideal place because it was no more than a twenty-minute drive for either of us and because it was a quiet place with some air of dignity; the emphasis was on the

69

quality of food and service rather than on the nudity of the waitresses or the outrageousness of decor and clientele.

Over a martini I remarked that he looked tan and fit except for his bandaged forehead.

"I'm lucky," he said. "I totaled out my Jaguar two weeks ago. Went over the center strip on the Hollywood Freeway trying to dodge a truck."

I expressed sympathy. "I hope Susan wasn't hurt," I said.

"No," he said, nibbling on his lemon twist. "She wasn't along. Susan and I are divorced."

I ordered more martinis as he sketched his difficulties with a new girl friend, and then I pressed on to what I hoped might be happier areas of conversation. "Your business is thriving still, I'm sure."

"You remember the time I called you to check out that house builder?" he said. "I called too late. I had already agreed to back him in a subdivision and we went broke. I'm still trying to settle with my creditors. It's like starting over again."

In a last desperate move I asked about an attorney who had been his closest friend. "You still see a lot of Hal?"

"No," he said. "Hal and his wife broke up too. He and Susan just got married."

The plight of my unfortunate friend suggests something pertinent to the nature of California. Its people are not widely prone to trading wives or losing fortunes in impulsive investments. But the Californian has a penchant for impermanence. Those people with whom he involves himself seem interchangeable. His social and business institutions are neither so entrenched nor so sacrosanct as in older regions of America. His approach to morality is flexible. He makes love or money or friends with a casualness that stuns more traditional Americans. He has scant interest in social class, and there is very little social stratification in California. Genealogy, to him, is a whimisical study that might be of interest to Mormons or to Daughters of the American Revolution or Sons of the Golden West. Tradition is something that he is busy establishing.

He is demonstrably different in the way he lives and sometimes even in the way he dies. He buys and sells his houses in much the same way that others buy and sell their automobiles, and then he moves on. He tends to live on the land, an affluent squatter, rather than to become a part of it. He does not sink roots easily. He drifts between communities of amiable strangers. He may be immensely affable with his neighbors, but he chooses to avoid personal entanglement; his closest friend may be twenty miles distant by freeway. He finds a sense of community with his neighbors only on the occasion of accidents, dog fights, wife beatings, fires, flash floods or earthquakes. But the Californian is as open as a Fuller Brush man. One morning my wife answered the telephone and a stranger asked if she had watched a drama on television the night before.

"Yes, I did," my wife said.

"Oh, good," the woman said. "I was watching too but I fell asleep, and none of my friends saw it. I decided I'd just dial numbers until someone could tell me how it came out."

"They got married," my wife said.

"Oh, I'm so glad," the woman said, and hung up.

That phrase from the musical *Guys and Dolls*, "a permanent floating crap game," describes many aspects of California life. This is the land of the urbane hustler, the professional nomad. He has come from somewhere else. He is not certain that he will stay. Will Rogers wrote of an imaginary group called "Old Settlers of California," whose meetings no one could attend unless he had lived in the state for two-and-one-half years. This and all the other jibes at the instant California native are apt. Yet when the Californian talks of home, he often means a place in Kansas or Illinois or New York. In the end, with startling frequency, he does return to that home. Air shipments of corpses from Los Angeles International Airport are over three thousand every year. Airlines employ full-time personnel to assist morticians and families of the deceased. While millions move to California from other areas of the nation and the world, there are many who can never bring themselves to call it home. They have insured that they will go home again in death. Their own sense of transiency is underlined by the policy of some California newspapers in printing only the obituaries of the well-known, or those who have lived in California for periods of twenty or twenty-five years.

Other regions of America have been settled by large numbers of people with related ethnic or religious backgrounds. But California has found its personality always being shaped and reshaped by new arrivals of polyglot background and origin. About seventy percent of Americans live in the state in which they were born, but in California the proportion falls to about forty percent. The California native is still an oddity worthy of comment, and those few who can trace their California heritage three or four generations back to the Gold Rush—no matter how disreputable their forefathers may have been—are likely to claim rank in a peculiar aristocracy that is incongruous and ignored by most who live in California today.

Most Californians have come from other American states and it has usually been impossible to categorize them neatly. There have, of course, been migrations from overseas. Coolies came from China to build railroads, and Japanese to farm. There are Irish and French and Italian along with the Chinese in San Francisco. Jews, many of them Russian, have sought out Los Angeles along with Japanese and Mexicans. Until recently Los Angeles had a larger Mexican population than any city of Mexico but the capital. California has the largest Oriental population of any state. Here and there are pockets of migrants from other nations. California is cosmopolitan in the ethnic sense, but even more important, it is all-American in its mixture of residents who have come from every corner of the United States. Many of the earliest Californians came from New England, New York and Pennsylvania. Others soon arrived from Ohio, Indiana and Illinois. By the time of the Civil War enough Southerners had moved to California that there was considerable agitation for the Confederate cause. Soon after the railroads were built, settlers were solicited with the lure of bargain fares—once as low as a dollar—by railroad representatives who canvassed the Midwest at the height of snowbound winters. During the Depression of the 1930's, migrant workers came from the Southwest dust bowl. An accelerated influx of Negroes has entered California during the racial upheaval of the 1960's. But with these exceptions, the number of people moving to California has been in surprising uniformity with the size of population of the states from which they come. Despite old jokes about mass attendance at Iowa state picnics in Los Angeles, or the predominance of the "Okie" in the aircraft plants, California represents a geographical cross section of America. A four-month sampling of migrants conducted by the California Department of Motor Vehicles in 1964 showed their origins as Ohio, Texas, Illinois, New York, Michigan and Pennsylvania, in that order. These six states are the top six in population, excluding California. The Californian has come from all the states, rejecting geographic regionalism and ethnic ties for a loose confederation with those having some affinity of status and aspiration.

So the mainstream Californian of today is a highly individualistic migrant. He has come alone or as part of a family unit, not with any group. Religious persecution and famine set off waves of migration in the past from Europe to the Atlantic seaboard, but the Californian is typically a loner, lured by climate, by the hope of economic advancement, and by his desire to be part of a nonrestrictive new society. There are sharp differences of character between Southern California and the San Francisco Bay area, and even stronger contrasts with the stable small towns in that northern one-third of the state above San Francisco. But there are striking common bonds among all new Californians, wherever they settle. Instead of ethnic traits, they share hallmarks like their startling mobility and restlessness, their excesses in the pursuit of leisure, their burgeoning affluence, their relative youth and slightly higher level of schooling, their social casualness and their dabbling in intellectual frontiersmanship.

Especially in Southern California, the new Californians exhibit small-town hospitality in a vaguely urban atmosphere. San Francisco is a somewhat more closed society. But even there, social clubs of every type spring up—for single people, for married couples, for divorced men or women, for widowed men or women. Making contact becomes an obsession. Many new arrivals have had no experience in a totally friendless setting, but they quickly find others who are a great deal like themselves. In many areas, well over half of the resident families have arrived in

California within the prior ten to twelve years. Some have moved west to escape neighbors and relatives who expected them to conduct themselves traditionally. Many are rebels. In a San Francisco suburb lives a successful liquor dealer; he is a former Roman Catholic priest who had been held in high esteem not many years ago in a Midwestern city. A one-time member of the Al Capone gang is a former member of the school board and a respected member of his community near Los Angeles. Suddenly unfettered and exploring new facets of their own personalities, such migrants often have an exuberant style of life. Their mood is contagious. It seeps from personal life into community institutions and business affairs. It is blitheness, unconcern. Youth senses it and exploits it, and begins to develop the theme further.

But at each generation level there is something synthetic in the relation of the Californian with his new environment. The setting intrudes more into his daily life than did the setting from which he came. But the seashores and valleys and desert and mountains of California are a capacious amusement park for him, not a part of his homeland. That attitude contributes to the outsider's feeling that California is not quite real, or that it is infantile and a little wanton, a sensual paradise where nothing weighty can be undertaken, from which serious people must eventually flee. The critic Edmund Wilson once wrote that "all visitors from the East know the strange spell of unreality which seems to make human experience on the Coast as hollow as the life of a troll-nest where everything is out in the open instead of being underground. This is partly no doubt a matter of climate: the empty sun and the incessant rains; and of landscape; the dry mountains and the vast void of Pacific space; the hypnotic rhythms of day and night that revolve with unblurred uniformity, and of the surf that seems to roll up the beach with a purposeless expressionless beat after the moody assault of the Atlantic."

The spell that Wilson describes is more incisively explained by what Carey McWilliams called the "highly imperfect cultural adaptation [of California], the general unrelatedness of things, the ever-present incongruity, and the odd sense of display." There is too little sense of the community consciousness that comes with age and its traditions. "Towns do not develop here," Sarah

Comstock wrote. "They are instantly created, synthetic communities of a strangely artificial world." Such a land encourages social vagrancy, and the vagrants who inhabit it show little inclination to change its nature. It is serving their purposes. It makes few demands on them. They are aloof to the land, and it seldom resists their presence with any outburst of blizzard or ice or heat. At the epicenter of the vagrant society, in Los Angeles, there is a bland land with benign climate, well suited to the nomadic life.

But such a life must take its toll. All is not well with the new Californians. The sociologist Carle C. Zimmerman wrote that "long-continued residence in any region or climate tends to bring about adaptations, customs and habits, violation or disruption of which brings strangeness of feeling and nostalgia." The new Californian has suffered just such a disruption in the move from his former home—the one that he may go on thinking of as his home. He says and does what he pleases, or what he presumes to please him, but he is not pleased. He is more self-oriented than he has ever been before. No one frowns at him. There are no intimate neighbors to gossip, no established reputations to be destroyed. The tolerance of the frontier still exists, but now it is a sociological frontier. Individuality and a lack of inhibition often characterize pioneer people: the Californian has those qualities, but he is uneasy about his freedom and unsure about his goals. If there are new social mores to replace those he has abandoned, he has not yet found them. His anomie becomes epidemic. It lurks unspoken behind the glossy but fragile façade of California. Yet it is measureable in many ways.

One of them is frenetic mobility. Californians travel substantially more, both in business and pleasure, than Americans of other regions. In recent years they have been buying about half again as many passports as the national average. They make up more than one-third of all the pleasure travelers in the Pacific beyond Hawaii. As domestic travelers, they are unrivaled. A survey by American Airlines showed that almost twice as many Los Angeles residents, on a per capita basis, flew between Los Angeles and New York as did New Yorkers. The idea of transcontinental commuting is less appalling to the Californian than to the New Yorker. Since the advent of jet travel, the Westerner is a familiar figure in the daily affairs of commerce and government along the Eastern seaboard. Dr. Lee DuBridge, science advisor to President Nixon, said: "It is common to see professors traveling back and forth to meetings in the East five, seven, ten or fifteen times a year. I see these same faces on the jets. Yet the Eastern educator who comes to California once a year thinks he has done a tremendous thing. Now it is the Easterner who needs to be educated. The Easterner has not learned that you can cross the country in four or five hours. He is the provincial one now!" Yet even in California, eyes are raised at the case of Edgar Paul Boyko, a lawyer with a family and a private law practice in Los Angeles, who periodically made the twenty-five-hundred mile commute to offices in Alaska where he served as that state's attorney general.

Another kind of mobility is the constant movement of the Californian from residence to residence. On a national average, one in five families changes its residence each year. In northern California the ratio is one in three. In Southern California, it is a startling one-in-two, meaning that every second family moves its residence, on the average, every year. A recent survey of San Bernardino County in Southern California, the largest county in the nation and one with a heavy military and aerospace factory population, showed that on an average every family moved every year. An Air Force officer who had moved his family twelve times in thirty-two months spoke with unconscious eloquence of social vagrancy: "It doesn't seem to matter much. We go from one tract house to another and they're all about the same. You get used to the next one after a week or so. There's always a good new school not too far away, and a shopping center where my wife can pick up the same kind of specials."

Somewhat more than half a million Californians, taking a more direct approach to their restless urges, live in mobile homes. They are spacious and expandable, costing up to $30,000. While they are seldom moved from one site to another, there is a considerable floating population who sell one mobile home and move to a different location. One in every five mobile home parks in

America can be found in California. They develop their own recreational facilities and in some ways provide more sense of community for their residents than is found in conventional residential areas.

The yellow pages of California telephone directories provide some hints to the eccentricities of the region. Not uncommonly there are as many pages for moving and storage firms as for physicians. Real estate agents and building contractors rank close behind. Far out in front, with no runner-up in sight, is the classification AUTOMOBILES. The number of additions, changes and deletions made each month in the telephone directories of California are far above the average for cities of equivalent size. Stops and starts of residential service by utilities companies and newspapers are more frequent than anywhere else in America.

Some entire cities are so new that real estate brochures and street signs commonly carry misspellings. Communities are built so rapidly that new schools become overcrowded before they are completed and classes spill over into nearby tract houses that are converted into two- or three-bedroom schoolhouses. Somehow no one ever seems quite settled, and construction sometimes has the make-shift quality of the mining camp. (One of the oldest Chinese restaurateurs in San Diego, who had occupied the same site for 21 years and had complained to the municipal water department for just as long about his excessive water bills, called a plumber one night to fix a water leak. As he left, the plumber said: "I guess you know the hotel upstairs is on your water meter.")

But such traits are surface symptoms of the California anomie. The more significant patterns are found in high rates of divorce, suicide, homosexuality, illegitimacy, drug addiction and crime, and the relatively low rate of church affiliation. Los Angeles is unrivaled as the bank robbery capital of the world; in 1967, fourteen percent of the nation's 1730 robberies of banks and savings and loan institutions took place in Los Angeles. The city ranks at the top of almost every listing in the frequency of bankruptcy, forgery and bad checks. Credit checking is difficult because of extreme mobility. A San Diego department store with seventy thousand revolving charge accounts must make three thousand address changes each month; half of its customers move each year. The high volume of tourists and military personnel adds to credit complexities. The sense of social responsibility is underdeveloped. In 1967 a private study group at San Carlos, expressing concern over moral listlessness in the California society, asked the San Diego police department to send a representative to its next meeting to speak on public apathy. Later the chairman telephoned the police department to say that the meeting had been canceled due to lack of interest. For the same reason, charity drives are relatively difficult to mount and to pursue in the newer California cities. Attitudes toward racial minorities and discrimination may carry the usual ugly tinge of irresponsibility, but there is also a unique sense of irrelevance. How can the citizenry of Whittier be persuaded to assume some constructive sense of guilt in the plight of their Negro neighbors in Watts when there is a general impression that almost everyone in both communities is newly arrived in the Los Angeles area?

"California," wrote Eugene Burdick, "has had to make a merit of the novel, the unique, the *sui generis,* the new, the rejected, the unarticulated, the emerging, the unformed, the rebellious . . . It is not easy. A pluralism imposed too quickly makes for subterranean tensions." With alarming frequency, those tensions become overt. San Francisco, which as a city seems more stable than the sunshine communities of the southern part of the state, erupts regularly with the highest rates among those cities of alcoholism, divorce and suicide. In rate of suicide, California is about one-and-a-half times the national average, and three of its metropolitan areas rank consistently within the top five U.S. cities of more than half a million population: Los Angeles-Long Beach, San Francisco-Oakland, and Sacramento. Alcoholism statistics are vaguer, but San Franciscans buy liquor at a faster rate than the people of any other U.S. city except Washington. Divorce is a staggering burden. Marriage has one chance in four of ending in divorce on a nationwide basis; in California, one in two marriages ends in divorce. In Los Angeles County there are about nine divorces for every eleven marriages; Los Angeles divorces each year affect close to fifty thousand dependent children. "Divorce," says the San Francisco novelist Herbert Gold, "is the last frontier. The only adventures left are marriage, adultery and divorce."

The social environment is more tolerant, and so some who might otherwise avoid divorce are encouraged to go through with it. Yet all California divorces cannot be blamed on such attitudes. There are many whose marriages are tottering when they migrate to California. They find that a change of scene does not help. A failing marriage can no longer be blamed on meddling relatives or small-town gossip. There is nowhere farther to go to escape each other, so the marital tie is abandoned in the divorce mills of the Golden State. More than half of those divorced in Los Angeles have been married outside California.

Divorce is so common that it is treated with casualness and good humor. In Mission Beach, two women who had been divorced from the same man found enough in common to take an apartment together. One girl, divorced and remarried, with a supply of engraved note cards from her first marriage, blocked out her old name and had a printer add the line, "*Under New Management.*" Tradition rules that the woman becomes the plaintiff, and the waiting rooms of divorce lawyers, filled with women of all ages, have a carnival atmosphere. Secretaries circulate among the clients handing out printed information sheets answering basic questions about divorce, lists of instructions, and check-off forms on which, with the flick of a pencil, the women can indicate which of a hundred transgressions their husbands have committed against their marriage vows. There is something for everyone, and on the pre-printed divorce forms later filed with the courts, it is all usually called mental cruelty.

Judges mete out decrees with only occasional efforts to impede the whir of disengagement. When his wife's attorney complained that she couldn't produce a witness to testify in court to his outbursts of anger, a suave San Francisco husband persuaded his new girlfriend to take the stand against him. At San Diego, an attorney represented a woman and her daughter who appeared together before the same judge, each seeking a divorce. First the mother testified to her son-in-law's drinking habits, and then the daughter told of her stepfather's aloofness. The actions were uncontested and the decrees were promptly granted, with mother and daughter leaving the court arm in arm.

Husbands display their bravado in the face of divorce by mailing premium stamps along with alimony checks, or delivering boxes of candy by private detectives who have been employed to trail them. Most are quick to remarry. At a Los Angeles wedding chapel, an organist reported that the song most frequently requested was "The Second Time Around." Some couples seem much better friends after they agree to divorce. A beaming couple entered law offices in San Jose and set a huge piggy bank on a lawyer's desk. To finance their divorce, they had pooled their savings for a year. The San Diego attorney John T. Holt had the pleasant duty of informing a husband and wife that the divorce they sought would be unnecessary because a search of records had revealed their marriage to have been technically unbinding. That did it; on the next day, instead of divorcing, they married.

Reconciliation efforts by the courts are seldom enough to stem the tide. In Sacramento, a wife told a judge that her trouble had begun soon after her honeymoon when her husband had insisted that she transfer all her property to them as a couple. "That's not an uncommon procedure," the judge observed. "But, Your Honor," the wife protested, "I barely knew the man!" San Diego judges established a counseling system in an attempt to reduce divorces, but the court-appointed marriage counselor was soon divorced and gave up his post. In Los Angeles another marriage counselor began to lose his clientele when newspapers reported that he had separated from his wife and five children.

Not all counselors are so ill-fated. One of the most authoritative is Paul Popenoe of Los Angeles, who traces the high incidence of divorce to the qualities of social vagrancy. He cites the lack of family ties, extreme mobility, high use of alcohol, the tendency of the Southern Californian to be lax in matters of credit, overemphasis on "shallow, shabby standards," and the frontier-like attraction that California holds for "the desperate and the unstable." There is a tie, too, between the high divorce rate and low church affiliation. Less than half of Californians are church members while the national level is estimated at about sixty percent.

In divorce as in much else, the gap between California and the nation begins to narrow. California permissiveness is spreading. "I think this country is at the beginning of an era of tremendous change in the social order," Dr. Melvin Brown, adviser to the San Mateo County Domestic Relations Court, said recently. "It is only happening here first." In the view of the behavioral scientist Richard Farson, the high divorce rate of California "may be a result not of wretched family life but of good family life. Husbands and wives have begun to solve basic problems of survival and have grown concerned over higher fulfillments. They have greater expectations from the relationship of marriage. If this leads them to seek new mates, it may represent a wider search for those things that mean most to the human being: love, creativity, and self-understanding." Both Farson and Brown sense that California society is in the forefront of an evolution that may in time make marriage a shorter-term, less close-knit institution. Farson talks of five-year marriages with options for renewal, and predicts shorter and shorter marriages within the existing system. Brown says, "We could become a society of temporary husbands and wives. Meaning will come not from the family relationships but from jobs, careers, creative endeavors. I see some of that here now." Mrs. Nola Stark, a longtime dean of women at UCLA, said: "I think an early divorce is often good for a girl. Even today she is often sold on the idea she will marry and live happily ever after. She expects to get married and drain the other person. It needs a jolt to get her out of it."

Women have occupied an unusual niche in California. At a premium in the mining camps of early days, they grew to have stronger legal rights than were granted elsewhere. In 1867 a visitor to California wrote that "a white woman is treated everywhere on the Pacific slopes, not as man's equal and companion, but as a strange and costly creature freed from the restraints and penalties of ordinary law." The Gold Rush brought a heavy proportion of males and led to a high divorce rate in the East and

Midwest among wives who had been left behind. Divorce came
to be looked on with favor in California and decrees were granted
casually. The plaintiffs, then as now, were most often women.
Finding themselves in demand, women of early California were
less hesitant to move on to husbands with more wealth or gentil-
ity. The legal tradition of community property, passed along from
the Spanish, pertains in California, giving the wife an equal share
in all property of the husband and wife. Coupled with alimony
grants which often penalize the male excessively, the community
property laws do much to make divorce more attractive for California women. Women may no longer be "strange" as in Gold
Rush days, but they are, in divorce as in marriage, quite often
"costly."

The uniqueness of the California woman has some origin in
early history, but it is probably more a result of contemporary
social patterns. She is at the forefront in the revolution of sexual
permissiveness. She may make her own living in many ways if
she chooses, be as aggressive as she desires, and challenge every
facet of the traditionally male-dominated society. "She is the
first really free woman in history," writes Dr. George R. Bach,
a Los Angeles psychologist, "the equal of the male in every respect." Many women have moved westward in search of sexual
freedom and they find it—bolstered by the advent of the birth
control pill—in the unfettered apartment communities for the
"swinging singles," at the all-night beach parties, or even as nude
dancers like one in San Francisco who reached some degree of
notoriety as the "topless mother of eight."

To determine if the California woman is indeed different, a
research sampling of four thousand women was made in 1967 by
the editors of the *Ladies' Home Journal*. Questionnaires went to
two thousand California readers and two thousand in other parts
of America. The results indicated some marked characteristics.
California women have more liberal attitudes toward sex and
birth control and prefer smaller families; fewer attend church;
they are more racially tolerant, more adventurous, attend more
cultural affairs, and seem to lead what they regard as "more
glamorous, more exciting" lives than other American women. Yet
more California women admitted to feelings of loneliness.

The Los Angeles woman in particular has obsessed journalists. *Esquire* characterized her as "possessing no sense of the past, no conception of history . . . possibly the first woman to be totally of her times, so plugged into the potency of the moment that nothing she says or does can be counted on to last." In a city where women make three times as many recorded suicide attempts as men, the magazine insisted, the Los Angeles woman thrives on fads and youth and is often washed up and worn out at the age of twenty-one. (It may be significant that the *Esquire* outburst was unsigned; its original author later charged that the magazine had distorted his concept by rewriting and he had declined to allow the use of his name.) Many periodicals seem to prefer to say nothing about Los Angeles unless it fits trimly into some wheezy old image like the one *Esquire* drew: a city whose contribution to the world has been "drive-in living, super-conservatism, guiltless carnality, elegant irresponsibility, Jax pants."

Soon after this appraisal, *Los Angeles Magazine* responded aptly in a less strident tone: "Like her environment, the L.A. woman is untethered by the past and uniquely free to devise new roles. Her educational opportunities are unmatched, yet her intellectual contributions are thus far unimpressive. Her mobility is unique, but so is her dissatisfaction . . . deriving from her awareness that she hasn't yet found the new birth implied in the new freedom she has."

In any case she spends a large part of every day away from her home or apartment—doing some of the usual womanly chores, but much more besides. In her quest to avoid being a satellite of her husband she pursues a new role, seeking answers in self-help group therapy sessions, health clubs, golf or tennis clubs, classroom workshops, and the consultation rooms of psychiatrists, astrologers, faddists, and even computer-run dating services. Sex is at the root of much of her flurry. The University of California Extension recently offered a lecture series on extramarital experience. It was well attended by women, but it attracted no unusual attention. Sex is snicker-free. In the city that has been the cradle of contemporary sex symbols, sexuality is divorced from prurience. In *The Day of the Locust,* Nathanael West portrayed sex in the Los Angeles orbit as so pervasive and obligatory that it became a bore. One senses much the same illusion these days in the pages of *Playboy*, where a startling proportion of nude "playmates" have been ascribed to the Los Angeles area.

Sex is, in fact, different in California. Restraints have never been present to the extent that they were in the regions of America settled between the landing of the "Mayflower" and the Gold Rush. California is a product of the past hundred or so years. Its sexual mores have been less inhibited from the start and they are being steadily liberalized. However amoral they may seem to some, Californians are fortunate in one respect; they are not burdened with alarm or guilt over the sudden collapse of sexual restraint. The existence of libido has always been acknowledged.

"From our youth to our grandfathers, there is more philandering in Southern California," writes Dr. Richmond Barbour, an official of the San Diego city school system and a columnist in the San Diego *Evening Tribune*. "There is a freer atmosphere. You sense it especially when you return from the East or Midwest. Here, there are looser clothes, looser behavior at parties, looser conversation. In some parts of the country only the *avant-garde* talk openly about sex; here, everybody does. People are freer to do things they only dreamed of doing before."

California has stood indicted over the years at every point of the moral spectrum. It has been called both a reincarnation of the Bible Belt and the world center of hedonism. Though it touches neither of these extremes, it conforms to fewer established patterns of behavior than most regions. The mood is "Why not?" In an unanchored society, the answers to such a question can be slow indeed in coming. When a "Why not?" question involving sexual liberty is asked, and there is hesitation about the answer, no one stays around to listen. "We have this wild sexual rebellion," wrote Merla Zellerbach, a San Francisco journalist who is herself a divorcée. "Everybody is popping in and out of marriage. Emotionally, we're not equipped to handle so much permissiveness." Yet with the same assiduous searching that has brought them to California, the divorced go on seeking new mates

in the conviction that marriage can be—or at least ought to be—
beautiful.

It is no wonder that the young people of California can be
found leading the way in America's changing attitudes toward
sex. They were born a long way from Plymouth Rock. California
is a tribal cemetery for antiquated social mores, and its youth
rejoice in serving as pallbearers at the interment of Puritanism.
"The atmosphere is wide open," wrote Gerald Kennedy, Methodist bishop of Los Angeles. "There is more promiscuity, and it is
taken as a matter of course now." The bishop even left an escape
clause in his general condemnation of premarital sex: "I wouldn't
stand in judgment. There would be exceptions." With their casualness toward sex, especially along the beaches of Southern
California, young people challenge the concept that sex play
must be in private; the beaches provide an all-year setting which
demands only the most minimum standards of privacy for youths
without cars. It is only because of the car-oriented society that
the beaches are not in greater demand; about one in every two
Southern California boys owns a car by the time of his high
school graduation. The Californian cannot legally buy liquor until he is twenty-one; but he drives at sixteen.

In high schools a marriage fad often gains momentum in the
spring. Sociologists have guessed that one in six American marriages is the hasty result of pregnancy. At the high-school level
in California cities, the proportion is surely greater. One Los
Angeles principal speculates that three in four marriages among
students stem from pregnancy or the fear of it. School counselors
call in parents of girls as early as the sixth grade to discuss their
sexual precocity. Separate schools are provided for pregnant girls
and those who have already had children. A Pasadena mother
increased her daughter's allowance at the age of sixteen to allow
purchase of birth control pills, and at a San Francisco high
school, a coed chose birth control as the subject of her term
paper. A week after turning it in, she dropped out of school,
pregnant.

"Little marriages"—involving sex relations between unmarried steady daters—are common in California. "I've had sex lots of times," says the heroine of a musical written and produced by the UCLA Musical Comedy Workshop, "but I don't mix love and sex at the same time." Another UCLA coed related: "I had a date the other night and we were sitting in a bar and this boy suggested we have some P.M.S. I thought it must be some fancy drink. It turned out he was talking about premarital sex." A more extreme development is promiscuity, the end result for a number of unrestricted teenagers. A Los Angeles newspaper noted that one sixteen-year-old boy was infected by a prostitute and in turn infected a fifteen-year-old girl. In two nights, she had intercourse with nineteen youths and infected nine of them. The reaction of many parental readers was to express surprise that a sixteen-year-old boy had resorted to a prostitute. The nadir of the youth scene can be found in the perversions of such renegade gangs as the Hell's Angels. The extent of their sexual deviations is marked by their insignia: variations of swastikas, wings and military patches bearing squadron or unit numbers.

Sexual freedom is not an easy burden for California youth. Teenage suicide often associated with drug abuse is increasing; already it is one-third higher than the overall suicide rate. There is no uglier pattern of social vagrancy than that which involves the unwanted child. With a rate of illegitimacy rising more rapidly than the national average, the people of California adopt more children than those of any other state, and still face the largest backlog of children seeking homes. Social workers find an increasing number of children are placed for adoption by young married couples who complain that an unplanned and unwanted child will interfere with their education or their leisure, and that they do not yet feel prepared for parenthood.

In the big new housing tracts of California, these young people are growing up apart from relatives or old family friends, often seeing their own parents only in brief interludes of going or coming. The world comes in to them by television, and in its moments of realism the screen provides a frightening glimpse of a life for which they sense they are not prepared. They take their doubts to their peers and together strive to arrive at acceptable patterns of behavior. They are improvising, often with total rejection of their parents. With the advent of The Pill, many of them have concluded—not without some logic—that their sexual instincts make up one of the less troublesome, more easily controlled facets of their young lives. Instead of guiding, many parents find themselves marveling over their teenagers' casual, uninhibited approach toward sex. It is often the parents who have wrestled with inherited Victorian restraints and lost, and are immersed in sexual diversions of their own with more doubt and guilt than their children can ever know. Many of the young have never been told what not to do, and now they have struck out to make their own code in the accommodating California society. In any case they do not follow the patterns set down by the generations that have preceded them. They are plotting their own world.

Parents watch their offspring violate sacred mainstays of their old codes; quite often, nothing tragic ensues. Intimidated by the cool intelligence of their children and their often superior educational achievement, parents resign their role and entrust the future to the fates of the new frontier. The rising roar of protest from the new generation against restriction of any kind provides the most eloquent testimony that unprecedented freedoms have been assumed by the California young. They, in the end, will provide the ultimate test of this vagrant society.

. 6 .

DESERT AND RIVER

The Colorado is an outlaw. It belongs only to the
ancient, eternal earth.

—FRANK WATERS

Most of the twelve million people of Southern California
live in a narrow coastal strip two hundred miles long. Despite
their affinity for mobility, they are held in a vise of two hostile
natural forces: the Pacific, at one side, and the desert at the
other. If you go inland thirty miles from the sea you have left
most of the people behind you. Ahead of you rise coastal
mountains that block the moisture-laden ocean winds and so
create the parched infinity beyond. Nine-tenths of the land area

of Southern California is mountain and desert, but it is the home of only one in twenty of its people.

"Desert is a loose term to indicate land that supports no man," Mary Austin wrote almost seventy years ago. "Whether the land can be bitted and broken to that purpose is not proven." Even as she wrote, men labored below sea level in one of the lowest cauldrons of the desert to harness the unruly torrent of the Colorado River. The continuing struggle to adapt the desert to man's use is a contemporary saga that is hardly less violent or desperate than that of the first California settlers two centuries ago. With massive ingenuity, man begins to tame the desert here and there.

The paradoxes of the Southern California desert are unending. But none is more bizarre than that this desert is the major source of water by which the megalopolis of the coast survives. When you have crossed the desert more than two hundred miles from the sea, to the point where California becomes Arizona, you stand beside one of the strangest of the world's rivers, the Colorado. Here in the searing desert it is no tree-lined stream with grassy banks. It rushes in a torrent through gaunt rock canyons or it grows deep and quiet behind some impediment to its flow where man has sought to make the river a tool of the Californian prosperity. Because of this river, desert valleys have become fertile farmland and windblown outposts have grown into cities. It supplies more than one-half of the water used in Southern California, and a major share of the electric power. Now its lakes are busy aquatic playgrounds, setting off the weekend spectacle of a procession of boats being hauled by trailer along desert highways.

In no sense is the Colorado an ordinary river. Starting as a small but spirited stream in the Rocky Mountains of Colorado, it cuts a jagged channel across the thirsty southwestern United States for fifteen hundred miles. Draining an unpopulous, wilderness basin of a quarter of a million square miles, the Colorado is one of America's three major water systems. It is the only river in the Southwest whose year-round flow makes it worthy to be called a river. Dammed, diverted and depleted by the demands of seven states, it flows finally into Mexico and its meandering delta at the head of the Gulf of California. Even in death it is an angry river; its collision with the waters of the gulf has in the past generated sudden walls of water that rose fifteen feet and higher, setting off lesser waves that swept rhythmically up the river for more than thirty miles. Such tidal bores have been matched only by the Hangchou Bore on the Tsientang River in China and that which occurs where the Tigris and Euphrates unite to flow into the Gulf of Persia.

From headwaters to delta, the Colorado flows at the foot of rock cliffs for nine-tenths of its route, including that renowned course it has slashed, the Grand Canyon. Its course was first traversed by man in 1869 when John Wesley Powell, a one-armed veteran of the Battle of Shiloh, set out from Green River, Wyoming, to conduct the last major exploration of unknown lands within the continental United States. Some of the river walls rise 4500 feet—so high that snow falling past them never reaches water level. Along its way the bed of the Colorado drops from a height of more than two-and-a-half miles to 248 feet below sea level. Its force as it reaches the desert is so strong that only the Tigris is a greater carrier of silt; each year the Colorado sends downstream enough soil to refill the Panama Canal. "Too thick to drink and too thin to plow," river buffs used to say of its flow. Those who swam in it, some said, dried off with a whisk broom. It was Mark Twain who said he had fallen into a California river and come out "all dusty." But now dams and desilting basins turn much of the river along the Southern California border into a blue lake.

The flood cycle of the Colorado is extreme. For years, the Imperial Valley of Southern California, a desert reclaimed with the waters of the Colorado, lay vulnerable to the whim of the river. It was threatened with inundation in summer months as the snow pack of upstream mountains melted and drained into the river. In fall, as the river slowed to a trickle, Imperial Valley faced drought. That has been changed now, but not until the Colorado totally deserted its bed and ran amuck for months in the Southern California desert. In those months, this desert and its errant river became irrevocably involved, each with the other. Yet even now they are uneasy companions.

The Colorado has already escaped one of man's tallest river traps, Hoover Dam, when its course turns south beside the Mojave Desert and California. Here it is a threading oasis in an austere, windblown landscape of sand and rock. The desert is pervasive and overwhelming; its vastness reduces the river to a shimmering sliver, incongruous and seemingly tenuous.

In this part of California man is no more than a tenacious intruder. The desert draws some men almost irresistibly by its challenging brutality, but when man is gone, the desert blithely erases his mark. Like the sea, but with more diversity, the desert bespeaks the mystic strength of unseen power. It has persistently been the setting for colonies of cultists, usually short-lived, and it is a favorite location for the sighting of unidentified flying objects. Rock-hounds and those who collect bottles or bits of glass poke about the desert, often reveling in their aloneness. To many others, the unlimited horizon suggests a sense of being free. As a desert road leads across the shimmering sand floor of a dry lake and up the sweep of an alluvial fan—with the route visible forty miles ahead and no habitation in sight—man is forced closer to nature. Even the tricks of the road warn him that he is in alien land. The most frequent mirage is a distortion of distances; the service station on the next rise may be twenty minutes away at high speed. In a seemingly flat desert, angles go awry: the whole horizon may be uptilted, and the driver trusts only the feel of his gas pedal to know if he is on a twenty-mile climb or a ten-mile straightaway descent.

It is a land of unending harshness, pushed up from chaos, its flatlands baked and its mountains gnarled and wrinkled. Across empty horizons there may seem no sign of life, and yet here live two birds in the shadow of a cactus, over there a painted lizard slips out of a crevice, and in the air a pair of buzzards swoop over some dying rodent. It is a society of fauna cunningly adapted to intense heat and cold, raw winds, and a parched land sometimes besieged by flash floods. I stood once on a crag in the high Mojave as the sky was slashed by lightning. Rain clouds moved overhead, but the electric dryness of the air milked them of their burden and no moisture reached the thirsty ground. Off in the distance, instead, wind devils sucked swirling sand up into the sky.

One's first desert sandstorm is unforgettable. The brownish monotone of the landscape grows gray and smoky and visibility is suddenly retracted. Even along the freeways, cars and trucks come as one to a halt. The desert floor, borne aloft by wind, strikes with a stunning savagery, sandblasting all in its path, blinding the eyes and filling the ears with the sound of grinding on each wave of its assault. In its wake the concrete of the roadway is rippled with waves of sand. Automobile insurance companies note the dates of such windstorms and await the filing of claims. Windshields and windows are pitted beyond repair, and enamel may be swept clean from the body of a car. As the air clears and the winds move on, the motorist in the shelter of his car looks with renewed respect on the occasional roadside service station or shack where man, like a burrowing rodent or the vulture, has learned to survive the desert.

To the untrained eye, the flora of the desert seem all sagebrush or cactus. Yet their variety is immense. In the upper Mojave the creosote bush is dominant—an odorous evergreen with wandlike, shining foliage that Indians have learned to tap for glue. Flood plains of the Mojave River, which is an underground stream except in time of rain, are marked by cottonwood groves and thickets of mesquite. The shaggy yucca, bristling with spikes, puts forth waxy white blooms. The Joshua tree is contorted into forms that suggest human anguish. The tall, haughty ocotillo bursts with crimson blooms in spring, sometimes with mutations in white or yellow. Generous spring rains may bring the barest desert floor alive with a carpet of California poppies, purple lupines, white primroses, pink verbena, and dwarfish cactus flowers of a hundred hues. By summer they have receded into the sand and left the desert drab again.

This desert is the backside of Southern California. It is divided into areas which both geographers and residents refer to as the high desert and low desert. The Mojave is the northern, and higher desert. The lower, even hotter desert is named Colorado for the river that flows beside it into Mexico. The Mojave lies north and east of Los Angeles; at its northern edge, opposite Monterey Bay on the coast, is Death Valley.

Even the snowy Sierra Nevada falters and dies out as its southern flank approaches the molten wasteland of Death Valley. Here is a 150-mile-long cleft walled in by bare rock mountains of savage colors named Panamint and Grapevine, Amargosa and Funeral. The smooth white salt floor of the valley is broken by patches of gray clay and yellow sand. In the area called the Devil's Golf Course, crystallized salt beds are covered with jagged, yard-high pinnacles and ridges to form a terrain more suited to nightmares. Yet Death Valley, which was established as a national monument in 1933, can be an absorbing place to visit in the temperate winter months.

Hardly twenty miles wide, the valley has served often as a human trap. It took its name following the winter of 1849–50, when a wagon train of immigrants pulled out of Salt Lake City along the Old Spanish Trail in September on their way to San Bernardino, near Los Angeles. Part of the group, seeking a short cut, saw the snow-clad Panamints and mistook them for the Sierra Nevada. They left the main party and found themselves struggling for their lives in Death Valley. Lacking water for their horses, they burned their wagons, slaughtered their cattle and walked out. Another part of the wagon train, carrying women and children as well as men, spent most of the winter in Death Valley while two leaders hiked on to Los Angeles and returned with help. In all, about ten persons died of heat and dehydration.

Early Shoshonean Indians called the valley Tomesha—"ground on fire." In summer months Death Valley temperatures soar so high that one's intake of fluid must be measured in gallons to offset loss of body fluids. About one-sixth of the 2981 square miles within Death Valley lie below sea level. In salt flats near Badwater is the lowest spot in the United States: 282 feet below sea level. If clouds do not intervene, and they rarely do, one looks from here across 85 miles to the peak of Mount Whitney, which at 14,495 feet is the highest point in the conterminous United States.

Southwest of Death Valley lies the heart of the Mojave Desert, a land covered by the sea at least twice in centuries long past. As its mountains rose and the sea retreated, the Mojave became the vast quadrangular bleakness of today, an area of more than 25,000 square miles—larger than Rhode Island, Massachusetts, Connecticut, and New Jersey combined. It reaches eastward from the Tehachapi Mountains and the Sierra Nevada to the Colorado River. Its short and rugged mountain ranges rise with random irregularity from high plains that are largely the result of ancient volcanic action. Between these ranges are close to fifty basin-shaped plains about three thousand feet high, some of them ancient dry lakes. Such lakes shelter the residue of old dead seas: salt, soda, gypsum and borax—a mineral, prized as a cleaning agent, which was formed when hot lava streams flowed into the saline lakes.

The history of man in the Mojave is sparse. Northeast of Barstow in 1968, Dr. Louis S. B. Leakey and other scientists found crude stone tools that they believed were made by human hands in the Mojave Desert more than forty thousand years ago. Other anthropologists believe that man's existence on this desert is relatively recent. The last of its lakes were drying up about the time that Columbus reached America. When the Spanish arrived in the Mojave almost three centuries later, it was settled spottily by Indians. Yet it was even then so empty that scant contest was waged over it between Indian and white. The discovery of gold and silver brought some development in the 1880's and 1890's, notably the open-pit Yellow Aster mine which yielded several million dollars in gold. The Rand silver mine at Red Mountain has been California's major silver producer, operating until after World War II. Railroads had come to the Mojave by the 1880's and villages sprang up along their route, but their growth was limited and some have disappeared. Without water the desert is simply unhabitable. Even today, along the Santa Fe Railroad east of the junction town of Barstow, water comes in by barrel and tank for the use of the railroad, for mines, and even for entire villages where wells cannot tap any underground supply.

Borax has been important in the Mojave from its discovery at Death Valley in 1881 until now. The twenty-mule teams which hauled borax ore were much more than legend; they were a unique means of transport formidable enough to cope with the natural hardships of the region. They were designed for the run from Death Valley through Wingate Pass to the nearest railhead at the village of Mojave, 165 miles distant. The round trip took twenty days, and those who drove the wagons faced disaster in the desert if animals or wagons broke down, or if the water tanks they pulled were cracked or looted. Harnessed together into hundred-foot-long spans, the teams of mules drew a water tank and two wagons, each holding eleven tons of borax ore. The wagons were immense, with rear wheels seven feet high and front wheels five feet high. Their steel tires were eight inches wide and an inch thick. Axle trees were made of fixed steel bars more than three inches thick, so that turning was always a process of skidding the wagons. Their route out of the valley led through the horrors of the Devil's Golf Course; Chinese laborers spent months using sledge hammers to flatten the yard-high salt extrusions into a wagon road for a distance of eight miles. It was impossible to mine borax in the heat between May and October. Yet borax was mined in Death Valley until 1927. Mining continues today at the settlement of Boron in the Mojave's Antelope Valley. The demand for boron additives in fuel has accelerated demand for the mineral. At Boron there is an open-pit mine more than two thousand feet wide, already so deep that a thirty-story building could be lowered out of sight. Ore comes out now by conveyor belt and rail into a twenty-million-dollar processing plant nearby, which looms like a mirage over the level desert floor. Miners and their families live in a company town called Desert Lake.

Elsewhere the Mojave yields minerals for the production of cement, which is shipped across the mountains to the west for use in the unending construction boom of the coast. Iron ore is mined at Fontana and tungsten at Atolia. Gypsum for plasterboard is harvested from the desert, and so are salts for table and industrial use. Here and there, where water lies underground, desert subdivisions and resorts spring up. Some proclaim the Mojave as an area into which Los Angeles will spill over. Yet it seems doubtful, even with abundant water and air conditioning, that this desert ever will have the residential appeal of the coastal strip.

Sometimes the Mojave has lured the eccentric to seek out homes. During the years of 1922 to 1924, one John Shea built a castle in Antelope Valley. His workmen tried to follow the lines of a Dublin castle from a magazine photograph that Shea provided. Once finished, the castle was furnished with a pipe organ and European antiques. But in the stock market crash of 1929 Shea lost his fortune and his castle and committed suicide, jumping to his death from an ocean pier at Santa Monica with the ashes of his wife in a chamois bag tied around his neck. Eventually the castle was bought by Thomas Lee, a Los Angeles sportsman, who designed a race course nearby and rebuilt the garage to shelter his racing cars. But Lee also committed suicide. Today Shea's Castle stands behind an eight-mile fence, empty and deteriorating under the desert sun, on its way to the extinction that the Mojave has dealt to many other of man's slight efforts.

Now the desert assumes new roles. In the midst of the Mojave, sixty-five miles from the nearest grocery store, stands little Baker, one of the desert villages that exist only to serve the passing motorist. It is on the main car route between Los Angeles and Las Vegas, a parched huddle of seventeen gas stations from which tow trucks may roam as far as a hundred miles to the aid of stranded motorists. Among the three hundred residents of Baker are many out-of-state transients who work in the gas stations, motels and cafes only long enough to pay off their own auto repair bills. Flat-broke gamblers on their way home from Las Vegas swap televisions, radios, jewelry and guns for gas. Ken George, a gas station operator in Baker, has said that "everybody in town at one time or another has been offered to share a wife in trade for gas or repairs."

Northeast of Baker is the two-million-dollar Turquoise microwave station, a link in transcontinental radio and television communications. A NASA tracking base operates now in Goldstone, a remote desert valley where gold mining went on for several years after a vein was discovered in 1916. A huge saucer-shaped radio antenna revolves in the sky above the relics of miners' shacks. To the south and east is Lake Havasu City, a real estate promoters' town of four thousand persons where the London Bridge, shipped from the Thames and reassembled, spans a finger of the Colorado River. Far to the west, the vast tunnels and aqueducts of the three-billion-dollar California Water Project bore under the Tehachapi Mountains and across the Mojave. A nuclear power station is to be built near the pumps to expedite the southward flow of water from northern California's Feather River. But of greatest significance in the modern Mojave is the military. Each service maintains at least one major establishment to exploit its space and its climate. Almost one-sixth of the Mojave is military land. Weekend jeep riders must beware of bombing ranges and more sophisticated explosives, as well as avoiding the rockets and jets of space-oriented test stations.

The reasons for the existence of Edwards Air Force Base, the nation's second largest, are inherent in the Mojave, which offers at least 350 clear flying days each year, an endless number of satisfactory emergency landing sites, and an unpopulous area in which the distress caused by sonic booms and crashes is at least limited largely to those who are professionally involved. From Edwards' three-mile-long concrete runway and out over Rogers Dry Lake, which is an almost equally smooth landing area, have climbed some of the fastest aircraft known to man, including the X-15 rocket ship. It was from Rogers Dry Lake in the fall of 1942, under wartime secrecy, that America's first jet aircraft, the XP-59A, took to the skies. Even in the grandiose scale of the desert, Edwards looks big. A single hangar occupies four-and-a-half acres and accommodates a dozen of the largest aircraft so far developed. There is a working population at Edwards of about ten thousand people, half of them civilian and half military. It is the heaviest concentration of population on the Mojave.

I took off from Edwards Air Force Base on one painfully bright spring day in the back seat of a TF-106 interceptor. The afterburner pushed our speed past that of sound and on past Mach 2, twice the speed of sound, somewhere around thirteen hundred miles an hour. The desert flattened into an unbroken tan carpet. Even the railroad junction town of Barstow looked, from forty thousand feet, like a spill of ashes on the desert rug, and its trains like burned-out paper matches. Westward over the San

Gabriel Mountains, Los Angeles seemed to nestle intimately beside the sea; it was an illusion I have never been able to recapture. To the east the desert spread bleakly to where the Colorado River ran along the horizon. South toward Mexico, the Mojave dropped off into the lower Colorado Desert. The resort city of Palm Springs was a sparkling speck crowded in at the foot of the sheer San Jacinto cliffs. Beyond like a mirage was a tiny oval, the forty-mile-long Salton Sea, a freak of nature that was formed when the Colorado River broke out of its bed in 1905; there is no odder testimony to the efforts of the Californian to water his desert.

The drop from the high Mojave to the low Colorado Desert is almost imperceptible to one who sees the desert only as sand and rock and sun. But it is a subtly different land. Nature's portal is the San Gorgonio Pass, a break in the San Bernardino mountain range along today's freeway route from Los Angeles to Palm Springs. More than one-fourth of the four thousand square miles of this Colorado Desert lies below sea level, including most of its towns. Hot dry air rising from the lower desert moves up into San Gorgonio Pass and collides with cool, moist air from off the Pacific. So there is constant turbulence at San Gorgonio. For a fleeting moment, even the freeway driver tightens his grasp of his steering wheel to battle a buffeting wind.

Still in its geologic youth, the Colorado Desert is younger than the Mojave. It is a sunken desert formed by the collapse of the rear slope of the coastal mountain range. At its heart is the Salton Sea, which seems at first look to be the nadir of nature's prodigal idiocy in Southern California. The measurement of its water level is an exercise in reverse arithmetic. At its highest, more than forty years ago, it reached about 195 feet below sea level. Its present, lower elevation is about 232 feet below sea level. Created by a runaway river, it lives on because the drainage from a vast irrigation project feeds it more water than the desert sun evaporates.

The Colorado Desert grows hotter even than Death Valley, up to 130 degrees in summer. Its rainfall, which may be as little as two or three inches a year, is even paltrier than that of the Mojave. Its vegetation is so sparse that not even sheep can graze without irrigated pasture. Town after town lies roasting below sea level. Calipatria, which claims happily to be the nation's lowest city—at 184 feet below sea level—has a civic flagpole 184 feet high; at Christmas, colored lights are strung all the way up to sea level. Throughout the region in summer, hordes of crickets may lie underfoot in such quantities that it is impossible to cross the street or even the floor of a public building without crunching the bodies of hundreds of them. It was near here that General George Patton trained his troops for North African combat. There is terrain to fit every person's image of desert, including the shifting sand dunes of the Algodones—white, rippling hills that rise up to three hundred feet in height and extend forty miles to the Mexican border. The Algodones are almost devoid of habitation unless a movie company is present on location. To moviegoers all over the world, the Algodones will pass for the Sahara Desert, for most of Hollywood's desert films have been made there. In the slant rays of sunrise and sunset, the dunes grow mysterious with shadow, reflecting the browns of the nearby Chocolate Mountains or the incongruous lavenders and purples that in half-light soften this Colorado Desert. It is a land of delicate colors contrasting with the grays and tans of the older Mojave.

The Algodones, just inside California on its southernmost transcontinental highway, offer one of the more bizarre approaches by which newcomers enter the state. The highway is a fast one, skirting most of the dunes, but the curious visitor finds traces of the one-way plank road that first made this desert passable to the automobile. The highway is busy on weekends with trailered dune buggies, those versatile but unwieldy desert vehicles that are another in a long series of devices with which the Californian has responded to his urge to move about over his varied land.

No such means of transport aided the passage of the first explorers in this awesome desert. It was not seen by white man until 1774, when the Spanish cavalry captain Juan Bautista de Anza sought an overland supply route from northwest Mexico to the California coastal mission chain. The Colorado Desert then was only an obstacle to be surmounted, a bad place to be crossed over. It would have taken immense audacity to imagine this desert as one of the most prolific agricultural valleys of the world.

That vision was first projected by Dr. Oliver Meredith Wozencraft, a physician who laboriously crossed the Colorado Desert on muleback in 1849 on his way from New Orleans to San Francisco. He exhausted his water supply and narrowly escaped death, but he was alert enough to note formations of silt on the then dry bed of the Salton Sea. He deduced that the Colorado River, flowing more than forty miles distant, must once have run away and filled this inland lake.

Wozencraft went on to San Francisco, served as a delegate to the first California constitutional convention at Monterey in 1849, and became an Indian agent in the Sacramento Valley. But for the almost forty years of his life which remained, he waged an unflagging fight for diversion of Colorado River water back into the desert sink. In 1859 he boldly asked the California legislature to assign him sixteen hundred square miles of land, almost the entire southeast corner of California; in return he proposed to build a series of canals to irrigate the valley around the dry sea bed with water from the river. By then the work of a brilliant young geologist, William P. Blake, a member of a federal topographic survey, had confirmed that much of the Colorado Desert lay below the level of the nearby Colorado River, a fact that helped to explain the river's errant path in past ages.

The California legislature blithely conveyed to Wozencraft the rights of the new state in the region. But federal approval was necessary, and Wozencraft went to Washington to persuade Congress to vote the land to him. The House Committee on Public Lands agreed. But when the bill came up for debate in 1862 it was shelved. Wozencraft's vision was derided. In California the humorist J. Ross Brown wrote: "I can see no great obstacle to success except the porous nature of the sand. By removing the sand from the desert, success would be insured at once." Dejected, Wozencraft went back near the edge of the desert and practiced medicine at San Bernardino, pleading intermittently with congress after congress. It was to no avail. He died in

Washington in 1887 while awaiting the introduction of yet another bill to irrigate the desert.

But he had set in motion one of the most remarkable irrigation projects of all time. In 1900 George M. Chaffey, a wealthy civil engineer with experience in Australian irrigation, became president of the California Development Company. He undertook to divert four-hundred-thousand acre-feet of Colorado River water through a devious sand canal that veered south into Mexico and north again, forty miles west of the river, into the area that was then bravely named Imperial Valley. Town sites were laid out and an advertising campaign was launched; the Southern Pacific Railroad built tracks and ran excursion trains, and settlers began arriving from all over the Southwest in the summer of 1900. At the start of 1901 the valley population had risen from zero to fifteen-hundred. Chaffey built his canal in five months, using old flood channels for much of the route. In May, 1901, water moved through the canals and the valley came to life. The water had to be strained of silt before it could be drunk, but it began to turn the valley green. At the end of 1903, more than a thousand miles of sub-canals served one hundred thousand acres of farmland. It was a new American epic with hardships that seemed, in their way, as great as those faced by any other settlers in the nation's history. Valley farmers regarded this as a last frontier. But its melons, lettuce, cotton, grapes and tomatoes, maturing earlier than those anywhere else in America, brought premium prices. The climate allowed growth of two or more harvests within the year on the same land—up to six harvests of alfalfa. Rich yields were common; soon an acre was yielding half a ton of cotton, about twice the national average.

The desert blossomed, but the California Development Company was in trouble. The newly established U.S. Reclamation Bureau challenged its right to water from the Colorado. Its canal silted; in a time of drought, farmers began suing the company for failing to deliver water quotas. With Chaffey retired, his successor, Charles Rockwood, an impulsive man, blundered. He cut a new and dangerous intake into the Colorado River in Mexican territory without building a headgate to control the amount of water that was to be diverted toward Imperial Valley. It was a desperate gamble to maintain the water supply. Rockwood had studied the river's flood pattern and noted that there had been only three winter floods in 27 years. But his cut into the river opened a gate to disaster.

A rare series of spring floods, fed by desert cloudbursts, came roaring down the Colorado in 1905. Now farmers were ready to sue the beleaguered company because too much water flowed to their farms. With dawning horror, the settlers realized that the wild river was out of control. The dry inland lake bed that Wozencraft had first observed was filling with water from overflowing canals, its level rising at the rate of several inches each day. Already, at its lowest point, 273.5 feet below sea level, it was a new lake. Worst of all, the usual summer flooding, fed by the melting snow pack from off the mountains far up the river, was yet to come.

Rockwood went to New York and appealed for help from Edward H. Harriman, whose Southern Pacific served the valley. Harriman loaned $200,000 and took control of Rockwood's company. But the Colorado had only begun to display its trickery. When summer flooding subsided, the Colorado turned away from its own bed and began to pour its entire flow through the artificial cut that Rockwood had made. Harriman sent in an engineer, Epes Randolph, to succeed Rockwood as president of his company. On his arrival, Randolph telegraphed Harriman that the cost of turning back the river and saving the valley might run to more than $700,000. His estimate was woefully low. But now it was Harriman, the iron-fisted railroad tycoon, pitting his empire against the force of a desert river. So began a three-year struggle against the Colorado, with Randolph feverishly building the first of a series of dams, floodgates and diversions. Day by day the Salton Sea spread ominously through the valley.

In November, 1905, another flash flood came down the Colorado. The river rose ten feet in ten hours. A new six-hundred-foot barrier dam was pushed aside like a postage stamp. By now the Salton Sea covered 150 square miles. The flood-fighters turned their hopes to a huge steam canal dredge to be built in San Francisco. A contract was let, but the dredge was never delivered. On April 18, 1906, San Francisco was dealt a natural blow of a different kind: its great earthquake and fire. From New York, Harriman rushed to San Francisco; from the Colorado Desert came Randolph. Both turned to the task of restoring the railroad's shattered operations. But before April ended, Harriman allotted $250,000 more to the fight to turn the Colorado back into its bed.

Mexican families were retreating homeless before the spreading flood in the river's delta. In the Mexican border village of Mexicali, where the poor buried their dead in a dry creek bed because the earth there was softer to dig, the frenzied waters swept away skeletons. To the north in Imperial Valley, disaster seemed imminent. A salt refining works lay under sixty feet of water by June, 1906, and the Salton Sea had increased its area to four hundred square miles. Southern Pacific tracks were submerged and rebuilt on higher ground. The rate of rise in the Colorado River was at its highest in years, and its entire force was bludgeoning the valley that lay forty miles away from its bed. As the volume of flow soared, the river began to erode new channels at random with the snakelike cutting-back of its waterfalls, moving more than four times as much earth as was later to be cut for the Panama Canal. The flood ate away at the twin villages of Mexicali, just inside the Mexican border, and Calexico, just above it. Sandbags and mud levees helped, but the Calexico railway station washed away in one wrenching jerk as Southern Pacific officials stood by helplessly. The lives and property of twelve thousand people lay at stake unless the river were controlled; yet if it were turned back entirely, the desert would reclaim two hundred square miles of town and farmland, the investment and struggle of six years. Meanwhile the dry Colorado River channel grew thick with bushes and grass.

In August, 1906, Randolph launched a new assault against the river, waging it on the scale of a small war. The railroad brought in all the rock immediately available from quarries within three hundred miles. Two thousand Indians were set up in a work camp under martial law. Three hundred side-dump railroad cars, known to railroad men as battleships, plied across a trestle at the site of the break, each dumping sixty tons of rock onto a brush mattress, one hundred feet wide, sewed with iron rope. The resulting dam was almost finished, a trap aimed at turning the river back into its normal channel. Then on the morning of October 11, 1906, as a band of weary engineers watched incredulously, a sudden surge of the river swept up two-thirds of the new dam and carried it off. Harriman had turned a million-and-a-half dollars into his fight against the Colorado. He was no closer to victory than a year before.

A former engineering professor, Harry T. Cory, took charge. He determined that only "rock and more rock" could turn back the river. A thousand men were in the fight by day and night, with six work trains dropping a carload of rock every five minutes. Cory's crew was building the barrier faster than the Colorado could sweep it away. At dawn on November 3, 1906, the waters of the river turned back into their ancient channel leading south to the Gulf of California. Cory worked tirelessly to seal his levees and rock dams to insure that they stood the test of floods. The farmers of the valley, finally reassured, went about the planting of winter crops. The battle seemed ended. But on December 5, 1906, after another cloudburst, the Colorado rose from a flow of 9,000 second-feet to 45,000. The new dam stood, but the river ate through the levee and turned downhill once again into Imperial Valley and its swollen, captive reservoir, the Salton Sea.

Even Harriman was at the end of his patience. He turned to President Theodore Roosevelt for help. But it was the era of Roosevelt's drive to break the corporate trusts, and the President was in no mood to ease the railroad's burden. So Harriman wearily girded for another battle. It was one of the rainiest winters in the history of the Colorado. Freshets repeatedly tore away trestle pilings as crews plunged them down below thirty feet of swirling current. When they were finally imbedded and a trestle in place over the break, Harriman placed the entire freight system of the Southern Pacific at the disposal of his crew on the river. Other railroads diverted trains to help. All of them brought cargoes of rock. Construction of Los Angeles Harbor was virtually suspended so that equipment from that site could be moved into the effort. In fifteen days, three thousand carloads of rock were dumped at the Colorado, a logistic feat unmatched in American railroad history. On February 10, 1907, the river, its channel raised eleven feet by the repair of its break, resumed its normal flow. A million acres of rich American farmland had been saved from flooding. The victory was hailed in headlines across the nation. The settlers promptly formed their own Imperial Irrigation District to own and operate the canal and levees. One of their first acts was to buy Harriman's interest in the development company. The railroad magnate had won his fight, but he wanted no more.

Trouble came from a new source. The canal passed through Mexico, and directors of the Irrigation District found they could service the canal only at the pleasure of border officials. So began long years of negotiation with United States agencies to build a canal that would not enter Mexico. Control of the Colorado River was too massive a task for private interests. With federal direction, the All-American Canal was completed in 1941 to link Imperial Valley with the Colorado River. A river of desilted water two hundred feet wide, it flows by gravity through the white dunes of Algodones, close along the Mexican border for eighty miles to its terminus just south of the Salton Sea.

With its accompanying storage reservoir on the Colorado at Imperial Dam, this canal answers the water needs of the 75,000 residents of Imperial Valley. The Imperial Irrigation District has developed three thousand miles of canals and drains—more water lanes than the total paved streets and roads within the entire valley. Each day two billion gallons of water roar through the system, making it the largest irrigation district in the Western Hemisphere. The agricultural richness sustained by this water supply is astonishing. Feed crops loom more valuable as cattle are shipped by the thousands into the valley to be fattened in small feed-lots on their way to market. Lettuce heads the list of truck crops, and cotton and sugar beets are of major importance. Just to the north in the smaller Coachella Valley, dates and grapefruit vie in dollar importance with resorts built around verdant desert golf courses like Eldorado, where former President Dwight Eisenhower was an early and active member. Across the Mexican border, the town of Mexicali has become the metropolis of the region, with more than three hundred thousand residents. Now it fights its own water battles, trucking in drinking water from the United States and drawing on the left-over flow of the Colorado River for agricultural irrigation.

The farm towns of Imperial Valley seem foreign to the throb of Southern California. With fewer than twenty thousand persons, El Centro proclaims itself to be the largest city below sea level in the Western Hemisphere. Like other valley towns, its skyline is low and its storefronts are typically arcaded. Farm machinery stores seem most prosperous. Even the simplest wooden shack must have its air cooler, and motels proclaim that they are "refrigerated." Yet there are front yards of raw earth with dust-choked tamarisk trees. Migrant labor camps are numerous, and minority residential districts are bunched in with shipping sheds and processing plants. The Mexican border comes to life at 4:00 in the morning as thousands of "green-card" laborers—commuting aliens—cross into the United States to work in Imperial Valley fields. The typical ranch is an owner-operated field factory of several hundred acres with modest farm buildings and plain dwellings. All life bends toward the field, and each town celebrates its own agricultural specialty. During the February harvests there is a tomato festival at Niland and a carrot carnival at Holtville. Brawley observes its autumn cattle roundup with a rodeo called the Brawley Cattle Call. Calexico, the cotton center, stages an April festival. The list of produce seems infinite. The valley grows a vegetable or fruit appropriate for every meal and seems to harvest such crops almost at will—from broccoli to pecans, tangerines, asparagus, garlic and melons. It is a fifty-mile-long valley now, with half a million irrigated acres. Yet it is still a harsh place to live. The 1985 population projection for Imperial County is less than one hundred thousand. In the mountains that rise above the valley to the west there are countless miles of the same cruelly magnificent land that challenged the first pioneers—including Anza-Borrego State Park, a half-million acre preserve that provides a winter refuge for hikers and campers.

The Salton Sea, created during those tense eighteen months of 1905–07, remains a source of alarm. It is rising again because of the return of used irrigation water, and damage suits are filed against the Irrigation District when its waters flood beachfront homes or marinas. Bird refuges have been created on the shore of the sea, and the throbbing wings of thousands of migrating ducks and geese are often heard. Fish have somehow survived the increasing salinity of the Salton Sea, and marina resorts have been built. Farmers who remember the terror of 1905 find it strange to see water-skiers and seashore subdividers busy exploiting the catastrophe of more than half a century ago.

The intricate web that history has spun between the Colorado Desert and its river seems likely to be eternal. The construction of the All-American Canal was possible because of the completion of Hoover Dam, which in 1936 established the key point for control of the rampaging river. That dam was by far the largest multipurpose dam in the nation, providing both water and power. Downstream is the source of the aqueduct owned by the Metropolitan Water District, providing water for 119 cities of Southern California. Snaking across the northern Colorado Desert from Parker Dam, the aqueduct was completed in 1939. It bores through 42 tunnels and employs five pump stations and huge siphons in lifting its flow over the coastal mountains. Yet the daily usage of water by the millions of city residents served by the pipeline is only about a billion gallons a day, half that of Imperial Valley. Such are the thirsty demands of the desert, and of agricultural water. In this region almost six acre-feet of water (close to two million gallons) are needed to produce one crop on an acre of land. These networks of water movement across the desert are constantly patrolled, on the ground and from the air. The sole air patrolman is Ed Hamilton, who flies daily watches in a light plane over the 250-mile aqueduct and its power lines as they cross Southern California. He may land on the desert floor to shake an eagle's nest out of a high voltage tower so that the aqueduct's pumps will not be shorted out. Erratic desert winds and temperatures that rise above one hundred degrees for eight months of the year makes his one of the roughest of air routes. "When the bird gets a bad case of violent shakes," he said recently, "I land somewhere and wait until the air quiets." Most of the people of Southern California are dependent for their water supply on the success of his daily patrols. The relative frailness of pipe and pump and canal—when seen against the expanses of the Southern California deserts—do much to enhance the air of impermanence that sometimes envelops those who live in the region. Despite the intricate systems of water movement, the modern Californian lives in a region where Indian cultures of the past have disappeared in times of drought without leaving any trace. So he looks toward both aqueduct and science to insure his future water supply—perhaps through desalinization plants along the coast, or progress in the reclamation of used water, or even weather control.

The California desert, where man still wages a constant war to stay even with nature, may yet be softened and placed at man's control.

.7.

THE LONG CAMPUS

> I now believe that what happens within the University of California will affect the future of the state, of the nation, and of mankind to a greater degree than what happens on any other campus in the world.
>
> —ROGER REVELLE, DIRECTOR OF THE CENTER FOR POPULATION STUDIES, HARVARD UNIVERSITY.

California is a community of campuses surrounded by a state. One trait above all binds Californians: their almost mystical faith in higher education. To oppose education in California is like damning tobacco in the Carolinas. Angry furors over public education reverberate from California around the world, but they occur largely because most education *is* public, or tax-supported, and Californians are intensely concerned with what they are buying.

Everywhere, universities are becoming more a part of the fabric of society. They are the reservoirs of expertise in an increasingly difficult world. Ivory towers crumble under the political and economic demands of the community, the state and nation. The university is in transition from the grove of academe to a role as a primary moving force that supplies the ideas and concepts that feed society. Nowhere is there a university more extensively involved with the world around it than the University of California, a nine-campus multiuniversity with more than a hundred thousand students, still so relatively young that it celebrated its centennial in 1968 at a time when California as a state had not yet observed the bicentennial of its first settlement by Europeans.

The public state university is not alone in the meshing of California campus and community. There are nineteen four-year state colleges, just a step down the ladder in academic excellence. They yield to few universities in size. Enrollment at Long Beach State College in the fall of 1968 was in excess of twenty-seven thousand students, and several others in the system had student bodies in excess of twenty thousand. The two-year public junior colleges, operated at the local level and designed to accommodate all students who do not qualify for higher institutions, have proliferated in California at an astonishing rate. In 1969 there were eighty-five of them and enough more were planned that three-quarters of all future high-school graduates in California are expected to attend such colleges. The two-year college was introduced in California in 1907, but its role in the public education system was not clearly affirmed until the landmark California Master Plan for Higher Education of the 1950s. Under that plan the top one-eighth of high school graduates may be accepted by the University of California, the top one-third by the state colleges, and the remainder by the two-year colleges operated within local school districts.

While public education is dominant, there are notable private colleges and universities. Stanford University, founded by one of the Big Four railroad builders in 1887, may not have achieved its benefactor's goal as a Harvard of the West, but it has reached a high level of academic and scientific distinction and a certain social status that is rare on Western campuses. At Los Angeles, the independent University of Southern California, established by the Methodist Episcopal Church in 1880, has shaken off its label as a football campus. Across the city at Pasadena, the California Institute of Technology—known more familiarly as Caltech—can draw many parallels with its Eastern counterpart, MIT. It reflects the philosophy of Robert Millikan, one of its founders, who said in 1948, on his 80th birthday: ". . . if Southern California is to continue to meet the challenge of its environment . . . its supreme need . . . is for the development here of men of resourcefulness, of scientific and engineering background and understanding—able, creative, highly endowed, highly trained men in science and its application."

It is not insignificant that higher academic achievement in the sciences is generally attained on California campuses than in the liberal arts. The taxpayer sees the results of scientific training and research more vividly than the subtler studies of philosophy and language or the arts; like science, he is oriented to the present and future, and he has little patience yet for the long look back at human history.

In his quest for the full life, the Californian looks to his educational system and in particular to the gargantuan University of California. He feels proprietary about it. He regards its hippies and radicals as interfering with his fulfillment. With a perception that falters rarely, he pays heavy taxes and endorses bond issues for its growth and that of lesser schools and colleges. He expects the University to do far more than educate his brightest sons and daughters, in a state where higher education is predominantly public. He assumes his university will somehow lift him in society, serving as his cultural custodian and the checkpoint for his continuing education as an adult. It will come to the rescue of his local and state governments when they admit a need for counsel. It will cure the pear grower's blight and show enologists in Napa Valley how to make a more velvety Cabernet Sauvignon. It will operate laboratories like Los Alamos and Lawrence at the outer fringes of scientific advance. It will continue to play the Nobel Prize numbers game, racking up astonishing numbers of Nobel laureates among its faculty, because California, he proposes, is to set the pattern for the enlightened world of tomorrow. The University, in the end, need only be the mirror on the wall to assure the Californian that he is the fairest of them all. So it is no wonder that when things seem to go wrong at the University of California, an angry cry rises up and down the state. For then the mirror is in danger of cracking.

Because of its rapid growth, California has experimented in crisis areas of higher education sooner than most other universities have been forced to do so, and often it has provided clues to problems and solutions that are later to become ordinary in education. The University of California began a century ago at Berkeley, across the bay from San Francisco. It prospered, and eventually Californians reasoned that if Berkeley's campus could become distinguished, so could others within the same system. Now there are nine campuses, still far from equal, but functioning within one bureaucracy and under one budget that far exceeds half a billion dollars.

The University of California encompasses two nuclear laboratories, nearly a hundred research and experiment stations, and an extension system serving more than a quarter of a million people. Not without some logic, it is called "the thousand-mile campus." In 1968 its total number of employees was about fifty thousand people. More than one billion dollars has been spent in capital improvements on its nine campuses since 1945. It was involved in overseas projects involving more than fifty nations. In excess of ten thousand courses were in its catalogs. More than five thousand babies were born each year in its hospitals. It has the world's largest primate colony and is the world's largest purveyor of white mice. It is also a supreme effort at higher mass education. Sheer size has compelled the University to challenge the tradition that academic excellence is endangered by rapid expansion. By the diversities of its campuses, the multiversity has hoped to avoid the chilling impersonality of vastness. They are all discrete total campuses, and yet few entire universities anywhere are larger than Berkeley or UCLA. "The University of

California is a very large and viable target," Clark Kerr once said. "Like Mount Everest, it is a perennial challenge to some types of people, just because it is there."

The origin of the University was not auspicious. A Congregationalist clergyman from Yale, the Reverend Henry Durant, opened an academy in an Oakland dance hall in 1853. Moving to the present university site, he named it for the Irish bishop, poet and philosopher George Berkeley, the author of a poem that holds special meaning for Californians:

> *Westward the course of empire takes its way;*
> *The first four acts already past.*
> *A fifth shall close the drama with the day;*
> *Time's noblest offspring is the last.*

Durant's academy became the University of California in 1868.

Three presidents have dominated the University. The first was Benjamin Ide Wheeler, a tempestuous autocrat who in the first twenty years of this century was the architect of the University's academic emergence. Under him grew a faculty so strong that its members revolted at the end of his reign and formed the prestigious academic senate, to which all professors belong when they achieve tenure status. The senate on each campus zealously controls the curriculum, degrees and selection of faculty. The faculty throughout the University exercises more control than in other state universities. But an increasing minority of the faculty believes the academic senates are not exercising their responsibilities as effectively as they are exploiting their privileges.

Robert Gordon Sproul became president in 1929. He shaped University expansion through a snug rapport with legislators. One of his early gambles was to raise funds for a young physicist, the late Ernest O. Lawrence, to build the nation's first cyclotron. The Lawrence Radiation Laboratory evolved from this, and today it receives a heavy share of the Federal research funding allotted to the University, which recently has exceeded a quarter of a billion dollars a year. Sproul survived in a bitter loyalty-oath fight within the University in 1949–50, but did not distinguish himself. If there was a victor, it was the protesting faculty: the oath is no longer required.

The University was at the edge of another abyss in 1958 when Clark Kerr became president. California educators were at war among themselves. Kerr figured in the much-copied California Master Plan for Higher Education, which held off chaos in an era of skyrocketing population. He daringly guided the evolution of new campuses at San Diego, Irvine and Santa Cruz. It was high irony when Kerr, as Berkeley chancellor and later as president of the overall University, sought more independence for students and faculty, only to become the target of both in the Free Speech Movement of 1964–65—an event which set the stage for his dismissal by regents in 1967 soon after Ronald Reagan, as governor and ex officio regent, had taken office. Kerr was succeeded by Charles J. Hitch, an academician whose flair for administration had been sharpened by a tour of duty at the Pentagon. The pressures of the presidency of the University had grown so massive that an Alumni Council member said seriously, "You can find a thousand people who could serve as President of the United States, but you can't find half a dozen who could serve as President of the University of California."

The domain over which the University of California president rules is both physically and academically the most complex higher educational system in the world. Its southernmost landmark is the white pier that juts into the Pacific from the Scripps Institution of Oceanography, a part of the San Diego campus of the University. Like about forty thousand other acres of admirable California real estate, this pier and the campus that rises inland from it at La Jolla (a corporate part of San Diego) are posted with white plaques denoting them as property of the regents of the University of California. Nearby at twilight, the sunset is reflected in the windows of the redwood-and-glass Institute of Geophysics and Planetary Physics. Farther up the sea cliff, twinkling through eucalyptus trees, are the lights of a cozy complex of student apartments.

It is a matter of local satisfaction that both these additions won architectural awards, and that fresh campus offices have been occupied by such residents as chemist Harold Urey and physicist Maria Mayer, both Nobel Prize winners. Yet, in this community so recently placid and stolid, only a few grasp the scope of the campus future: either its physical range or the scientific frontiers being probed. The campus is spreading across a eucalyptus-dotted mesa above the sea to provide for a student body of 27,500 by 1995.

This embryo campus—the first four-year class was graduated in 1968—is envied for its research budget and its renowned faculty. It is a campus that, in the opinion of Clark Kerr, "started at a higher level of distinction than any university campus since Johns Hopkins in 1876, and Chicago and Stanford in the early 1890's." The genesis of the campus was the oceanographic institute, which became part of the University of California in 1912. In 1960, its director, Roger Revelle, inaugurated a Graduate School of Science and Engineering. The persuasiveness of Revelle and of the setting, combined with a burgeoning research-and-development complex (Salk Institute and Gulf General Atomic are nearby), lured a faculty top-heavy with scientific genius. Under the later tenure of the historian John S. Galbraith, undergraduate emphasis swung to the humanities, but with a sturdy compulsory schedule in math and science.

At the heart of the campus today are the first three of twelve colleges, planned on a variation of the Oxford college system in England. A provost will guide each college with its maximum of 2500 students, sixty percent of them undergraduates. For each college there will be separate residence and dining halls. Students cross over into other colleges to pursue specialties. The hope is to combine the intimacy of the small college with the varied resources of the University.

The mood is euphoric. "You get the feeling that big things are about to happen," a student told me. As chancellor until he departed for Cambridge University in 1968, Galbraith pressed for experimentation and innovation. "The old forms, not the new, must defend themselves here," he said. "We propose to challenge every assumption of higher education." The mission at the San Diego campus continues to be to show that instruction in the sciences and humanities can be interlocked meaningfully for all, and that monarchs of the laboratory can and will teach undergraduates effectively. But as the ivory tower crumbles, there is growing tension between town and gown. In the fall of 1968 a new chancellor, William McGill, stepped into the midst of a raging debate over renewal of the teaching contract of Herbert Marcuse, the aging Marxist revolutionary. The demonstrations of militant students and the pronouncements of Marcuse had stirred deep resentment in San Diego, an area with a strong military community and roots in the conservative tradition.

Two centuries ago, a Franciscan priest named Junípero Serra launched California, for better and for worse, with the first of a chain of 21 missions separated by a day's journey on horseback. Suddenly there are twenty million people in California, and the thought of many is to save souls with shrines of learning linked by six-lane freeways.

Beyond the oceanographers' pier at San Diego, on those electric-blue days when California is working right, one can look sixty miles up the coast to a bluff near which the freeway to Los Angeles divides into coastal and inland routes. A huge freeway triangle results; within it is a 93,000-acre ranch extending fifteen miles from coast to foothills and blocking, for the moment, the human torrent that spills southward from Los Angeles.

This is the Irvine Ranch, which urban planners see as Mecca: one of the largest undeveloped areas within a megalopolis. On part of the ranch, not far from a shack where cowboys lived into the 1950's, a flood of University of California students attend classes on a campus that has surged up out of bare, rolling hills in conservative Republican Orange County. Fifty thousand neighbors pledged support if this site were chosen as a campus by the University board of regents. That it was chosen, despite dogged opposition by Edmund G. Brown, the Democratic governor when the decision was made, is evidence of the constitutionally guaranteed independence of the regents.

A superb master plan from the architect William L. Pereira points this campus toward a look of airy traditionalism, but the academic plan is spelled out in unfettered terms. To draw academic talent from the inception of the campus, Chancellor Daniel

G. Aldrich, Jr., a trim, tennis-playing idealist, allowed top men to initiate their own "dream curricula," ignoring artificial departmental structures. There are many courses at the Irvine campus for which no appropriate texts had been written, so textbook publishers camped eagerly as the University campus got under way in 1965.

"The professor who wants to grow old gracefully in ivy-covered buildings is not at ease on this campus," Aldrich has since said. "This is no wooded glade. We are here to train people for responsible interaction in a crowded urban world." His point was illustrated by James G. March, who came to Irvine from Carnegie Tech. "What has happened in the last ten or fifteen years has made me and a good many other social scientists obsolescent," March said as he chewed on a corncob pipe. "It is hard to say what our disciplines are today. The economist is in engineering. The sociologist is in environmental planning. We need educational and organizational innovation. At Irvine we deemphasize departments."

His students take a heavy math load, emphasize project studies of flexible length, and go into research in their senior years on specific social problems. Independent studies are the norm instead of simply the name of a course. "The students who seek us out at Irvine are a bunch of academic revolutionaries," March said.

One strength of the Irvine faculty is in urban planning, appropriate to its location in a vast model community in one of the most rapidly urbanizing areas of the nation. Irvine faculty members seek ways in which their campus can benefit society. "Typically," Alrich said, "universities serve through agriculture, engineering, medicine and the law. I say that every element of this campus will relate to the community. Our men in the humanities help their neighbors with their searches for aim and perspective. Every dimension of the University should communicate in some way to people outside the campus gate. So watch out, here we come!"

There will be plenty of coming and going, for Irvine adds students each year toward its maximum of 27,500. As it grows, the campus will become an oasis of expanding circles around a spacious centrum (no cars admitted), with a campanile affording a view of the Southern California gold coast. The outer ring of buildings will include a theater and a library. Oats and barley grow on much of the townsite now, but soon it will house a hundred thousand people. So says its chancellor. "What has taken Berkeley almost a hundred years and UCLA forty," he adds, "we must do in twenty."

East of Los Angeles, beside the freeway to Palm Springs, the tall palm trees of the University of California at Riverside signal an impending off-ramp. "The campus is a little bit out in the tules," a student said. "You have to go a mile for a beer." Sterile buildings rise in the hot sun at the desert's edge. Barren hills erupt behind the campus, their scrubby foliage interrupted only by naked granite boulders. The face of greatness is not yet here. I feel a strange loneliness each time I visit the Riverside campus. Of all the University of California campuses it most resembles an instant campus. Yet it is not. Riverside began in 1907 as a University citrus-experiment station. It flirted with academic nobility when a small College of Letters and Science opened in 1954 with a notable importation of young professors, largely from the Ivy League. The dream was swept out for a time in the student avalanche that soon followed. The college was to build toward a maximum enrollment of 1,500 students by 1970; instead, with new graduate schools, the number will be closer to eight thousand. Yet it is traditionally the last of the nine campuses to fill its entrance quota, and it receives students turned away from crowded University of California campuses elsewhere.

One night I sat in a tree-shaded old barn that had been happily converted into a temporary student lounge. With the president of the University present, Riverside students sang their favorite school song, to the tune of "Davy Crockett," and every student in the hall seemed to roar out the final words of the chorus:

> *River*,
> *Riversi*-ed,
> The *bas*tard of the *multiversi-tee*.

As the big-city campus, the University of California at Los Angeles is the most deeply enmeshed in community affairs. At times UCLA appears to regard itself as responsible for southern California's welfare. It means no harm; like the citizens of the region, it is overwrought with a restless urge to be at something, to keep moving about, to arrive at an attitude or reach a condition it can assert to be unique. Like the city itself, UCLA is maligned and underrated—not for grace or style, in which both are deficient, but for dynamism and purposefulness.

As the "Southern Branch," it was not accepted into the University until 1919, and it was another eight years before it could get its own name, then two more years before it arrived at its present site. The UCLA yearbook is still called *Southern Campus.*

Former Chancellor Franklin Murphy of UCLA, one of the strongest in University history, regarded the traditional scorn of Berkeley for UCLA as "rather like the old man who suddenly recognizes his son is an equal." The UCLA library, with about two and a half million volumes, is the largest research library in Southern California. In enrollment, UCLA has surpassed Berkeley; it is far past its theoretical maximum of 27,500 students, with a campus far newer but more crowded than Berkeley.

From UCLA one takes away images of stark red-brick walls without ivy interspersed with more modern structures, acres of parking areas with no unoccupied spaces, and intent, intelligent young people who do not regard themselves without humor. The absence of tradition is noticeable, too, as in the Faculty Club at lunch—a democratic scene lacking the usual claques of younger men who tend to gather around revered figureheads. Athletic tradition is minimal. UCLA now has an on-campus sports arena; no on-campus stadium is yet available as home ground for the vaunted UCLA football team.

But Murphy did much to build tradition. "He was a force of nature," said Dean Lawrence Clark Powell, the librarian, "that came spinning to us out of Kansas like a comet, with phosphorous glowing on its tail." Murphy came in 1960, and it is not entirely coincidental that there was an unprecedented cultural gain for Los Angeles in the following years. The son of a concert pianist, and by profession a doctor of medicine, Murphy is at his most intense as a connoisseur of the fine arts. He left the university in 1968 to become board chairman of the Times-Mirror Company and was succeeded by former vice chancellor Charles E. Young who, at 36, was the youngest of the nine university chancellors.

UCLA has excellent departments in brain research and African studies. It has unusual depth in chemistry, geophysics and languages. There are dynamic men on the faculty. But to many Southern Californians, the strength of UCLA is its ability to trouble-shoot rapid growth. UCLA professors have been prominent on major Los Angeles commissions and civic boards. Corporate executives attend week-night classes and weekend conferences at Palm Springs or Lake Arrowhead under the Graduate School of Business Administration. Through institutes and grants, UCLA is studying the Mexican-American population, urban encroachment, Los Angeles transit, smog and California water shortages. Now, almost too late to salvage the local scene, there is a School of Architecture and Urban Planning.

The campus seems as busy at night as by day, because of Southern California's vast commitment of leisure time to learning through University Extension. At last count more than one hundred statewide Extension specialists were at work creating six thousand educative "products," or courses. The students are typically college-educated. Few study for credit, and they pay substantial fees for advanced learning. Extension programs range from the superb theater group headquartered on the UCLA campus to invitational seminars in private homes for the study of interracial affairs. By correspondence, students of more than sixty nations study at the University of California. By the usual standards of measurement, UC Extension has the largest enrollment of any extension program in the world.

Another two hours along the freeway, often beside a languorous, hazy sea, the tempo of the University slows. North of the city itself on a handsome wooded beach, there is little in Santa Barbara's setting to offset its nagging reputation as a sports-car-and-bikini campus. Residence halls have large picture windows facing the Pacific. Snow dusts the gentle Santa Ynez Mountains to the east. Some old frame buildings remained until recently from an era of Marine Corps occupancy, but permanent buildings of pleasant sizes and shapes are rising, all capped with red-tiled roofs. The University of California at Santa Barbara is not the best, but its student body has recently been growing at the greatest rate of the older campuses.

The relatively easy pace of Santa Barbara was ordained not by rurality but by heritage. This was a teachers' college until World War II, and then an undergraduate college of the University until 1958. Now it has its own academic senate, as the other campuses do; this gives the faculty virtually sole power to hire, promote and fire, but until recently the senate was dominated by professors entrenched in tenure from the teachers'-college days. Gresham's Law worked here: poor faculty drove out the good, and it is only recently that scholars of stature have been attracted to Santa Barbara. Such campuses benefit most from the strength of the big University system, which automatically attracts both superior faculty and students to a campus while it is emerging with a reputation of its own.

One thing firmly established some years ago at Santa Barbara is the loyalty of the community toward the campus. Far from any major city, and with few alumni, the fledgling Santa Barbara campus needs friends as well as gifts. When he was chancellor here before departing for the East in 1962, Samuel B. Gould helped to organize the Affiliates of UCSB, an active group of adopted alumni. Dame Judith Anderson regularly paid her annual dues, as do some Santa Barbara plumbers, and as did the late Thomas Storke, who published the local newspaper so long and well and helped to establish the University campus here.

There are sights to see at Santa Barbara, but none more astounding than the community of Isla Vista, which has sprung from the earth next to the campus. It is unincorporated (thus without police) and beyond University jurisdiction, a mile-long jungle of neat two-story stucco apartment buildings with names like Eldorado East (and West), Cortez, Tahitian and Balboa. It is Volkswagen and walk-up country. Rent is low, and thousands of students live in the apartments. For a university community, Isla Vista is such an astonishing little caricature of suburbia that I wondered if anything ever happens there. Chancellor Vernon Cheadle, a botanist, put my mind at rest. "Once in a while," he said, "on a Sunday morning, I get a call from an outraged apartment owner saying I should make my kids behave. These are all warm-blooded young people living close together, but Isla Vista is *not* part of the University."

Above Santa Barbara, a tailfin of the Tehachapi mountain range curtains off Southern California's milling hordes, and then comes no-man's California. For a time there is the easy breathing of open space. To the northeast lies the trough of the Great Central Valley. In the three hundred miles between Santa Barbara and San Francisco, until the fall of 1965, there was no University of California campus. Now there is Santa Cruz. Not since medieval Heidelberg have educators had a setting of such natural eloquence in which to build a university.

My first visit to the Santa Cruz campus was on a bright Sunday just before the first class of students arrived. I drove through Santa Cruz, an easy-going and unsophisticated beach town first celebrated by John Steinbeck. It is built on the northern arc of the great coastal indentation known as Monterey Bay, a town that seems to have remained oblivious to any sense of purpose between the eras of its old boardwalk casino and its new hilltop university. It is a familiar story in California, and one that has startling visual effects: new era atop old.

Chancellor Dean E. McHenry is the prototype of the academic persuader. He was president of the student body in his undergraduate days at UCLA and later a political scientist there. By now he is resoundingly bald, a hulking man who speaks and moves as gently as a kitten and with as winning a manner. He needed it to persuade regents that he could build this campus of twenty or more separate liberal-arts residential colleges, for seven or eight hundred students each, at a cost to the taxpayers no greater than that of conventional campuses. On its success rode hopes for retarding the gap between student and faculty that has seemed so inevitable in the massive multiversity. Despite gloomy warnings from those who insist that this small-college plan is anachronistic and will not attract distinguished faculty,

Santa Cruz has prospered. There is disenchantment here, as on every campus, but it is offset to a great degree by a high level of earnestness.

I walked with McHenry that Sunday through a virgin stand of redwood and oak, fir and California laurel and madrone. Almost hidden among the trees are the first campus buildings: massive, low-set, not vying with the trees to reach the sky. Upper limbs of firs, stirred by breezes, brush the eaves of a three-story science building. The matched redwoods that flank the entrance to the library were protected during excavation by hundreds of feet of lumber. Down a wooded trail is a limestone quarry, its kiln weathered from 85 years of disuse, now finding a role as a natural amphitheater. "We think students who want to learn will be happy in this setting," the chancellor said that day. Since then there have been Santa Cruz students who have seemed riotously unhappy; campus revolution reaches even within the stately forests above Monterey Bay.

The farmers of the Great Central Valley look with awe on the faculty of the northernmost campus, at Davis. From here, since it was created in 1905 as the University Farm, has come the agricultural technology that lifted California's farm income above the four-billion-dollar-a-year level. The Davis campus was built close to the soil, with a tradition of service. Its faculty does not consider it academically disgraceful to bring together theory and applied sciences. Horses and cattle, barns and green fields close around the vast, tree-shaded quadrangle. Students smile as they pass, and relatively few members of the faculty have found it necessary to require appointments for office visits. It is a small-town campus, but the mood is misleading.

The Department of Applied Science at Davis occupies one wing of a building that not long ago housed agricultural equipment—tractors, cultivators and harvesters—in a high-ceilinged hall. The equipment gave way to two levels of offices and scientific laboratories. I found Dr. Edward Teller in his office on the second floor, above where the tractors stood. As a University professor-at-large, Teller dashes between Davis and Berkeley and the Lawrence Radiation Laboratory at Livermore, campuses separated by close to a hundred miles. I found him interviewing one of the several hundred seniors he observes each year in order to choose about fifty whom he undertakes to teach to be inventors. His goal is to educate the rounded "Renaissance man" who can move confidently among several scientific disciplines. His laboratory headquarters at Livermore is a bleak nuclear-weapon design facility operated by the University for the Atomic Energy Commission (much like the so-called Tenth Campus at Los Alamos, New Mexico). Teller's classes are scheduled with lengthy half-hour breaks because when lectures end, heavy questioning usually begins.

Engineers of the Davis campus continually help to design and modify the complex California water-transport system. Agronomists are all over the state coaxing new miracles from the soil. A department that concerns itself with the growing of grapes and production of wine is unrivalled on any campus. The kennels at Davis, teeming with beagles, are part of the Atomic Energy Commission's life-span studies in radiation. At last count in 1968 the animal population of the Davis campus was eighty thousand, almost nine times the student population. Within a hundred buildings and half a million square feet of corrals adjacent to the campus were housed fifty-three species of animals, from dingos to Mexican coyotes. Veterinarians were breeding Shetland ponies with Rocky Mountain burros to produce a versatile mini-mule.

Davis, with almost four thousand acres, is plantation-sized. The campus includes an airport and is bisected by the Southern Pacific Railroad and by two freeways. That, of course, is not notable in California; each of the nine University campuses is involved in present or proposed freeways.

One of the freeways from Davis funnels fast traffic into the San Francisco Bay area and to the two other University campuses. The midget campus of the system is the Medical Center at San Francisco, a competent but restive combine of four professional schools on the slopes of Mount Sutro. A venerable school by West Coast standards, it ranks somewhat behind the medical school of UCLA; neither is yet of the topmost caliber. In the training of medical men, the conflict of quality and quantity reaches an acme; it has been one of the thorniest continuing conflicts facing the University.

From high up at the Medical Center in San Francisco, one sees far across the Bay, against the hills, a spire much like that of St. Mark's in Venice. This is the Campanile of the troubled heartland of the University, the Berkeley campus. It is the home of such academic notables as Mark Schorer, George R. Stewart and Thomas Parkinson in English; Harold Weaver, the radio astronomer; biologists Daniel Mazia, Curt Stern and Howard Bern; physicist Edwin McMillan; economist Robert Aaron Gordon; William Fretter of the College of Letters and Science, and chemist Melvin Calvin.

At Berkeley, twice in modern years, such incredible strife has erupted that the academic world marvels that the University has survived at all. In 1949 and 1950 there was the academic war over the regents' demand that professors sign loyalty oaths, an ugly backwash of World War II and McCarthyism. In more recent years, and with bizarre parallels, there has been a tawdry jumble of fuzzily focused student rebellion, faculty belligerence and administrative bungling. Like a foredoomed monarch, Clark Kerr anticipated the cracks in his system before they showed. In scholarly books and lectures he described the nature of the protagonists most likely to lead the rebellion. But when it came, late in 1964, he seemed stunned and helpless to change its course. Emboldened by the tacit approval of civil disobedience in the South, a philosophy student named Mario Savio and his followers tried to use the technique, and the momentum it had gained, to change policy at Berkeley—notably, to win permission for on-campus advocacy of activities that were illegal off-campus.

"We seemed to forget how to talk to each other, how to listen to each other, and were content to yell at each other," historian Raymond J. Sontag recalled in the baccalaureate address at the close of that nearly wasted academic year. The central issue was not free speech; the real issue was one of changing roles within the large university. "There is a traditional three-way balance of power among the regents, the president and the academic senate," concluded the scholar George Stewart. "Do the students today constitute a fourth power? I don't think so." But Savio, and those who carried on after he was jailed, did think so. With new leadership, the Berkeley campus weathered its storms well enough to underline its prospects for continuing greatness, and the wave of student activism swept out to engulf the rest of America, leaving Berkeley as another prime exhibit in the great advance testing laboratory that is California.

Berkeley has become a womb for youthful nomads from all over America: drug-users, refugees from the chilling blight of San Francisco's Haight-Ashbury or New York's East Village, naive idealists, militant dissidents and avowed revolutionaries. Repeated attempts to disrupt civil affairs have brought these street people under surveillance from local and federal authorities; they have succeeded in blacking out much of Berkeley for a few hours and in dynamiting a naval reserve facility on the campus. Yet the chaotic attempts at organization by these street people have been as futile as those of professors and clergymen to direct them, or of law enforcement officers to control them. The leading New Left student group at Berkeley and across the nation in 1968 was Students for a Democratic Society (SDS); within its national membership of about 35,000 were conflicting anarchist and Marxist factions. The SDS leaders at Berkeley scorned the street people as nihilistic anarchists, as opposed to revolutionary anarchists. So did Berkeley leaders of the Young Socialist Alliance (YSA), the youth arm of the traditional Trotskyist Socialist Workers Party, which seeks Marxism and opposes anarchy. Perhaps the closest to a spokesman for the Berkeley street people in 1968 was an Iranian graduate student, Hajj Razavi, 30, who described himself as "the pimp of the revolution" and the leader of a shadowy group he called the Berkeley Commune. He told a reporter that he lived by tutoring Iranian students in English and by a $40 bimonthly allotment from an inheritance in Iran. He had a full dark beard and piercing green eyes, and he wore a red skull cap and walked about with a cudgel in the manner of an old man. His critics called him a saboteur and an anarchist; he spoke of them only in unprintable obscenities, and described the role of his followers merely as "to do something together, to give first aid, whether it be for a scratch, a hit on the head or the clap."

Even the congregation of bizarre and calculatedly grotesque youths such as Razavi cannot mask the appearance of Berkeley as the only campus of the University that visually approaches Eastern specifications of tradition. South Hall, the first University building completed, in 1873, stands proud in its four-story Victorian cliches, raised groupings of chimneys and formal vaulted windows. Nearby is the superb library, well on its way toward its four-millionth volume, with its Louvre-like main reading hall. One of the architectural gems is the rambling redwood Faculty Club. The modernistic Student Center is exciting. The contemporary College of Environmental Design, known to some as The Thing, must be there to shock its students into doing better.

Californians have more than their stake as taxpayers in these buildings: one-third of them have been built with non-public funds, mainly private gifts. It is traditional in California that public institutions are proper objects of private benevolence. More often than in the East, individuals of wealth and influence are state-university graduates.

Such intense personal involvement between community and public campus provides the University of California with its capacity for greatness—a stature that is continually attributed to it and, quite naturally, just as often in jeopardy—and also with its potential for educational disaster. "What I want is a society that is *all university!*" cried a university official on the eve of the centennial. "The state of California must be a campus in which everyone's life is touched by the University and it is brought into every home and community. We should never leave the University and the University should never leave us. The whole *state* is the university!"

That is the dream. But like most of the grandiose visions of this new world beside the Pacific, it is sullied. One afternoon at the Santa Barbara campus I sat across from an elder statesman of the University, a keen Welsh-born economist who had already gone through several careers in this vast educational complex. Three of the chancellors at that time were his former students, and the University had awarded him two honorary degrees.

Lowering his head, he sighed and said, "I suppose you have noticed. Around our campuses, one stumbles over an increasing number of broken dreams."

As he left the San Diego campus for a sabbatical year in England in the fall of 1968, the former chancellor John S. Galbraith summed up the plight of the University:

> It is a battleground for an ideological conflict, and battlegrounds typically are very messy places to be. There are forces of the far right which believe that the University should inculcate what they call sound moral values and develop good citizenship. At the other extreme is the activist fringe of the New Left, which believes that the University should be the staging ground for attacks upon the established order. These two elements are alike in the sense that they believe the University should be an instrumentality for the prosecution of their views. Many faculty members tend to sympathize with the New Left because of its avowed idealism, and also, perhaps, in part because 'Left' is assumed to be closer to liberalism than 'Right.' The fact is that the New Left is no more 'liberal' in its outlook than the John Birch Society. Both are essentially narrow, intolerant and antagonistic to the democratic process. Both, if they had their way, would destroy the University as a center of free inquiry and debate. Both must be resisted if the University as we have known it is to survive.

On campuses around the world such issues are being painfully clarified. The peculiar nature of the California culture has helped to bring the conflict into early prominence up and down the state. Its shock waves, and those that will be set off if the battle is to be resolved, seem likely to shake Californians and their University as violently as any of nature's earthquakes.

. 8 .

SAN DIEGO AND SERRA

San Diego: The odds-on favorite 'most livable city.'
Prevailing Pacific winds blow away automobile-
caused air pollution, but about eight times a year,
breezes die down and residents suffer from a Los
Angeles-type smog that burns the eye and irritates
the throat. Heating is done with natural gas, considered a 'clean' fuel, and 12 years ago the city set up
careful controls over its heavy industry. San Diego
pipes its treated sewage 2½ miles out to sea, and buries
its refuse neatly in unused canyons. There is no major
water-pollution problem.

—"AMERICA'S HEALTHIEST CITIES," *Ladies' Home Journal.*

It is not so much a city, somehow, as it is a good place to be. Some of the city things happen. Street crews inexplicably rip up the pavement with air hammers at those seasons when traffic is thickest. City councilmen ridicule each other, admitted murderers plead innocent, and there are fevered dialogues between black and white leaders at city hall. But it is hard in San Diego to be quite so angry, quite so harried, so desperate or intense.

San Diego—not Los Angeles or San Francisco—is the kind of place that those in other parts of the world are most likely to think of when they picture California: a bucolic setting of sunshine and water, not yet shrouded in smog or grown into anonymous infinity, still full of dreams, still obsessed with the hope of greatness tomorrow.

It is a community that sprawls out with a placid, low-key feeling over the hills that rise from its Pacific coastline and the shores of its two bays. In its size and the gentleness of its face, it is not unlike Lisbon. With similar ease it mixes past and present, always facing the sea. There is a disarming modesty about Lisbon, and I feel it when I am at home in San Diego. These are not the biggest cities of the world, and they never will be, and their people seem glad of it.

A quirk of geography also links Lisbon and San Diego. One is near the southwest corner of Europe, and the other at the southwest corner of the United States. Both are off the mainstream and a little self-conscious about it. They lack the frenzy of the waypoint between one place and another. If one is in Lisbon, he means to be there. If one is in San Diego, it is because he has sought it out. That reduces the howl and scream of transiency and supplies a certain substance and solidity.

In Southern California, that trait sets San Diego apart from the bedlam of Los Angeles. The metropolitan area of San Diego approaches 1,500,000 in population, but the visitor wonders where they all are. He looks in vain for trademarks like the conventional urban core. There is a cramped and dreary downtown plaza with a tarnished fountain along a Broadway that looks—except for some quite recent structures—like Norfolk honkytonk or Wichita sincere. The courthouse is here, the newspapers, a huddle of high-rise office buildings, and a proud new community concourse with one of the world's best-designed civic theaters.

Far out on Broadway, the city dissolves into miles of sun-baked homes with their lawns and their walled patios in the rear, a low-level stucco wilderness that rolls up to the foot of the coastal mountains and merges into rural lanes that have the feel of back-country and back-time.

In the other direction on the harbor front, at the foot of Broadway, San Diego becomes all nautical. The stolid concrete hulk of the headquarters of the Eleventh Naval District rises here, and a supply depot that serves the Pacific fleet, and piers where Navy ships tie up to welcome taxpayers aboard for Sunday afternoon open-houses. Crews of more than two hundred Navy ships call San Diego their home port, more than along all the rest of the West Coast combined.

But this Broadway is no longer the main street of San Diego. The city rambles fifteen miles south of Broadway to the Mexican border, and twenty miles north along the Riviera-like coast, past the fabled suburb of La Jolla, toward Los Angeles. Along the way it becomes a decentralized metropolis of a score of communities whose people are united only in allegiance to sun and clear skies and the most benign climate of any major American city. Yet these people seem pleased that educators and researchers and tourists are increasingly among those who have come to share this allegiance, and they become instantly a part of the scene as surely as if they had been thrown up on the mesas when the Pacific receded eons ago.

Standing at dusk against a wind from off the Pacific atop Point Loma, at the portal to the city's boot-shaped main harbor, one looks back at an inky velvet waterway that becomes the real main street of the city. In the desert-like absence of humidity, the lights of communities over the forty-mile span of the city sparkle in patterns of varying intensity that outline the scattered sub-cities. Some are part of the San Diego municipal structure and some along the edges are small cities of their own. But with this pattern, so typical of both San Diego and Los Angeles, Southern Californians have maintained some of the small-town sense to which so many of them were accustomed before they migrated here.

The twilight view from Point Loma shows the setting of the city at its finest. The sky grows bright in the north with the haze, comfortably distant, of Los Angeles reflected against its cloud cover more than a hundred miles away. The Laguna Mountains to the east, sometimes capped with snow, form an austere backdrop for the city. To the south the blaze of San Diego gives way to the lesser lights of the Mexican border city of Tijuana, the truncated silhouette of Table Mountain, and beyond, the emptiness of an eight-hundred-mile desert peninsula over which Spaniards marched two hundred years ago in the first settlement of California. There to the south along Baja California's dusty trails, little has changed. San Diego, once the wilderness outpost, is now in the reverse role. It is the end of the line going south. When I first saw the city as a green Navy ensign late in World War II, I was astonished that the train on which I arrived backed into its station—to be ready for its turn-around trip to Los Angeles. This geographic position has shaped San Diego's history and its character. The city has grown rather steadily, often doubling its population each decade, but still at a rate which in California seems almost calm and natural. San Diego absorbs some of the leisurely pace and dignity of its Latin neighbor; the passion for bigness so prominent in the psyche of Los Angeles, on its northern side, seems tempered by the Mexican spirit. San Diego has remained an unexpectedly pleasant and leisurely metropolis, cradled between the land of mañana and the city of colossal.

But the shadow of Los Angeles has loomed large over San Diego almost since its beginnings. With boisterous glee, some San Diegans pass out printed cards that read: WE DON'T GIVE A DAMN WHAT THEY DO IN LOS ANGELES! The joke is a local one, but it is revealing. The cry rose first among San Diego businessmen who were piqued when their prices or practices were contrasted with those of the aggressive metropolis to the north. But more than economics is involved: the vigor of youth has taken hold in San Diego, tempered by an innate conservatism that prevails against the onrush of the bizzare.

Make no mistake: San Diego is *in* Southern California, but it is not *of* the same land that spawned Aimee Semple McPherson and igloo-shaped ice-cream palaces. It is the city where California began, and it intended to be in all ways the first city of California. But there was scant gold here, and the builders of highways and railroads found better passes through the mountains from the east, leading into San Francisco and Los Angeles. With one of the nation's finest natural harbors, San Diego surrendered maritime supremacy first to San Francisco and again later to Los Angeles, when the latter city built its own unnatural harbor.

Half a century ago San Diego leaders insisted that they did not want their city to boom, but they hired experts to tell them why it did not. They glowered while Los Angeles became a runaway megalopolis, and only now are they beginning to realize that they were blessed by their early failures. Lacking crowding and smog and the other badges of industrial triumph, San Diego has become the playground for Los Angeles millions, a kind of weekend patio for the Southwest. In the era of affluence and mobility, when tourism brings in the least troublesome dollars, San Diego remains unspoiled and alluring. The hubbub to the north was shrugged away and tacitly ignored for decades. Now San Diego, brimming with parks and golf courses and aquatic playgrounds, is finally in vogue.

San Diego's problem of identity has been like that of the conglomerates of the corporate world. Both are suddenly large, motley in composition and lacking any immediately recognizable tag. Like a blander San Francisco, San Diego is a city of hills and bays. Its hills are less dramatic, and there are two distinctly separate bays. One is dominant: San Diego Harbor, seventeen miles long and bristling with naval vessels. Tuna clippers base here for their southward runs below the Equator, while thousands of pleasure boats overflow from its yacht clubs and marinas.

Mission Bay, to the north, is separated from San Diego Harbor only by the hooking ridgeline of Point Loma. It is designed solely for leisure, a seven-square-mile aquatic park. It was created by the city as a civic playground and resort center on the site of noxious mud flats that had lain dormant ever since early explorers mired down in them and named the place False Bay. By the time visionary city planners came up with a design for creating playground islands and channels for water sports, the name of False Bay had given way to Mission Bay. For on a bluff overlooking the bay, in

1769, the first European settlement of California had been made
—a mission founded by Father Junípero Serra, a frail and diminu-
tive Franciscan priest who is one of the most gallant figures in the
history of the American West. It is because of his indomitable
will that Californians celebrate their bicentennial in 1969.

Most Californians are remarkably vague about the history of
their land. The prevalent image is a nebulous jumble of exploited
Indian, romanticized Spanish missionary, and jaunty gold-hunter.
The shifting nature of the California populace is nothing new. Its
history is still short, but it has followed a weaving course.

The first vagrants were the Indians: probably about one hundred thousand of them when the earliest settlers arrived, before
their ranks were decimated by the white man's firepower and,
more deadly but unintentional, his diseases.

California remained the Indians' land for more than two centuries after the first white man stepped ashore. Because of the
nature of the Baja California peninsula, early Spaniards thought
California to be an island. From the center of New Spain at
Mexico City, explorers roamed far to the south, into the Andes
in search of Inca gold. To the north, into what is today the
American Southwest, they ventured rarely. California was a savage wilderness.

For a short while in 1535 the conquistador Hernán Cortés
established a tiny pearl fishing colony far to the south of San
Diego at the Baja California harbor called La Paz. A romantic
novel was in vogue just then in Spain. Written by Garcí Ordóñez
de Montalvo, it was set on a rich island near the Indies whose
only metal was gold. The island was ruled by a black Amazon
queen named Calafia. The Spaniards knew nothing of California
gold, nor did their pearl colony survive; but California took its
name from that legendary queen.

In 1542 the Spanish explorer Juan Rodríguez Cabrillo sailed
into San Diego Harbor and became the first European to touch
the soil of the California of today. There was no thought of
colonization then. Cabrillo was the Columbus of California, seeking a Northwest passage to link the Atlantic and Pacific. This
was a time of Spanish glory on the seas and the hunt was for

quick riches; nothing in the California shoreline suggested wealth. But Cabrillo was high in his praise of the natural harbor of San Diego.

Sebastián Vizcaíno sailed along the Southern California coast for Spain in 1602 and named San Diego, Santa Monica, Santa Barbara and Monterey. In his log he so embellished the virtues of Monterey as a safe harbor that the next white man on the scene 167 years later, a Catalonian nobleman, Don Gaspar de Portolá, marched past without recognizing it.

With missionary fervor, the Church pleaded through these years for settlement of California and the conversion of its Indians. But the star of Spanish greatness was soon in decline and a campaign in so remote a region seemed too costly to the Spanish viceroy at Mexico City. Manhattan Island may have been bought from Indians for twenty-four dollars, but for many years Europeans did not seem to care for California at any price.

Overland explorations by the Spanish from Mexico had revealed California to be set apart by desert and precipitous mountains. The approach from the sea was little more inviting. Prevailing northwest winds blew against explorers who sought to beat their way under sail up the California coast. No ship entered San Diego harbor to disturb the placid indolence of the Indians from Vizcaíno's visit in 1602 until its settlement in 1769.

Spain moved finally toward California with reluctance, intent only on heading off Russian fur traders who were reported sailing out across the Aleutians and down the coast of northwest America. As it had elsewhere in the half of the world that it then dominated, Spain moved forward with both the sword and the cross. It seemed unthinkable to launch a military campaign with such long supply lines against hordes of Indians who still lived in the Stone Age. It was more reasonable to lend modest military support to mission priests who wished to Christianize the heathen, and incidentally hoist the flag of Spain.

In 1697 Spanish priests had moved across from the mainland of Mexico at San Blas to Loreto, far down the Baja California peninsula, and established a mission. Loreto, a dusty Mexican village then as now, became the capital of all California, an unknown empire claimed by Spain and ranging almost eighteen hundred miles north to what became the Oregon border. It is one of the classic studies for the geopolitician that Loreto remains a Mexican village of about fourteen hundred people, almost inaccessible except by small plane or boat, and that as it has slumbered, the prodigious force of American California has helped to reshape the world.

A lonely desert string of missions was slowly built up in Mexican Baja California, their outpost about three hundred miles short of today's United States border. The Spanish viceroy assigned José de Gálvez, an Andalusian who had become an adviser to the Spanish king, Charles III, to investigate the Russian menace to California. There was not much menace, but Gálvez saw an opportunity to advance his career. He sailed to Baja California to organize a force that might settle Monterey, which had been regarded as the prime California site since the glowing reports of Vizcaíno so many years earlier. The Franciscan mission priest, Junípero Serra, had just been named to head the missions of Baja California, and he was eager to push the mission chain northward. On the ambition of Gálvez and the zeal of Serra the settlement of California hinged.

It is hard to imagine a less likely candidate than Serra to survive the ordeals of a desert frontier. He was already fifty-five years old when his challenge came. He was no more than five feet, three inches, in height. He suffered incessant chest pains as the result of his fervent evangelism, not uncommon in that day: he struck himself with stones and chains as he preached, and held lighted torches to his body. His legs and feet were given to severe swelling, making him often almost a cripple. He was humble and meek, deprecating his abilities. Yet his spirit was so intransigent that all who dealt with him knew him as a formidable adversary. A distinguished theologian and teacher of philosophy in his native Mallorca, Serra had abandoned the academic life at the age of 36 to come to Mexico as a missionary.

In their goal of blocking Russian advances toward California, Carlos III and José de Gálvez could have had no more intrepid champion. It did not matter that their interests were divergent; the great crucifix which Serra wore day and night would lead the way, and the Catalonian captain, Don Gaspar de Portolá, in his bedazzling uniform, would carry the sword.

Although the American colonies were then on the verge of their revolution for independence, surprisingly little was known yet of California. In 1768, the year before the expedition to San Diego, the first edition of the *Encyclopaedia Britannica* referred to California as "a large country of the West Indies," and called it "uncertain whether it be a peninsula or an island."

San Diego was chosen as the first California base for the expedition because of its harbor and its position as a halfway point from Loreto to Monterey. Gálvez assigned two overland parties; Serra was to march with Portolá. But Portolá, skeptical of Serra's chances to survive the march, urgently entreated him to withdraw. Serra refused.

Three packet ships were outfitted to sail toward San Diego, and tragedy haunted all of them. They bore sailors and soldiers, seed and farm implements, foodstuffs, and cargoes of vestments, sacred vases and ornaments. One ship, the *San Jose*, vanished entirely. Scurvy prostrated the crews of the *San Antonio* and *San Carlos* during their tedious beat northwestward into the wind.

Leading one of the two overland expeditions, Portolá and Serra came three hundred and fifty miles with soldiers, muleteers, several hundred head of cattle and a pack train through a desert described by Father Juan Crespi, diarist of the expedition, as "sterile, arid, lacking grass and water, and abounding in stones and thorns."

Portolá's fears for Serra proved valid. In his diary for May 17, 1769, Serra wrote: "By now the swelling has reached halfway up my leg, which is covered with sores . . . I was afraid that before long I should have to follow the expedition on a stretcher." The company ran out of food; friendly Indian servants deserted or died. Portolá led his men up into the desert mountains to kill geese and rabbits, and back to the Pacific shore for clams and fish. Water was scarce; they went for three or four days without finding water holes, and their stock went without water for almost twice that long.

After six weeks, Serra saw on the horizon the white sails of the *San Antonio* and *San Carlos* in San Diego Harbor. But the tragic little camp he found at the mouth of the San Diego River brought tears to his eyes. The *San Carlos* had wandered lost off the California coast, finally arriving in San Diego after 110 days. Those of its crew who survived scurvy were unfit for duty. Perhaps sixty of about ninety crewmen of the two packets were already dead, and more were dying. Even ashore, in a land that was soon to grow green with the cultivation of fruits and vegetables, the natural preventive for scurvy, there was no help. Serra and Portolá set to burying their dead and caring for the survivors.

To his friend and later biographer, Father Francisco Palou, Serra wrote: "I arrived here at the fort of San Diego. It is beautiful to behold and does not belie its reputation. Here I met all who set out before me, whether by sea or by land, but not the dead." He had time to note that he had reached his destination in a pagan land among Indians who were shameless in their nudity, "a harvest of souls that might easily be gathered into the bosom of Our Holy Mother the church and, it would appear, with very little trouble." It was the fervent dream of a missionary, but it bore little resemblance to the terrors that still lay ahead.

In the beginning the Indians were shy, but they quickly grew bolder and began to steal—even the sheets off the men dying of scurvy. One party of Indians rowed out to the *San Carlos* and attempted to steal its sails. They did not respond to Serra's evangelism. The soldiers who were able to stand guard built a stockade of simple logs and thatch and watched warily.

Two weeks later Portolá led a group of men he referred to as "skeletons who had been spared by scurvy, hunger, and thirst" on an overland march to seek out Monterey Bay. Serra stayed behind and on July 16, 1769, he dedicated a small brushwood hut as the first California mission. The *San Antonio* sailed back to San Blas for supplies with eight men aboard, all that remained of her original crew of twenty-eight; only two of these survived the trip to San Blas.

That first winter almost ended the Spanish effort to colonize California. Food supplies were exhausted. Colonists lived on fish and geese, and corn that they could wheedle out of the Indians in barter. Portolá returned from a grueling and futile march north as far as San Francisco Bay during which he and his men had been reduced to eating their mules.

Early in March, 1770, with the little San Diego presidio and mission at a desperate ebb, Portolá set a deadline for abandoning the colony and returning to Mexico unless supplies should arrive. Serra's protestations were to no avail, but he declared that he would not depart under any circumstances. Portolá's deadline approached, and the priest began a novena, a nine-day devotion of prayers.

The final day came and there was no ship on the horizon. Portolá began to prepare for departure. At three in the afternoon sails were seen on the horizon, moving north. It was the *San Antonio*, on her way with supplies to Monterey, where her captain assumed Portolá had succeeded in establishing a camp. Cheered even by the sight of a passing ship, Portolá agreed to delay his departure. Four days later, in what seemed to Serra an answer to prayer, the *San Antonio* reappeared, this time entering San Diego harbor. Her crewmen, going ashore for water near Point Conception, had learned from Indians that Portolá's expedition had returned to San Diego. Her supplies saved San Diego. Until his death, Serra celebrated a high mass on the nineteenth of every month in memory of the vigil which preserved the first settlement in California.

Serra moved on from San Diego to Monterey and went about the work of building the chain of twenty-one California missions that was completed, years after his death, in 1823. Serra was not present at San Diego on the night of November 5, 1775, when Indians, aroused now to the expulsion of the white man, attacked and burned the mission. Soldiers fought them off but Serra's successor at San Diego, Father Luis Jayme, was lost. He pushed out into the midnight melee with his hands upraised and called to the Indians, "Love God, my children!" He was clubbed and shot full of arrows, the first martyr of California.

By that year there were five missions and two presidios along a four-hundred mile strip of California coast, and only seventy-five soldiers on guard. It would have been a simple matter then in a united Indian effort to erase all the tedious efforts of a decade. But the Indians of the California coast, softened by a relatively easy existence, were not fighters. Soon they began to drift into the missions as converts, led by gifts and attracted by singing. When baptized, they moved into the mission compounds and were ruled under rigid regulations. They could not leave the mission community without permission. They were taught the rudiments of Christianity, along with farming and mechanical crafts.

Death came to Junípero Serra in 1784 at the age of seventy as he clutched the foot-long crucifix he had brought up from Mexico fifteen years before. There were 4600 Indian converts living at his California missions. The land was held in theoretical trust for the Indians, and Serra's passion for improving the lot of the heathen seemed established on a sound basis. Yet in another fifty years the mission system would be destroyed.

The missions and their vast surrounding farmlands grew verdant with wheat and vineyards, usually under irrigation. Many priests felt it unseemly to operate great ranches and supervise machine shops, but it seemed necessary to the support of their prime function of winning souls. The missions developed a powerful commerce, trading hides, tallow, wine, brandy, olive oil, grain and leatherwork for manufactured goods brought increasingly by trading vessels. Yet the frequent appearance of Yankee ships from New England suggested the doom of California as a Spanish colony. The new republic of the United States was beginning to press westward.

From the start, historic tides caused sudden wrenches of the California culture. The Spanish mission system was challenged by Spanish-Mexican settlers—two generations of whom had by now grown up in California. These were the *Californios*. Because the land was held under the mission system, the Californios could not own property. When Mexico declared its independence from Spain in 1821, another cultural jolt was in store for all of those in California. The cry arose for secularization of the missions as the only way to open land to private ownership. In 1830, only twenty-one parcels of land were in private hands. The order came in 1833 and over the next sixteen years the mission ranches were parceled out by the government of Mexico to political favorites. Greedy land settlers moved in from both the United States and Mexico. The Indians suffered. Through each era, like tragic children, sometimes angry and cruel, the first Californians seemed to come out last.

On the eve of the breakup of the missions, prosperity had grown startlingly, as evangelization and slavery had been conveniently merged. More than thirty thousand Christian Indians tilled the soil under the direction of sixty padres and three hundred soldiers at twenty-one missions. They herded 396,000 head of cattle, 62,000 horses, 321,000 hogs, sheep and goats, and harvested 123,000 bushels of grain in one year. If in no other way, the record of the Franciscans was extraordinary: sixty-five years earlier, there had been in all of California no grain of wheat, no cow, horse, hog, sheep or goat. But not many years were to pass before the chapel that Serra built at Carmel was to be used for hay storage, and pigs were to be quartered within the San Fernando mission. Not until after 1900 did the missions, by then in crumbling ruins, draw the attention of enough Americans to bring about their restoration as antiquities.

The official end of Mission San Diego de Alcalá came in 1846, when, unable even to support a parish priest, the mission and more than fifty-eight thousand acres of land were granted by Mexican Governor Pio Pico to a government favorite, Don Santiago Arguello. Nothing remains today of the original San Diego presidio and mission except humps of earth beneath which lie the bones of their founders and crumbled adobe remains of walls, now yielding important artifacts to archeologists. The subsequent mission, built seven miles to the east in 1774, has been charmingly restored both as a place of worship and a tourist attraction.

First in history, San Diego lacked the location and the aggressiveness to maintain rank as the metropolis of California. It was far off course in the Gold Rush. It became a border community with the Treaty of Guadalupe Hidalgo at the close of the Mexican War when California was ceded to the United States, with the international boundary drawn just south of San Diego.

Gold brought the rush for settlement in northern California; in the south it was land speculation. But growth did not come so swiftly nor build so solidly as in the north. At the end of the Civil War, after several years of drought which left Southern California rangeland sere and cattle dying under the sun, fewer than two hundred people lived in the community at the base of the old San Diego presidio.

"I would not give you five dollars for a deed to the whole of it," cried Alonzo Erastus Horton, a settler from Wisconsin, in 1867. "I would not take it as a gift. It doesn't lie right. Never in the world can you have a city here."

Horton proposed instead to build the city three miles to the south, the site of the present downtown San Diego. He bought 960 acres at an average price of 27½ cents an acre and left San Francisco to establish a San Diego land sales office, proclaiming San Diego as the city of the future. It was a minority opinion.

The rivalry between San Diego and Los Angeles began early. Before the Civil War had ended, Rufus K. Porter reported in the San Francisco *Bulletin:* "The Los Angeles folks do not look with favor at anything tending to promote the prosperity of [San Diego]." David M. Berry, who later helped establish Pasadena, was appalled by San Diego. "The people are all in the real estate business," he wrote, "and will not dig wells and irrigate the land and develop the country . . . even the ice they use is made in a factory in Los Angeles. . . ."

Los Angeles began to pull ahead of San Diego in the 1870's, providing the Southern Pacific with a site for a rail depot and a $600,000 grant to bring its lines into Los Angeles from the north and east. Until then it had been assumed that San Diego would be the regional hub. After abortive efforts to make San Diego a transcontinental rail terminus, its citizens settled in 1891 for a spur line from Los Angeles. A railroad over the precipitous mountains east of San Diego was finally completed in 1919, too late to challenge Los Angeles' supremacy as a transport center. By then Los Angeles had created a man-made harbor, overcoming its handicap in maritime commerce.

Yet there was no easing of hostility between the two Southern California cities. In a special edition soon after the turn of the century, the *Los Angeles Times* presented a map of the region on which San Diego did not appear. Los Angeles had been moved twenty miles westward on the map (before it did indeed annex its way to the Pacific shore) and shown as a port city. San Diego harbor commissioners retaliated with a sketch of San Diego Bay showing 174 nonexistent piers, all busy with traffic between railheads which had not been built, and Pacific shipping lines which in fact did not stop at San Diego.

San Diegans tried futilely to emulate Los Angeles in development of transport and industry. But it was the military that slowly and irrevocably shaped the San Diego future. With World War I, San Diego emerged as a naval bastion offering clear weather for flying and a deep-water harbor. Those who believed the future of San Diego lay in development of its harbor as a world port proved to be only half right; it was the Navy which grew to provide the bulk of its maritime commerce.

Tourism prospered. Resorts in the suburbs of Coronado and La Jolla grew popular. The Mexican border town of Tijuana became a major tourist attraction during Prohibition, operating wide-open with such blatant lures as "the longest bar in the world." Until a ban on Mexican gambling in 1935, Agua Caliente, a luxurious casino built at a cost of ten million dollars, catered to the film colony and other free-spenders of the era. In its day, the high-life of Southern California swirled as much around Agua Caliente as it does today around Las Vegas. Most of all, two San Diego expositions—in 1915–16 and 1935–36—brought hundreds of thousands of visitors, and some of them never left. The expositions also established a superb architectural nucleus in 1400-acre Balboa Park with the neo-Spanish buildings of the architect Bertram Goodhue; many of them today house galleries, theaters and museums that are at the cultural heart of the city.

Charles A. Lindbergh had come to San Diego in 1927 to supervise the construction of his *Spirit of St. Louis,* and the city soon developed a stake in the burgeoning aircraft industry. In 1935, Reuben Fleet, the president of Consolidated Aircraft Corporation at Buffalo, New York, made a decision that was pivotal in San Diego's later emergence as an aerospace center. With a contract to build flying boats for the Navy, Fleet was hampered at Buffalo by icy waters and stormy skies. He moved his factory equipment and his employees to San Diego in special trains. His firm became the foundation for Convair and subsequent divisions of General Dynamics Corporation at San Diego.

In the years since World War II, San Diego has found its civic niche. The shadow of Los Angeles is still recognized in the businessmen's plea to "Try San Diego First." But the community has grown into a university center with a core of extraordinary scientific research institutions including Salk Institute, the University of California's Scripps Institution of Oceanography, Gulf General Atomic, Scripps Clinic, Lockheed's oceanographic facility, and the Western Behavioral Sciences Institute. Education provides more jobs than aerospace.

For years San Diego was divided in a battle of "smokestacks versus geraniums." Some fought for industrial development while others—the geranium faction—strove to maintain San Diego as a placid residential and retirement city. The issue is compromised. Without smokestacks, the aerospace and electronic industries now provide the backbone of San Diego's manufacturing payroll of about $1.2 billion. There are an increasing number of corporate headquarters in San Diego, including that of the respected newspaper chain owned by James S. Copley, whose hillside estate is in La Jolla.

The military stands high in economic importance. San Diego ranks with Norfolk as the nation's largest Navy city. About one in every four San Diegans is involved with the Navy or Marine Corps—on active duty, as dependents, or as civilian employees. The armed forces have close to two billion dollars in property in the San Diego area, including about one-sixth of the entire plant value of the United States Navy. Twelve billion dollars' worth of ships and planes are based in San Diego. Among the facilities is the largest naval hospital in the world. It has two thousand bed patients and close to five hundred physicians. San Diego has evolved into a metropolitan area by the steady process of migration of men such as these; about one-half of the civilian physicians in San Diego first came to the area as navy doctors.

The coming of educators and scientists has been most marked in the years since 1950. The nature of the newcomer has undergone a considerable change; the highly-skilled engineer or technician is more common than before, and the migrant tends to be younger. It gives San Diego a sense of continual escalation. It is no longer the oppressively restrained conservative and isolated community of the 1930's, nor the drab and crowded staging area of World War II.

Now there is freshness, vigor, and an increasing degree of sophistication and emphasis on the amenities. In 1968, new construction at the University of California campus at San Diego was proceeding at a rate above two hundred dollars a minute in value. "When I started here in 1945," recalled a University Extension official, "two of every one thousand new people coming into the city were interested in what we were doing. Today our polls show twenty of every one thousand make contact with us." Laymen sit in at seminars with scientists and are stirred with pride as they leave laboratories and campuses. After one such session, a San Diego attorney related that he had been present when a NASA official, planning allocations of some fifty pounds of the moon's surface which astronauts proposed to bring back to earth, had asked the Nobel laureate Harold Urey: "How much of the moon do you want?"

San Diego lures growth by its climate, its roominess and the momentum of its absorption in futurism. "There is a surge of new life much like the frontier spirit," says Dr. Frederic de Hoffman, president of Gulf General Atomic. "There is a recognition that this area lives by its wits. If you are to make a good life in this part of the West, you realize it will be by having intellectually bright enterprises that will constantly stay up with the future. Everywhere I go in the West, this sort of world is much more in evidence than it is in the East. There is an excitement here in San Diego, an alertness. The people of San Diego voted six to one to deed three hundred acres of city land to us for this laboratory. This has made an enormous difference in our effort in recruiting people. It told them that here was a community that understands; not just the city council, but eighty-five percent of the people."

The newness takes many forms. In 1967 the average age of San Diego city councilmen was under forty. The San Diego Unified School District, twelfth largest public school system in the country, had been in existence for 111 years—but three-fourths of its facilities had been constructed in the previous fifteen years. The city had recently acquired professional major league teams in football, baseball, basketball, and hockey. It had lively local opera and ballet companies, a rapidly improving symphony orchestra, and a notable Shakespearean summer festival.

In tourism, San Diego races ahead. It claims more hotel rooms than San Francisco or the entire state of Hawaii. Its incomparable zoo is a major attraction. So is adjacent Mexico. It is a strange quirk of numbers that more U.S. citizens visit Tijuana than all other foreign cities combined, in excess of twelve million persons annually. Tijuana is a wide-open city, dirty and unattractive to many visitors, that offers every sensual indulgence so far conceived by man. But it is Mexico—and the most accessible foreign town to a large proportion of Americans. For those who are not searching for sin, the city offers pockets of interest and charm.

Considerable ingenuity has gone into the development of San Diego for the tourist. Islands have been dredged up to provide exotic settings for recreational facilities. Marinas and resort hotels and new restaurants spring up everywhere along the spacious waterfronts: both San Diego Harbor and leisure-oriented Mission Bay, and the seventy miles of San Diego County coastline. The almost-island of Coronado and its Victorian hotel, long shared by tourists and naval officers, is being linked to downtown San Diego by the first bridge to span San Diego Harbor. The suburb of La Jolla, graceful and serene along the cliffs of the curving coast, is the favored summer spa of a host of the establishment from the Midwest and Southwest. With twelve months of sun and warmth, more than forty golf courses open to play every day of the year, and the gamut of aquatic amusements, San Diego emerges as a casual and ingenuous Riviera of the West.

Driving along an interstate freeway today between Presidio Hill, where Serra and Portolá established the first California camp, and the restored San Diego mission seven miles to the east, the visitor finds a valley that runs like a spinal column through the expanding confines of the city. It has no conventional urban air about it. There are a dozen sprawling new hotels in styles ranging from bogus-Las Vegas to Old Mission. There are golf courses, gargantuan shopping complexes, and a handsome new civic stadium. There is also a dairy that has not yet been forced out, and a tunnel built beneath the freeway for cows. There are haymows and sand and gravel works and roadside rural stands that offer produce and dairy products. Yet on all sides of this valley, San Diego spreads out in fresh, clean and immensely livable communities of uncrowded homes and schools and churches and shopping complexes. The geographical center of San Diego population is not far distant from the site of that Mission Valley dairy.

San Diego is growing up without the brashness of Los Angeles or the narcissism of San Francisco. It offers climate and freedom. It is the oldest but in some ways the newest city of California. It seems to have the best chance for becoming the city of tomorrow, augmenting the amenities of the good life with firm cultural roots and a highly selective base of commerce. The civic character of Los Angeles and San Francisco is already set; San Diego's is only now developing. It is within the power of its people to bring greatness to the community that was first settled two hundred years ago by the doughty priest with the big crucifix.

.9.

GOLD SHAPED THIS LAND

> Today's Californians, like relay racers handed a
> tremendous lead by their first teamsman, have a con-
> fidence that sometimes alarms strangers. They are in
> the habit of having great expectations, of entertaining
> roseate hopes and seeing them come true.
>
> —JOHN WALTON CAUGHEY, *Gold Is the Cornerstone.*

There are two distinct California gold countries: then,
and now. Then it *was* California, and it was everything: raucous,
new, lusty, intense, determined, courageous. Now it is gentle and
sleepy, too corporeal to be thought of as a ghostland, but so nebulous in focus that it is difficult to imagine it as the catalyst of
modern California.

On a Saturday afternoon in early December not long ago, the pale winter sun shone through a haze that hung over this gold country, a corridor of rolling foothills from forty to sixty miles wide that lies north and south for almost three hundred miles between the San Joaquin and Feather rivers in northern California. The air was chill and brushed with the smells of green woods. The oaks and poplars and maples were at their best, their leaves turned bright golden and vermilion.

Wood smoke swirled from chimneys of frame houses on the back street that climbs toward California's oldest courthouse in Mariposa, the southernmost of the gold towns, not far from the portal to Yosemite Valley. A few cars were parked on the main street, snug up against high curbs along the empty sidewalks. Inside a dry goods store a woman was measuring out twelve yards of cotton flannel in a blue flower print.

In a bar next door, a lone old man sat hunched over his beer.

"There's a fortune in gold still hid up there in the Nellie," he was saying. There were only the bartender and my wife and me to listen, and none of us had asked. He talked anyhow.

"Up there on Mount Bullion, out past the little county airstrip, that's where the Nellie is. You can see it without too long a hike. What happened was we run out of water. I took a crew back in there and we patched up an old rocker and made it work and I took out enough gold to keep from going bankrupt. But we run out of water."

He took a long hard swallow and pretended to force himself to go on.

"I guess I put more than a hundred thousand in the Nellie and I took out maybe sixty. If I had water up there I'd go back and take out a fortune. Nellie's rich, still plumb rich. I'll mine her again some day, you wait."

The bartender yawned and dropped a quarter in the jukebox. We paid for our beers and another for the man who might once have been a miner. Outside there was still no movement. We turned a corner past the old Odd Fellows Hall and walked up the courthouse hill.

The houses of Mariposa are like those of aging country towns in so many parts of America: only the oldest and the newest of them hew to any recognizable style. Those in the throes of motley middle-age seem to have gained a room or two here, lost a porch there, and yielded in general to the demands of changing families and times.

Cats slumbered in patches of sunlight or prowled around stacks of firewood. Sheets and clothing flapped on lines. The people of Mariposa were inside, out of sight. There aren't many, anyhow. It is the central village of one of California's least populous counties, with just over six thousand people in an area a little larger than Rhode Island. They raise apples and some cattle, chickens and turkeys, and rather casually serve the tourist who comes to see what it is like these days in the Mother Lode country, now that the Gold Rush is ancient history.

Before California became United States territory, Mariposa was the center of government for a vast area that extended east across Nevada to the Utah border and south to Los Angeles County, more than three hundred miles away. Now its affairs of state are limited to a two-story white frame building with its tall, slender bell tower, a specimen of transplanted New England architecture that has served as courthouse in Mariposa since 1854. In California such longevity is regarded as droll.

But there seemed nothing self-conscious about the four men we saw at the Mariposa courthouse on that Saturday afternoon, with their pick-up trucks parked out front, as they raked leaves and climbed ladders to hang strings of Christmas lights in two big incense cedars. Inside, benches like church pews were lined up in a plain courtroom whose walls were built with dovetailed joints and held together with locust pegs. The jurist's chair is occupied, when court is in session, by a man remembered fondly in San Francisco from days when he led a hotel dance band.

We stood and watched as the lights went up. The clock in the bell tower rang twice. The men on their ladders did not seem to hear. In this part of California, time is not very important.

The sense of California destiny is not found in its restored missions, nor on the few fields of its paltry battles. The Franciscan padres did not shape the future; gold did. There is no Bunker Hill, no Shiloh nor Gettysburg, for in California the war was more often man's fight for survival—usually against the frontier, and sometimes against his fellow man. To understand California, you go back to the Mother Lode.

The southern half of the three-hundred-mile gold country was named the Mother Lode; the northern mines were higher, and a little later. The Mother Lode begins in low grassland, only a few hundred feet above sea level, and climbs higher; the northern mines soar close to 6700-foot Yuba Pass, whose pines and firs are clad much of the year in snow. Throughout its length, the gold country is today part of the quiet California, its villages startlingly foreign to the hustle of the cities.

Their urban ties, both by geography and history, are to Sacramento and thence to San Francisco; in their regionalism can be found the core of the divergence between the California north and the California south, a schism that is historic. The back country of Southern California is an often barren mountain country giving way to the harshest of deserts; in the north, behind San Francisco and across the Great Central Valley, there lies this softer land of tumbling hills that are the step-stones to the majestic Sierra Nevada.

The land has a heritage of verve and daring. But its passions are celebrated by the few who remain in a bland and offhand way that makes its people seem less like descendants of the Forty-Niners than voyeurs to the history with which these hills are impregnated. About five hundred mining camp towns were born here between 1848 and 1860. Because they were located usually along streams or rivers, their main streets were seldom straight. At first they were villages of canvas and rough plank shacks clinging to a hillside. Always there was a store and saloon and a hotel of sorts. If the gold lasted there would be stronger buildings, perhaps a Wells Fargo express office built of stone with iron door and shutters because it served as a repository for gold.

Time has wiped out all trace of about two-thirds of these towns, some surviving only in signposts or stone ruins or bronze markers. A historic plaque at Second Garrote points out a nearby hanging tree. Another identifies the site of Jenny Lind, a mining town named in honor of the "Swedish nightingale" about the time she was touring the United States with P. T. Barnum. Here and there, as at Bridgeport, one still finds a covered bridge that knew the clatter of the stage.

The population of the gold country is static. Its charm is associated with its lack of people and the absence of those terrors of urbanity that tend to make all the world alike. The faded villages make up a living forum not much more than a century old.

The evolution of those towns that have survived has been strange. They hung on for decades as relics, not quite ghost towns; California was too young and its Gold Rush too recent for them to have become museum pieces. Then they drew life from the surge of interest in history that swept California with the centennials of 1948 to 1950—celebrating the span from discovery of gold to statehood. Since then there have been historical committees and plans for restorations.

At Coloma, where it all began, John Sutter's sawmill has been reconstructed and an admirable state park museum commemorates the discovery of gold in 1848.

At Columbia, once known as "the gem of the Southern Mines," about $2.5 million was invested to transform the entire community into a state park. Both frame and red brick commercial buildings and their iron shutters have been restored to make Columbia a showplace of Mother Lode architecture—a blend of New England with the covered porches of the Mexicans. College students perform as a repertory company at Columbia in summer. Signs proclaim sarsaparilla a featured drink, but in the dim, windowless old bars, always replete with frontier atmosphere, the drinking is hard.

There is even greater appeal to be found in villages that have hung on without outside help. One is Jamestown—which miners knew as Jimtown. Before World War II its narrow main street and its handful of balconied frame structures were known to good-time Charleys for much the same attractions that Jimtown had offered in the Gold Rush. Its high-stake poker games drew farm and city sports instead of miners, and so did its rows of prostitutes' shanties. But increasing traffic began to bring in too many inquisitive outsiders. The law put a stop to the big poker games, and military authorities moved in on Jimtown prostitution.

Now Jamestown offers the visitor plank-floored saloons that are authentic to the mining era, and antique shops and an ancient locomotive that has come to rest on a siding near the center of the village. "One half minute to Jamestown," says a sign leading off the highway. In its accessibility, the Jimtown of today bears no resemblance to the miners' village of which Mary Austin wrote, "It is said of Jimville that getting away from it is such a piece of work that it encourages permanence in the population."

Some towns offer the visitor a chance to stay overnight in old hotels like that of the locust-lined main street of little Murphys. The registers bear the signatures of illustrious visitors dating back to 1856—Mark Twain, U. S. Grant, Henry Ward Beecher, Horatio Alger, and even the notorious highwayman, Black Bart. The hotel remains much as it was. A fine iron railing runs along the second-story balcony. Iron shutters hang at the windows. An iron safe stands behind the bar, and horsehair sofas and red plush are found in the best rooms. Bits of wire cable, once used for hitching horses, can be found outside in the trunks of Chinese heaven trees.

The St. George Hotel in the village of Volcano is a wistful double-balconied wooden structure that has stood since 1862; its vine-covered facade greets the visitor as he drives along a country lane across Sutter Creek and turns a sudden sharp curve into the main street of Volcano.

About ninety million dollars in gold came from the hills around Volcano. For a while it was a big town, with seventeen hotels, thirty-five saloons, three breweries and two temperance clubs. Now there are only ninety-six residents. Its main street is lined with crumbling stone buildings that once housed saloons and the Wells Fargo office. Down the block is a decaying cannon called "Old Abe" that Union volunteers smuggled into town in a horse-drawn hearse during the Civil War to quell a rumored Confederate uprising. An old express office is now the village store. Tombstones in the cemetery on a hill above Volcano, like those in most old California cemeteries, stress the origins of the immigrants. Volcano was settled by numerous Swiss and northern Italians, and sentimental tributes to faraway homes are found above their graves.

The pattern of life in these gold country villages can be found in almost any conversation with a resident.

"The population of Volcano has been just the same all eighteen years we've lived here," Jock Thebaut told me at Volcano, where on weekends he operates a tourist bookshop called the Eagle Bandstand. On weekdays he commutes to more distant points as a parole officer.

"Our biggest industry is the Volcano Telephone Company, an independent company that serves the town and countryside about halfway over to Jackson. The phone company hires six people, and that takes care of six families and that's a major part of the population.

"You can dial anywhere in the world from Volcano, but for a while there was a bottleneck in Jackson. We went to all-digit dialing but Jackson still had a manual system and you had to go through Jackson. Now we have everything in Volcano that they've got in New York, if you take away professional people like doctors and lawyers. We go to Jackson for them."

Jackson looms as a giant to the people of Volcano. It is the seat of Amador County, with a population of about two thousand. In the three-hundred-mile stretch of the gold country, it must be classed as a metropolis along with Auburn, Grass Valley, Nevada City, Sonora and Placerville, none of which has more than about seven thousand residents. Such towns, large enough to merit the attention of commerce, are suffering the normal attrition of visual garbage: gas station signs, dreary concrete block post offices and supermarkets and motels, mobile home parks, and blinking neon.

At Nevada City recently, the California Division of Highways overrode fevered objections by the citizenry and built a seven-mile freeway to Grass Valley. It slices through Nevada City, looming large above the banks of Deer Creek, the site of a gold strike in 1848 that lured ten thousand miners to work every foot of ground within a radius of three miles. Showing that the miners' penchant for vivid names is not lost, the residents of Nevada City named the freeway Calamity Cut. It is true that the road between these two towns was once the most heavily traveled route in California, but that was at a time when San Francisco was still a clapboard village and Los Angeles a cow town.

Now one sits and meditates within the century-old National Hotel in Nevada City, its rooms faithful to the period when five or six stagecoaches jolted to a stop here each day. Instead of miners, freeway builders stand up to a bar made of Honduras mahogany that was brought around Cape Horn by sailing ship. At night, freeway lights cast their bluish glow over the board sidewalks along hillsides where many-gabled white frame houses pile one above the other. In towns like Nevada City there is no effort at quaintness in maintaining such style; it is simply that the community lives on in proud memory of a more dazzling past.

Such pride is well expressed by the *Nevada County Nugget,* a weekly newspaper whose masthead reads as follows:

> Serving the communities of Nevada City, Grass Valley, Red Dog, You Bet, Town Talk, Glenbrook, Little York, Cherokee, Mooney Flat, Sweetland, Alpha, Omega, French Corral, Rough and Ready, Granitesville, North San Juan, North Bloomfield, Humbug, Relief Hill, Washington, Blue Tent, La Barr Meadows, Cedar Ridge, Union Hill, Peardale, Summit City, Walloupa, Gouge Eye, Lime Kiln, Chicago Park, Wold, Christmas Hill, Liberty Hill, Sailor Flat, Lake City, Selby Flat, Grizzly Hill, Gold Flat, Soggsville, Gold Bar, Lowell Hill, Bourbon Hill, Scotch Hill, North Columbia, Columbia Hill, Brandy Flat, Sebastopol, Quaker Hill, Willow Valley, Newtown, Indian Flat, Bridgeport, Birchville, Moore's Flat, Orleans Flat, Remington Hill, Anthony House, Delirium Tremens.

A few thousand feet north of Nevada City on the edge of the Tahoe National Forest, the sudden freeway ends as abruptly as it began and the visitor is back on the lazy, winding little Highway 49 that traverses the gold country from Mariposa at the south up to the high-country camps in the edge of the Sierra near Downieville. I doubt that any other route in America offers such a profusion of historic markers, or so subtle a galaxy of sideroad villages that exist in the most engaging settings with no visible means of support.

It is more apt to see the gold country from the narrower confines of Highway 49. The freeway may become a monument to another era, but it is foreign in the Mother Lode.

The Spanish had sought vainly for treasure in California. In the short and chaotic era of Mexican rule that followed the expulsion of the Spaniards, nothing new turned up to make California seem worth much of a fight. Yet Mexican control was casual, and the region was vulnerable to seizure.

The Oregon Trail lured the early overland settlers from the United States—about four thousand of them between 1843 and 1845. Most were farmers. There was no stampede to California; by 1845 the colony of U.S. settlers that had taken the south fork of the overland trail toward California still numbered only seven hundred. Then came the U.S. declaration of war against Mexico in 1846. The main contention was over Texas, but Washington had shown interest in California, even to the extent of an unsuccessful mission to Mexico City to buy the region. Now the more abrupt approach was used.

Despite the serious attention that some historians have accorded it, the course of the Mexican War in California seems almost as farcical as a Gilbert and Sullivan operetta. There was a great deal of discussion and even some moments of gallantry, but there was not much warfare. Even before the war began, a U.S. Navy commodore had astonished Mexicans by raising the American flag over Monterey; sensing finally that he was ahead of schedule, he had hauled down the flag, apologized and sailed south to Los Angeles, where the Mexican governor accorded him the honors of a formal ball.

The last of the Mexican governors, Pio Pico, wrote an eloquent letter that displayed his understanding of the collision of the two cultures: "We find ourselves suddenly threatened by hordes of Yankee immigrants . . . whose progress we cannot arrest. They are cultivating farms, establishing vineyards, erecting mills, sawing up lumber, building workshops, and doing a thousand other things which seem natural to them."

The pathos of the Mexican role was evident in the final irony. On February 2, 1848, Mexico signed the Treaty of Guadalupe

Hidalgo, ending the Mexican War and ceding to the United States all of present-day California, New Mexico, Nevada, Utah, most of Arizona and part of Colorado. Only nine days earlier in California, James Wilson Marshall, a carpenter who had come from New Jersey, had picked up bits of bright metal at a sawmill he was building along the American River on a site the Indians called Coloma. A mill employee wrote in his diary: "This day some kind of mettle . . . found in the tail race . . . looks like goald."

It was. Marshall gathered up three ounces of gold and took it to his employer, Swiss-born John A. Sutter, at his ranch head-quarters and fort at New Helvetia, which later became Sacra-mento. Marshall seems to have been agitated because his con-struction crew thought he was crazy; now Sutter, applying the test of specific gravity with information he gleaned from an old volume of the *American Encyclopaedia,* confirmed that the metal was gold.

Sutter, who had set himself up as baron of a vast central Cali-fornia land holding, rode back with Marshall to the sawmill and urged the workers to keep their discovery secret for six weeks while they finished building the mill. His plea was naive, and in the frenzy that followed, Sutter lost control of his empire. A teamster paid for brandy at Sutter's Fort with gold from Coloma. The storekeeper wrote the news to his employer, the merchant and Mormon elder Sam Brannan, in San Francisco. Brannan published the report as an inconsequential item on the second page of his newspaper, *The Californian,* on March 15, 1848. But his enthusiasm grew with conviction; late in May, displaying a quinine bottle full of gold, he ran through the streets of San Francisco shouting: "Gold! Gold! Gold from the American River!"

The Gold Rush was on. The military governor of California, Colonel R. B. Mason, visited Sutter's Mill in July and filed a report attesting to the richness of the strike. Sutter appealed to Mason for title to the lands he had settled. But the United States had only just taken title by treaty; there had been no time even for surveys. Sutter turned in desperation to the chief of the Coloma Indians and bought a three-year lease of the land around the mill in exchange for a few articles of clothing and some flour.

It was a futile gesture. By August the hillsides rising from the

American River were strewn with canvas tents and bush huts and boarding shacks. Four thousand miners were at work, and more were spreading up and down the Mother Lode. San Francisco and Monterey were vacated so abruptly that even the innkeepers left without collecting their rents.

The Californian suspended publication with the complaint that "the majority of our subscribers and many of our advertisers have closed their doors and places of business and left town . . . The whole country, from San Francisco to Los Angeles and from the seashore to the base of the Sierra Nevada, resounds with the sordid cry of 'gold! Gold! GOLD!!!!' while the field is left half planted, the house half built, and everything neglected but the manufacture of shovels and pickaxes . . ."

In his message to Congress in December, President James Knox Polk termed the reports of California gold as of "such an extraordinary character as would scarcely command belief, were they not corroborated by the authentic reports of officers in the public service." Horace Greeley's New York *Tribune* proclaimed, "We are on the brink of the Age of Gold." Other headlines recognized the historic irony: THE EL DORADO OF THE SPANIARDS, cried one. THE DREAMS OF CORTEZ AND PIZARRO REALIZED, read another.

Now the rush began from the East. From the start, the cost of getting to California ruled out the poor. The passage by sea around Cape Horn—a journey of about sixteen thousand miles— took from four to nine months and cost about five hundred dollars. Many chose it. Others, more impatient, sailed to Panama and took the hazardous overland journey across the Isthmus by canoe and muleback—later by railroad—only to seek another boat for San Francisco. The hardiest chose the overland route, two thousand miles long, usually going by covered wagon and sometimes by mule train, moving at a rate of ten to twenty miles a day. It was a route along which cholera proved to be a greater killer than Indians or thirst.

So began the year of the Forty-Niners, the most flamboyant chapter of the American frontier. "The cowards never started," it was said later in the gold camps, "and the weaklings died by the way."

In five months during 1849, 549 vessels arrived at San Francisco bearing gold miners—the vanguard arriving in June and the height of the influx coming in September. Close to forty thousand came that year by sea, perhaps half from the East Coast and the others from Europe and the Orient.

But the Forty-Niners of the California Trail—less numerous than those who came by sea—are those on whom history looks with keenest gaze. They pressed the American frontier westward from the banks of the Missouri to the Pacific shore.

They came from farms and cities, driven toward California by mass hysteria that was part greed for gold and part passion for adventure, accented by the social and economic maladjustments of men returning from the Mexican War. "Five years was the longest period any one expected to stay," the poet Prentice Mulford later wrote. There is a plethora of diaries and letters to testify to the high rate of literacy of the Forty-Niners. They were typically young men; in 1850, only one in thirty Californians was female, and children were seldom seen. The dangers of the trip and the inhospitable reputation of the California wilderness made it a rush, not a migration.

Those who chose the California Trail had to await the spring of 1849 so that there would be grass along the way for their oxen and mules. In March they began to assemble at the frontier departure points: Independence, St. Joseph and Council Bluffs. During the winter, more than twenty overland guide books had been rushed into print, some crammed with fatal misinformation compiled by men who had never been west of the Missouri. Trail maps at first were sketchy.

Merchants at the departure points grew rich on the bonanza of equipping the Forty-Niners. The lesson was there to be learned, but only a few observed it. Those who came on to California to hunt gold rarely made fortunes, but some who set up in business to trade with miners at the inflated prices of the gold camps later became the aristocracy of California.

The first of the wagons drove out late in April from Independence and headed for the Mother Lode, two thousand unknown miles away. The trail led out across the Platte River to Fort Laramie and on to South Pass, where the Forty-Niners crossed the Continental Divide over gently rolling high plains and then chose among alternate routes to the Humboldt River valley of Nevada. It led, in turn, up into the Sierra Nevada and over the passes of Carson, Lassen, Truckee or Donner to the gold fields.

The diaries of the trail are as absorbing as the later chronicles of the gold camps. There was little sense of loneliness. The string of wagons toward the horizon was as great, one traveler wrote, "as if a mighty army was on its march." Another diary carries this entry: "This evening we have somehow got into a perfect nest of emigrants. If I was to guess, I should say there was one thousand head of cattle within a mile of camp." Continuous lines of up to five hundred wagons were reported. The major bottlenecks were the river crossings, where wagons waited their turn to board makeshift ferries.

For every wagon that had crossed the prairies a year earlier, now there were fifty, usually with three or four men to a wagon. Most of the emigrants were novices at trail life. They were over-burdened with supplies and the California Trail grew littered with abandoned equipment, wagons, dead mules and oxen.

About six thousand wagons began the trek before the summer ended, their white canvas covers stark like sails against the Mid-west skies. From a path that had been a vague double wheel track, the California Trail grew into a sometimes dusty, sometimes muddy roadway beaten forty feet wide.

Perhaps a thousand of the wagons that started on the trail failed to reach California. But attrition among the gold seekers themselves was not so great. Despite the legend of later fiction and film, fewer than a dozen were killed by Indians. Drownings and shootings claimed fifty to a hundred lives during the long summer, and upwards of five hundred died along the trail from illness, principally the cholera that had become almost epidemic along the frontier.

As they drove westward, the young and the old, the city slicker and the farmboy soon became frontiersmen of a common cut. A hundred days of hard camp-out tends to make every man look much the same.

"It is difficult to judge of the character of men on the road by external appearances," the Illinois migrant, Alonzo Delano, wrote in his diary. "A Mexican hat, a beard of twenty days' growth, an outer covering soiled with dirt and dust, a shirt which may have seen water in its youth, will disguise anyone so that he may look like a ferocious brigand, while at the same time his heart may be overflowing with 'the milk of human kindness.' " It was the same incongruous camouflage that Bret Harte later made part of his gold camp stories.

To speed their journey and ease the strain on their wearying oxen and mules, the Forty-Niners doubled up in wagons more and more, and many began to walk. As autumn approached those in the last wagons faced critical hardships: lack of water and grass, heat in the desert and cold in the Sierra, and diminished provisions. Those already in California raised a relief fund of $100,000 and military authorities sent out rescue parties with provisions and fresh animals to bring in the stragglers. It was a charitable climax to an epic march. Its unique nature foreshadowed traits later associated with the Westerner. Individuals planned and organized the march—not military, civil or corporate leaders. This was the essence of the frontier.

Only a few struck it rich. The easy pickings had begun to disappear by the time most of the Forty-Niners arrived. Miners endured extreme discomforts to which many of them had never been accustomed. Swinging picks on river banks or standing with their gold pans in icy mountain streams under hot summer sun, they toiled long hours with poor food and scant shelter.

"Really," wrote Louise Clappe, the wife of a gold camp physician, in her delightful *Shirley Letters* of 1851–52, "everybody ought to go to the mines, just to see how little it takes to make people comfortable in the world."

But miners staked out their claims and pitched their tents and went at it. Gold sold then for $16 an ounce; the average miner's take was probably not above $100 a month. His costs were appalling. In Sacramento boots cost $100 a pair and a blanket cost $40. At a time when a loaf of bread in an Eastern city cost a nickel, the price in San Francisco was fifty to seventy cents. In the gold camps it was worse. Bourbon whisky sold at $30 a quart, eggs for up to $50 a dozen, and apples for as much as $5 apiece.

Disenchantment quickly set in. California gold seemed to be a fraud. The wisest emigrants turned to farming, merchandising, or transportation. In 1849 a German near Sacramento earned $30,-000 from his crop of melons. The demand for beef brought huge herds of cattle up from the ranches of Southern California. In Coloma, a miner came home to his wife with four weeks' take in gold; she laughed at him because in the same month she had earned twice as much by washing shirts at one dollar each.

The world prefers to recall the stories of the big strikes, the glory holes, the golden nuggets that lay waiting to be picked up in the Mother Lode. But the more typical life of a miner was like that of Ananias Rogers, a Wisconsin man, already past middle age, who left behind his wife and family and set up a crude sluice-box mine with several companions near Bidwell's Bar on the Feather River.

In a cheap ledger book he kept a log that is preserved in the Huntington Library. This was his entry for November 6, 1849:

"Rain, rain, nothing but rain & mud for this & the most part of the day. I am witness to much suffering. Many of the emigrants are much worse off than we are. Having no shelter, whilst our tent keeps most of the rain from us, but it is very damp & chilly. Many are troubled with Bloody Flux. . . ."

Almost three years later, sensing the futility of his hunt for fortune, he wrote:

"I am solitary & alone. Am I never to see my loved ones again. If I had determined to make a permanent residence in this valley I might now have been well off and have had the means to bring my family out, but disliking the country that I was in & firmly believing that it was a poor country to settle in, my whole anxiety was to make a sudden raise and return to my family. This I undertook to do by mining. This is certainly the most uncertain of any business in the world. . . ."

Not all the sounds of Gold Rush life were in so minor a key.

The *Shirley Letters* tell with distress of a "perfect Saturnalia" at Rich Bar that began on Christmas night with a feast accompanied by champagne and brandy. Lacking women, the men danced with each other, the female partner designated by a handkerchief tied to his sleeve. The party went on for four days until the miners were "past dancing, and, lying in drunken heaps about the bar-room . . ."

Gambling, drinking and whoring were the routine diversions,

but the Sabbath was widely observed as a day of rest and clean-up. The work was too hard and gold fever ran too high for rowdyism to be the prevailing state. Even the legends of lynch hangings have been magnified by time and retelling. Soon the camps were toured by performers like the smouldering Lola Montez, and later Edwin Booth and Lotta Crabtree. Many of the miners were, after all, men of culture and attainment.

But thousands of disappointed emigrants returned to their homes. For others, the spell of California was at work; some sent for brides or families. Usually they were attracted by rich farm-lands or the chance for high income in business. The Big Four who opened the Central Pacific Railroad in 1869 had been mer-chants in hardware, groceries and jewelry at Sacramento; they had neither mined nor invested in mines.

The peak year for California gold was 1852. The Gold Rush was soon over. By 1854 the easy placer gold, available to the lone miner with gold pan or cradle and rocker, was almost gone. Mining moved into the hands of companies with capital enough to tunnel shafts and erect timbers within bedrock, or to bring in the flumes and heavy machinery for hydraulic operations that ate away the hills with powerful water nozzles and silted the rivers until finally such mining was prohibited by law in 1884.

Along with such scars on the land—the eroded hillsides, the miles of ugly tailings, the gaping holes in the earth—the miners left behind them dying towns. The ghastly scene began to heal slowly under cover of chaparral and digger pine and valley oak. Professional gold-hunters moved on to the Comstock lode in Nevada and to other strikes around the West and as far away as Australia.

In thirty years following Marshall's discovery at Sutter's Mill, about $1.2 billion in gold was taken from the earth. At the end of a century, the figure was close to $2 billion. Mining became almost completely dormant in California after World War II.

The mainstream of California moved on from the Gold Rush to new and more lasting locales and pursuits. But gold had shaped all of California life, setting off social and economic currents that otherwise would have been delayed for generations.

Gold made California cosmopolitan. Thousands came to the

mines from Mexico, Chile, the British Isles, Germany, France and Spain—and lesser numbers from Hawaii and Peru. The Chinese were most numerous of all, with more than twenty thousand in California by 1852. Those who stayed formed the first large migratory wave on which all others have built. The gold pan became the melting pot.

The laborer became the capitalist. California went from a minor pastoral economy to one based on agriculture, industry, services and commerce. The total yield of gold from California has been less than half the value of a single year's farm production these days in California.

The Gold Rush made the name of California known to all the world and gave it a magic quality that it has not entirely lost. It catapulted California into statehood, in 1850, and helped to give the state an eminence above others in the West which it retains today.

Gold was the impetus for speedier transport across America. San Francisco at first was only a way point for mail ships that plied between the East Coast and Oregon; soon it became the western terminus. Stage lines, the Pony Express and finally railroads broke down the remoteness of the West, welded the nation and gave America its window toward the Pacific and the Orient.

Some of the wealth of gold went to spur cultural undertakings that now seem unprecedented in a land so recently redeemed from wilderness. San Francisco quickly became the center of a literary tradition made universal by Bret Harte and Mark Twain. The finest bookstore west of the Alleghenies was soon in business at San Francisco. Within twenty years after the discovery of gold, that city was hailed by many as a cultural rival of Boston and a financial center second in America only to New York.

The momentum that gold gave to California has never subsided. The flamboyance and self-confidence associated with the miner are part of the California temperament, and so are his speculative excesses. Above all, perhaps, there is the image of the miner cut adrift on a frontier where almost no one cared. That was the genesis of the vagrant society.

. 10 .

SAN FRANCISCO

> I have never found a city so girlishly charmed and
> delighted by its own absurdity or so calculating about
> inventing absurdity when it ceases to generate itself.
>
> —THOMAS R. EDWARDS IN *Partisan Review.*

Several years ago I spent some pleasant weeks in San
Francisco gathering material for a book about the American West.
It was my first opportunity to settle down in the city, and it was
a fascinating sojourn—one that I have resumed intermittently as
often as an excuse presents itself. I was trying to measure the heft
of San Francisco against that of other cities in the West. A week
or so seemed to do well enough for my purposes in Denver, a
few days more or less in cities like Phoenix and Seattle and Port-

169

land, and of course repeated assaults on Los Angeles—made necessary more by the bulk of that city than its complexity. But to understand the subtleties of San Francisco, I rationalized, would require full and prolonged concentration. It was and is *the city:* the citadel of the West.

The people of the city were thoughtful and attentive, perhaps because I asked them to talk about themselves; almost anyone in San Francisco seems willing to drop whatever he is doing to discuss the city. But beneath the dazzling beauty of the setting and the euphoria of the people, San Francisco was in trouble. The city wore its regal mantle smugly, almost oblivious to the growing cry of racial rebellion, to the intrusion of ugliness over its golden hills, to the pollution of its air and water, and to the erosion of the civic virility and spontaneity that gave San Francisco its élan.

So in that book I wrote of the city as narcissistic, untroubled by conscience, blind to the human miseries that increasingly haunted its majestic landscape. I chided the sycophants—both within and outside the city—who chanted homage to the San Francisco that had been fading, a cultured and fun-loving city. My cry was less shrill than sad, for I have always been among those who hold San Francisco as a symbol of verve and beauty. The Angry Sixties had scarcely begun when my book appeared and San Francisco, like most American cities, was yet to be aroused to what was already a rapidly worsening urban crisis everywhere. It was still the vogue to pay tribute to San Francisco as fairest of the fair, and San Franciscans received such adulation with childlike innocence.

Friends warned that my views about San Francisco would arouse hostility. So I was surprised when the book was reviewed generously in the city and even more when it sold well there. My indictment of narcissism came to be accepted with enthusiasm. The word went around. There was a spate of essays and lectures and civic searchings for the roots of self-love. Its causes were ferreted out, fondled, condemned, and fondled some more.

On a televised seminar one evening the theme was underlined so heavily by local commentators that I found myself, as a guest critic, arguing back that the natives were overstating the case. I spoke in defense of the civic conscience. San Francisco couldn't

be all *that* bad. I had become the outlander turning to support
the homeland. San Franciscans, always striving to be passionate,
had grown passionate in the search for narcissism.

It was only at that moment that I first began to understand
something very basic about the city. Like a vain and beautiful
woman she is amused to be the center of attention while she pro-
fesses to remain aloof from criticism or approbation. Those of us
who offer it are hard-pressed to do so in moderation. Impervious
to such excesses, often accepting them blithely, San Francisco
feeds on her own image. Self-mockery is an acceptable pastime.
She has the poise to laugh at herself and does not chafe at the
laughter of others. No matter how she is castigated or adored, she
is her own best audience. So she remains grand.

Frank Lloyd Wright once told a local audience that "San
Francisco is the only city I can think of that can survive all the
things you people are doing to it and still look beautiful." The
good looks of the city, despite a thickening jumble of steel and
concrete that threatens to close off its airy vistas, are a source of
constant reassurance that things cannot really be as bad as they
seem—or that if they are, Armageddon will engulf a society that
is laid out in pearls and satin for viewing by the bereaved.

"Make no mistake, stranger," wrote Bernard De Voto. "San
Francisco is West as all hell." Born with the California Gold Rush
and nurtured into early brownstone magnificence by the wealth
of Nevada's Comstock Lode, the city quickly took on an air of
provincial elegance. Its pioneers sought to establish an outpost
of cosmopolitanism, and they succeeded well enough that San
Francisco has not yet lost its exaggerated image as an oasis of
amenities on a barren frontier. As they went about building, these
early San Franciscans must have had the look of barbarian invaders. They did not have time to establish their character or
reputation or to measure out their expectations. They came as
speculators, often from sophisticated backgrounds. From this
era came the tradition of playfulness in San Francisco, and the
capacity for self-ridicule; it cannot have been unassociated with
the fact that those pioneers who took wives in the city between
1849 and 1865 were being married—by odds of five-to-one—to
prostitutes. Yet the city they built along the rutted and hilly

streets of a wide-open town achieved poise and grace. Its people chose not to gloss over such aberrant detail but to dwell affectionately on it. From the start, San Francisco was like no other town in America. It is young and therefore affirmative, but it was born old and wise, an instant city that nourishes recollection of its past. It has been spared most of the embarrassing arrogance of the robust and rosy-cheeked young cities of the world.

The youngness of San Francisco can be measured by the red towers and trusses that bridge the Golden Gate. This great gap in the California coast and the sanctuary of sheltered water behind it awed early explorers. The gap was bridged only in 1937; until completion of the Bay Bridge to Oakland in the previous year, the city had been accessible overland only from the south. With the Ferry Building at the foot of Market Street, and along the wharves below Telegraph Hill, the forty-mile long San Francisco peninsula comes to an end. Here is the hub of the city, but it is only a pin prick in the confluence of water and land that makes up the community known as the San Francisco Bay Area. The bay, 450 square miles in size, extends forty-two miles north and south and unites a populous area the size of New Jersey. The city of San Francisco has only about 750,000 residents, but the Bay Area population is in excess of four million.

Unlike many of the nation's metropolitan centers, the area has several major centers and sub-centers—including those of Oakland and Berkeley on the eastern shore of the bay, and San Jose at the foot of the peninsula. North of the Golden Gate the towns of Marin County make up a relatively sparsely settled upper rim of the metropolis. There is heavy industry and manufacturing in the East Bay and in the Palo Alto-San Jose area, but the city of San Francisco itself accounts for seventy per cent of the total employment of the region in finance, insurance and real estate, and fifty per cent of the jobs in services, transportation, communication and utilities. More than one-fourth of the jobs within San Francisco are held by commuters from outside the city.

Social San Francisco, on the other hand, begins in the north at windswept Stinson Beach, which is scarcely an hour's drive from the city but is as close as most San Franciscans venture toward Oregon. Here, along the foaming and often angry surf, is an acceptable place for a weekend house. The southern limit of San Francisco society is Pebble Beach, south of the city on the Monterey Peninsula. In season, of course, the right people surge out to Squaw Valley (skiing, bridge and dominoes) and Lake Tahoe (sailing, bridge and dominoes). For the rest of the year, except for jet hops here and there, proper San Franciscans follow a zigzag north-and-south course along the peninsula. By some standards, the discrete valley of Ross, on the north side of the Golden Gate in Marin County, is a proper address. Southward the route of propriety sweeps through the establishments of the Pacific Heights sector of the city and down the peninsula to the estates of Burlingame (the Burlingame Country Club is still *it*), Hillsborough and horsey Woodside. The wooded preserve of Atherton, all gnarled oak and flashing diamonds, is presumed by some to be in jeopardy because, even in a fresh society, it is regarded as new. Such matters are debated at great length in San Francisco. Sometimes, as Stephen Birmingham once wrote, San Francisco society seems a trifle overenthusiastic about itself; but it must be forgiven, for here society is fresh and "still fun."

To a very real extent, the city of San Francisco is the stage on which the high drama of the region unfolds. The reputation of the city for urbanity lies in the hands of a relatively few residents and commuters; the rest are supernumeraries. The true San Franciscan rolls his eyes when he speaks of the "mysterious East Bay," and recalls that Gertrude Stein said of Oakland that "there is no there there." He insists that Los Angeles begins down the peninsula, somewhere south of Stanford and probably in the vicinity of San Jose, where the sprawl of new subdivision on flat valley floors gives the land a dreary anonymity.

Now the bridges that link the city to north and east, and the lone freeway that leads along the bayshore down the peninsula, are all choked with cars. The Golden Gate Bridge is critically overloaded. A rapid transit authority that seeks to serve the bay area has been plagued with rising costs and is falling far short of its original scope. It is as if those who manage the stage of San Francisco were lurking in the wings to control the setting; you approach the city still over one of its great bridges, savoring the jutting skyline and the hills in the distance, or along the free-way from the south, where a sudden curve reveals the downtown skyline like a magician whisking away his silk scarf from in front of a tray of rabbits.

San Francisco looks like a city; it is densely settled and com-pacted within an area no more than seven miles across. It is a sensuous city, forever caressing with its smells of sea and water-front, its soft and changing light, its sounds of cable car and ocean liner, and always its views: the big sweeping vistas from atop its hills or bridges, and the cozy little scapes that dazzle and surprise at street corners. There is no other city where a gentle physical environment intrudes so constantly into the life of its people. It is so benign a setting that even triteness takes on an amiability; long rows of squat bay-windowed houses are not tiresome because they are tiered up steep hillsides, and some Victorian mansion gains charm because recent owners, instead of trying to mask its ungainliness, have lovingly accentuated its baroque lines with dark gray exterior paint and olive drab banis-ter trim. Its high-domed city hall is among the most stately public buildings in America, and its sumptuous opera house is a worthy descendant of Gold Rush opulence. Civic furore erupts when there is a threat of tinkering with some such civic land-mark. At a cost of more than seven million dollars in public and private funds, about eleven times its original cost, a crumbling 1915 exhibition hall known as the Palace of Fine Arts was restored in 1967; only then did San Franciscans settle down to seeking a use for the hall. Yet in the view of the California photographer Ansel Adams, its restoration was "one of the silliest and most adolescent gestures imaginable," an act of veneration for a structure that had not been admired even by its designer, the architect Bernard Maybeck.

Elsewhere in the city, there is far less hesitation at abandoning the old. The end of the 1960's brought a downtown construction boom that is changing the face of the city. It was more than half a century after the earthquake of 1906 before San Franciscans dared to erect any structure higher than twenty stories; then came the fifty-two story Bank of America world headquarters, and a host of others only slightly less imposing, including the thirty-four story home of the Pacific Gas & Electric Company, the nation's largest gas and electric utility. Ground was broken in 1968 for David Rockefeller's Embarcadero Center, known to some as Rockefeller Center West. It is the most ambitious building construction project in California history, and its impact on San Francisco when completed sometime during the 1970s will be greater than that of Rockefeller Center on Manhattan in the 1930's. Three tremendous office towers—soaring as high as six hundred feet—are to be built in a phalanx on a landscaped podium that encases a two-thousand-car garage extending for four blocks through the heart of the city; the completed center will include a city-built plaza, theaters, and an eight-hundred-room hotel, all embellished by a series of elevated plazas and esplanades serving as displays for fountains and sculpture. Along with the Golden Gateway, a $100 million complex of 22- to 25-story apartment buildings, and a host of new hotels that will add five thousand more rooms to downtown San Francisco, this new construction will provide the city—within a single decade—with major buildings costing more than the total value of structures lost in the earthquake and fire of 1906—in excess of half a billion dollars.

"San Francisco," wrote the novelist Herbert Gold, who lives there, "ranks high in alcoholism, divorce, tennis, fresh air, suicide, egg rolls, seafood, free verse and experimental prose." But, he went on, the city lacks the central anxious energy of New York. Eugene Burdick, who lived across the bay in Berkeley, contrarily spoke of "an almost palpable sense of energy and tension and effervescence." "If you're alive," William Saroyan once wrote of the city in which he has been very much alive, "you can't be bored in San Francisco." Not, that is, unless you are bored by a city whose favorite topic of conversation is itself. The rage for self-analysis is developed to rare heights. The San Franciscan, from longshoreman to banker, is possessive about his city—all of it, not simply the waterfront or the West Coast Wall Street known as Montgomery Street. "It is as if the entire city came from common parents," a Hollywood writer once quipped. "F. Scott Fitzgerald and Isadora Duncan."

Because there is such an insatiable audience for analysis of San Francisco—both within the city and all over the world—it has been dissected and analyzed to the point that, with a lesser city, would be sure to provoke the flatness of overkill. San Francisco has grown into a fetish, and perhaps inevitably so; it is impossible to think of another city that has become so much so fast, and still continues to cast so warm a spell.

Yet in recent years San Franciscans have begun to face up to the flaws in their comely façade. When the hideous Embarcadero Freeway began to encapsulate its waterfront with an elevated band of concrete, the progress of the freeway was halted in mid-air and it remains a hapless monster seeming to lead nowhere. Few other cities are blessed with such a widespread awareness of architectural esthetics, and those who perpetrate monstrosities on the skyline are doomed to constant nagging in the press.

For a city with historic appreciation of the performing arts, San Francisco has had a paltry role in the development of contemporary theater, and its two legitimate theaters are in tatters. Its repertory company has clung only precariously to its existence. It has managed always to mount a brief annual opera season of stature, and more recently to send its Western Opera Theater, a stepchild of the San Francisco Opera, on missionary ventures to school campuses and musically underprivileged communities as distant as the Watts area of Los Angeles. Yet as Howard Taubman observed, the city has seemed "increasingly like a complacent aristocrat looking down at the bustling activity of the plebians around him," willing to swim in memories of a lively and glamorous past, doing little to foster the new ideas and movements that keep a city culturally aware. "San Francisco has wealth, prestige, and the power to swing things," the novelist Wallace Stegner said. "Instead of a good city, it should be an absolutely spectacular city. The opera and symphony are fine, but why shouldn't they be among the best in the world? Our cultural agencies are too self-contented."

This is the city that introduced to the West its standards of good taste in music and art, in clothing and jewelry and food. Its literary life was launched by men like Mark Twain, Bret Harte and Ambrose Bierce. West Coast jazz early established its unchallenged base here. The tradition of San Francisco poets is carried on by several hundred relative unknowns while their dean, Kenneth Rexroth, regards San Francisco as home no matter how far or how often he travels. Yet the movement is not exactly vibrant. "As in New York, where all young girls undergoing arrest for anything at all call themselves models," the critic Lewis Nichols wrote, "all young men getting arrested in San Francisco call themselves poets." San Francisco novelists are better known, from Gold to Stegner, Niven Busch, Kay Boyle, Wallace Markfield, Barnaby Conrad, Erskine Caldwell, Mark Harris, Mark Schorer and Calvin Kentfield. Something has gone wrong in the worlds of painting and sculpture, where for lack of a serious audience of collectors, the thrust has moved southward to Los Angeles. In the opposite direction, a surprising volume of film production has defected from Los Angeles to San Francisco, where backgrounds are unquestionably more interesting to the directors of the current main-street school of cinema. "Los Angeles is too overwhelming," said the London director Richard Lester as he went about San Francisco on location for *Petulia,* based on a story that had been set in Southern California. "I don't think you can tell a sad love story in Los Angeles. The background just swallows up the story. San Francisco is more sensitive."

"As New York is not the United States, San Francisco is not California," the columnist Herb Caen wrote. "The San Franciscan, gloriously insular on his peninsula, doesn't think much about California." The San Franciscan concedes that Los Angeles has outpaced his beloved city in size and sinew, with all the vulgarity that bigness entails. He is willing to grant Los Angeles its booming, if peculiar kind of cultural community. He admits that there are even two or three restaurants worthy of a visit in the southern city. He is happy to note that ten or so San Franciscos could be fitted into the vast conglomerate of Los Angeles. Having done so, he is grateful to forget Los Angeles.

Even though the southern city begins to achieve more of the amenities, and the Bay Area sprawls more and more like Los Angeles, the San Franciscan is insistent that the twain shall never meet. To him the issue is almost as precise as in *The New Yorker* cartoon that delighted Californians several years ago. A

tourist couple in their open convertible were driving among syl-
van glades beneath a Corinthian temple where dancers, musicians, artists and scholars plied their arts on the greens. In the
background was a fence, and beyond it a babble of vulgar signs,
conservative political billboards, temples of off-brand sects, and
cranes setting up crackerbox houses inexorably toward the horizon. "I don't think I ever before realized," the driver was telling
his wife, "the distinct difference between northern and southern
California." The San Francisco trial lawyer J. W. (Jake) Erlich
offers a similar over-simplification: "You have a different kind of
people down south. They are against everything."

Los Angelenos have grown secure enough in their new en-
lightenment to praise San Francisco these days when they feel
the city to the north deserves it. But at the official level, few
opportunities are lost to exploit the regional schism. In 1968
Mayor Joseph Alioto of San Francisco declined an invitation to
join in signing a Los Angeles County proclamation designed to
alert Californians to the inroads of pornography. It set aside
seven days in April as "D For Decency Week." Alioto predictably
insisted that to do so would leave the "distinct impression that
the other 51 are indecency weeks in San Francisco . . . . The
notion of Los Angeles playing holier than thou bears some ex-
amination." The San Francisco *Chronicle* followed the tradition
of its fun-loving constituency when it praised the mayor for
declining to sign the resolution and urged his continued aloofness
to such overtures "lest San Franciscans be made to believe that
they lack the maturity and intelligence to select their own reading
matter, and must have it censored and passed in Los Angeles."

There is much in the census tracts to support the theory that
different kinds of persons migrate to Los Angeles and San Francisco. The San Franciscan has more often come from another city
or is in search of the urban feeling. The flavor of Los Angeles is
set in large part by migrants from the South, the Midwest and
Southwest, many of whom have lived on farms or in small towns.
San Francisco is an older community and its sophistication is
more entrenched. Los Angeles is an easy first-generation city; in
San Francisco, it is the third and even the fourth generations who

are accused of sitting on their wallets and their reputations as they fend off the newcomer.

The tradition of San Francisco fosters open-minded tolerance of the foreign and bizarre. It was no coincidence that North Beach became the haven of the beatnik movement of the 1950s, and the Haight-Ashbury district was the domain of the hippies of the 1960's. The weight of public opinion was not favorable to either group, but San Francisco endured. Nor was it accidental that students left the campuses of Berkeley and Stanford in disproportionate numbers for civil rights protests in the American South, and that San Francisco college campuses later became centers for militant student movements. A certain *laissez-faire* attitude characterizes San Francisco. The shock waves of social change in the West eddy out from San Francisco. The mood is more permissive.

Yet the record of the city in racial affairs is spotty. It is true that there are San Francisco Jews in the Social Register, and that Jewish debutantes have been presented at the city's Cotillion, a white-tie gala that has been the major social event since its inception in 1932. (To qualify for introduction to society, the debutante or at least one of her parents must be a native Californian.) Hotelman Ben Swig, a Jew who came west from Boston, spoke of San Francisco as being freer of prejudice than any other American city.

The plight of the Negro in the Bay Area has been less publicized than in Los Angeles, but despair and rebellion walk the streets of Hunters Point and the Western Addition and Oakland just as they do in Watts to the South. Oakland is among the handful of American cities that will be predominantly black by 1983 if present trends continue. In 1968 Negro infants in San Francisco were dying at twice the rate of white babies, largely because of a lack of prenatal care. A group of four hundred physicians and health workers joined forces at about that time with a militant Negro group, the Black Panthers, in an attempt to provide emergency medical attention for the black community. Members of the Human Rights Commission noted that the city

ranked high in dissatisfaction among black people in a survey
made by Brandeis University, and urged increased effort by
government, business and labor to relieve the despair among the
blacks. At the campus of San Francisco State College militant
blacks momentarily assumed control in a series of explosive con-
frontations that resulted in dismissal of the college president in
1968 amid a continuing atmosphere of violence.

But it is the Chinese community that is unique. It is the largest
Oriental settlement in the western world, in excess of seventy
thousand in 1968, and growing at the rate of several thousand
each year within a densely settled ghetto having the highest
suicide rate of any area within a city known for its extremely
high suicide rate. The pagoda roofs that tier up along Grant
Avenue behind Old St. Mary's Square are one of the tourist
attractions of San Francisco; yet they shelter some of the most
pressing social problems of California.

Escaping the poverty of their own land, the Chinese began
pouring into San Francisco after the discovery of gold. By 1860
there were nearly thirty-five thousand of them, many of whom
had been conscripted by labor contractors in as tawdry a trade
as the African slave traffic. Most of them dreamed of returning
to China after they had amassed their fortunes. Some did; but
more of them stayed on, fortuneless, rather than lose face by
returning penniless to their families. At first they worked in the
mines, and later on the railroads in labor gangs. At a time when
the frontier was expanding and cheap labor seemed vital, the
Chinese were building the West. Yet they were never accepted
as part of the West. To most early Californians they were coolies,
and the "yellow peril" seemed very real.

As the Chinese helped to build California, a wall of exclusion
grew up around them. They did the jobs that no one else would
do. They washed clothes, dug in the fields, moved earth in baskets, drained the tule marshes of the delta region, and planted the
vines of Colonel Agoston Haraszthy's pioneering vineyard at
Buena Vista. The Chinese houseboy became a symbol of domestic style. As late as the mid 1920's in San Francisco it was common
for middle-income families to have a Chinese houseboy—often
in his fifties or sixties—who cooked, served meals, laundered, and

watched the children during a long work day for which his wages might be thirty dollars a month. His starched white jacket and his slate blue cotton pants made him, in the eyes of the Californian, much what the African had been to the Southerner. He lived typically in a dark, rough-boarded room in a dank basement corner. Somehow, from his meager earnings, he was able to send to his homeland each month a sum of money that seemed immense to his relatives there.

The settlement of the Chinese is an ugly facet of California history. Discrimination grew in the 1870's as the Chinese tried to compete in the general labor market. In 1881 the American Federation of Labor recommended exclusion of Chinese from unions, and in subsequent years underlined the nativist arguments common to that time with warnings against the "silent and irresistible" racial peril of the Oriental. In 1882, at a time when anti-Chinese riots were common in California, Congress halted immigration of Chinese, the first such blanket restriction to be laid down. Many left California to return to their homeland. Those who stayed drifted away from factory and farm into restaurants, laundries and stores. In 1890, more than one-third of California's Chinese were huddled in the tiny enclave of Grant Avenue, and by the turn of the century, the Chinatown of San Francisco had grown into a mass of tenements. Chinese were denied the right to own land and their testimony in the courts was declared void. Chinese pupils were denied permission to enter public schools as late as 1884, at a time when the Chinese were spending about fourteen million dollars annually in customs levies, taxes and general business, largely in San Francisco. Asiatic children in San Francisco attended a separate school as late as the 1890s, and Oriental schools were authorized by law until 1936.

Anti-Chinese feeling began to calm after 1943 when President Roosevelt signed the repeal of the Chinese exclusion act that had by then been in force for more than sixty years. Soon San Francisco's Chinatown was broached with high-rise cubicle apartments erected by a civic housing authority. At the time of World War II close to twenty thousand Chinese lived in a twenty-block area along Grant Avenue, often with ten or twelve people crammed into a single basement room. The tuberculosis rate was scandalous, and even today is more than three times greater than among Caucasians in the city.

Between 1950 and 1960, Chinatown population rose from about 25,000 to 36,455. When President Kennedy opened immigration gates in 1962 to about fifteen thousand refugees from Hong Kong and Taiwan, more than six thousand of them settled in San Francisco. The immigration quota system was abandoned in 1965 and in the years since the flow has gained force. Newly arrived immigrant families live in tenements, often four or five families with more than twenty individuals sharing a community kitchen and bathroom. Now Chinatown grows at the rate of five thousand persons annually, and the city's International Institute estimates that forty percent of the area's population would qualify for poverty program aid.

But not even militant unionism has penetrated the insularity of the community. About three thousand Chinese women work at sub-standard wages at sewing machines in almost two hundred small ladies' garment factories scattered through Chinatown. Many are recent immigrants from Hong Kong and Taiwan and have not learned English. There is a minority within a minority: the Chinese-born, who do not speak English, are the low caste in the view of the American-born Chinese. There are more young people than ever before—thousands of Hong Kong-born youth who do not speak English and have no work skills.

The abacus is still in use in shops along Grant Avenue instead of the cash register. From the basements comes the clatter of dominoes, the traditional pastime of the Chinese. The tourist visits the herb shops and temples, and sees the daily Chinese language newspapers. The Chinatown telephone exchange is housed in a pagoda on Washington Street, and Chinatown is ruled still from a building on Stockton Street that houses the Six Companies—the representatives of Chinese families who attempt to control community affairs under the more formal name of the Chinese Consolidated Benevolent Association.

But the ethnic character of Chinatown has begun to deteriorate. Young couples who are financially able are establishing their homes outside Chinatown. The pressures on those who cannot move out grow fierce. Late in 1967 work began on a Chinese cultural and trade center housing a theater, exhibit halls and meeting rooms within a 27-room hotel that is designed to support the activities of the center. Its construction was pushed by Justin Herman, head of the San Francisco Redevelopment Agency, the arm of urban renewal, as the follow-up to construction of a Japanese cultural and trade center in the smaller Japanese quarter known as Nihonmachi—a center which includes the first Japanese hotel of premium quality within the continental United States.

Within the new Chinese center there are to be continuous exhibits, lectures and English-language classes for immigrants. It is an admirable example of urban renewal, but it can be at best no more than a token of the will to help solve the social crisis of Chinatown. The growing determination of the American to show his oneness with the Eastern world meets a stern challenge here in this picturesque ghetto on the hillsides of San Francisco.

The landmarks of the San Francisco past are gold, railway fortunes, the sea traffic of its port, and the ebullience of the city's restoration following the earthquake and fire of 1906. Few of the fortunes that shaped modern San Francisco came from the mines. The classic example is The Big Four: the Sacramento merchants Charles Crocker, Mark Hopkins, Leland Stanford and Collis P. Huntington, who invested $15,000 each to launch the Central Pacific Railroad. Their names are inescapably entwined with San Francisco. The Nob Hill mansion that serves today as the Pacific Union Club, the sanctum of the city's merchant princes, was built as the home of James Flood, a San Francisco saloon keeper who made it with the richest vein in the Comstock Lode but parlayed his winnings into a banking fortune.

Modern San Francisco—its shape, its mood and its social structure—draws its roots from the great restoration that followed the catastrophe of 1906. It was a calamity shared equally by all, and the egalitarianism of San Francisco stems from the soup lines where banker and Chinese stood quietly together. Some historians go further, and suggest that the fire purged the city; that the two hundred thousand or so who fled the city cleansed it of the irresponsible and irascible, and that those who remained to rebuild were those of character who inherited their place on the hills. In any case the city emerged as a more structured and orderly society. The mining camp died in the ashes. A powerful trade union movement grew to develop its own elite so that eventually the radical longshoreman Harry Bridges would stand on the same podium at Civic Auditorium in a public debate with a shipowner and later mayor, Roger Lapham. Three decades later, a retired San Francisco longshoreman named Eric Hoffer had taken rank as the nation's favorite pop philosopher, a counselor to presidents. Discrimination is bad manners in the San Francisco code, and if that code is not universally practiced amid the fresh tensions of a swollen metropolis today, San Franciscans are likely to insist that they are at least doing better at it than most of America's similarly beleaguered cities. In fact, they probably are.

The columnist Herb Caen talks of the end of his city's Belle Epoque and says: "There is a moment of truth for all cities, a time when it must stop in the midst of its mindless self-involvement and take a long, hard look at itself. Such a time has come for San Francisco, the pampered darling of American cities, the sacred enclave that lived so long beyond reality, head in the sky, feet on an extremely steep and, as it turns out, slippery hill." With such pronouncements Caen calls time on San Francisco's narcissism.

The establishment has in fact grown impatient with civic bumbling and evasion. The Bay Area Rapid Transit District stumbled along in debt and controversy that left its ambitious route system curtailed and in doubt long before the first car rolled. Great hope rested with the organization charged with formulating the first steps toward regional government—the Association of Bay Area Governments—yet its second-in-command stood charged with absconding with half a million dollars in funds, well over half of the organization's annual budget. The San Franciscan points with affection toward once magnificent Golden Gate Park, yet bond issues for vital maintenance and improvement faltered at the polls, hippies laid claim to its rolling lawns and a freeway threatened to bisect it. The crown jewel that more than any other fact of nature makes San Francisco different

—its immense bay—lies dying with the burden of a daily inflow of nearly four hundred million gallons of treated wastes, enough to cover Golden Gate Park to a depth of one foot. Powerful interests go on filling the shallow parts of the bay, reducing the strength of tides that flush wastes from its waters and decreasing the oxygen supply of the water that is vital to neutralize the burden of wastes. Now comes a threat from the Great Central Valley: a proposal to drain vast irrigation projects from behind the San Luis Dam so that saline waters will flow into San Francisco Bay and further complicate its delicate ecology.

Perhaps this time it will not take an earthquake and fire to rejuvenate the city that knows how. There has been a marked swelling of the civic breast since a new mayor stepped out in front of the crowd in 1968. Mayor Alioto is a millionaire lawyer whose father was an Italian fisherman in North Beach. He has brains and courage and seems determined to build a reputation in politics by rescuing the city from the threat of mediocrity. Elected at the age of 52, he observed that he was "bored with making money," and was ready to devote his full attention to what he regards as "one of the few cities in the world one can be truly affectionate about."

Alioto has an impressive captive constituency. There are ten Joe Aliotos in San Francisco, the mayor and nine relatives. Four Aliotos own restaurants. In other ways Alioto fits the local pattern. An opera buff, he plays the violin; for his inauguration as mayor, he passed up the usual rotunda ceremony at City Hall and moved the proceedings to the ornate Opera House. Shortly after his inauguration, his college-age son served the first weekend of a twenty-weekend jail sentence for driving with a revoked operator's license. Another son, 22, was author of a so-called "psychedelic play," and his father the mayor was present at its opening in a North Beach cabaret.

His fight against mediocrity began in his own office. His executive secretary is John DeLuca, a scholar with a doctorate degree, who said, "Many pluralistic groups in San Francisco, as in other cities, are hostile to each other. There is no dialogue between the business community and the ethnic groups. Joe feels he can bridge the gap and get them talking to each other." Alioto moved rapidly in that direction. Backed by labor, he promptly chided union leaders for their reluctance in hiring blacks, and urged use of union pension funds to invest in rebuilding ghettos. He called on bankers to join in the project. He went directly to major employers and won pledges of large increases in minority employment. For himself, he named the first Negro to serve in a San Francisco mayor's cabinet.

With other projects he reached out to improve minority education and to bring San Francisco youth into his administration. In the cultural area he found backers to finance annual competitions among sculptors and painters and enlisted his neighbor Yehudi Menuhin to help in planning for use of the restored Palace of Fine Arts as a conservatory of music.

He launched a program for mini-parks, helped settle a long San Francisco newspaper strike in 1968, and named a blue-ribbon crime commission that was to spend eighteen months and $100,-000 in a systematic inquiry into law enforcement and the administration of justice. Noting that about $33 million is spent each year in San Francisco on services for non-resident commuters, he set off his first major imbroglio with a proposal for a commuter tax. Turning to the Port of San Francisco, which had been owned and operated by the State of California since Gold Rush days, he began prodding port leaders to buy the harbor back from the state. His pace and the temerity of his programs captivated a usually blasé constituency. Even the San Francisco Junior League fell in behind him, setting loose 80 two-woman teams across San Francisco to call on businessmen, to create jobs for minority youth. "We've never moved so fast," said the League woman who was chairman of the program.

In the gut language of a San Francisco columnist, the new mayor had begun to "put some class back into what used to be a classy town." About the time that Alioto took office, a magazine writer attempted to sum up the temper of San Francisco by reporting he had found there a "general agreement that, as the game is lost before it starts, one had better keep grinning to show it's all in fun." As happens so often to those of us who try to write about San Francisco, he had tuned in on yesterday's mood. One is hard put to imagine a city with more dynamic strengths than

San Francisco, in wealth and beauty, in learning and sophistication. It is rich in reserves. The chapters of its past demonstrate its rare capacity for responding to adversity. Its future, if it cares enough, could be to break a trail for other troubled cities to follow. The urban dilemma of today cannot be more total than that which San Francisco overcame in 1906.

. 11 .

THE LEISURE RACE

Donner Lake Memorial State Park, 2 miles west of Truckee on U.S. 40, covers 353 acres near the site where the Donner family became stranded during the winter of 1846. These pioneers, en route from St. Joseph, Mo., were without food. As members of the 85-person party died, those remaining resorted to cannibalism in desperation. Only 45 were rescued. [Facilities now available here for] *Picnicking.*

—FROM THE CALIFORNIA-NEVADA TOUR BOOK OF THE
AUTOMOBILE CLUB OF SOUTHERN CALIFORNIA.

At Los Angeles International Airport an elderly woman walked toward the departure gate for a Mexican flight. She was bent under the weight of an air tank on her back. An airline attendant moved quickly toward her but then stood aside when he saw that she carried the rest of a skindiver's equipment: face plate and fins. Here was only another Californian out to have a good time.

"Have fun!" the Californian often says in parting, and he is more earnest about it than most. His capacity for leisure becomes as specific a syndrome as a hyperthyroidism. "Anyone not having fun," writes Remi Nadeau, "is suspected of being a malcontent." Sociologists make tentative forays into the phenomenon, speaking of "inventive and zesty searchings for nonconformist leisure" by the Californian, and suggesting vaguely that the quest may yield a "new central pivotal focus for tomorrow's good life." Others wonder, like Joseph Wood Krutch, if society can survive the fun explosion; when pleasure becomes the *summum bonum,* its pursuit grows compulsive and mechanical. Yet much of the Californians' leisure time is spent in meaningful pursuits: in conservation and community beautification projects, in family explorations, in study, and in solitary or communal cultural advancement.

With his high income, his benign climates and his explorations into irresponsibility, the Californian is always ready to eat out and see a movie, buy a camper or a boat, join a club, build a fence or plant a garden, visit an amusement park, or go away for the weekend or longer. With him goes his camera; sales of film and photographic equipment are half again as high in California as nationally.

Usually without thinking it through, he equates leisure and environment. Television audience ratings are generally lower in California; these are leisure activists, and less time is spent in the home. Nature provides playgrounds, and Californians have cars to get there. (If they don't, they rent; car rentals are double the national average.) The sun makes the seashore, the mountains and the desert—and the increasingly cramped park systems—into amusement areas that are available even to those whose budgets (if they lived in other parts of the nation) would not allow them to regard themselves as a leisure class.

So the people of the Golden State swim, dive, ski, water ski, sunbathe, sail, picnic, skate, ride, climb, hike, fly, sky-dive, soar, hunt, race, fish, shoot, dig, plant, pick, prune, barbecue, paint and play innumerable games—out-of-doors as often as possible, for to be outdoors means to escape from the setting of work. They are also among the most omnivorous of spectators. Civic bond issues for luxurious athletic stadiums win enthusiastic approval, and the amount they spend on their own equipment for leisure is imposing.

The home swimming pool has become such a staple in Southern California that it is not uncommonly found in the back yard of a family with $10,000-a-year income. About one in every sixteen California families now has its own pool.

In 1966 there were thirteen thousand private aircraft registered in California with seventy thousand active pilots. There is a horde of powerless gliders and homemade gyrocopters that are best described as soaring living-room chairs.

On a winter weekend during 1966 in the sand dunes of the Colorado Desert, about ten thousand people appeared with about one thousand dune buggies, curious racing machines with soft tires and fuel-injection engines of up to a thousand horsepower that will climb 50-degree sand slopes and tear across desert drifts at a hundred miles an hour.

California has almost three times as many par-three golf courses as the second-ranked state, and only a slightly lesser multiple of regulation courses. About one in five California men plays golf, and probably one in fifteen women. New tennis clubs are appearing constantly. The state has the largest share of both fresh water and ocean fishermen, their gear ranging from trout lures to fast cruisers for the pursuit of marlin. The saddle horse population of Southern California alone is estimated at half a million; through the aristocratic heartland of the San Francisco peninsula, stables house impressive collections of polo ponies that are moved south to the Southern California desert in winter.

Californians own more than half a million boats. Their lavish beach equipment includes surfboards, water skis, fins, snorkels, face plates, and all kinds of inflatables. Now the second or third boat is in vogue. A survey by *Sea*, the magazine of western boating, showed nineteen percent of its readers owning two or more boats. The youth are no less affluent. In 1967 a charter flight from San Diego to Honolulu was delayed for five hours while airline personnel worked out a system for stacking more than one hundred surfboards inside the luggage compartment.

Outdoor sports go on twelve months a year in California, as the mild climate has spared most Californians such chores as shoveling snow or cleaning furnaces. In a land where one may ski in the snow and surf and lie beside a desert pool on successive days, there are some who find it irresistible to do them all. The pace grows frantic.

So in a first-night audience at a San Francisco theater one is only mildly surprised to find a patron in white tie and tails with a transistor radio plugged into his ear so that he can keep up with the follies of his beloved Giants at Candlestick Park. At Disneyland or at Sea World, the aquatic amusement park in San Diego, it is not unusual to see large families keeping in contact by walkie-talkie radio as they split off for various attractions.

The good life is more a California trademark than an obsession. But its pursuit, in the hedonistic environment of its playgrounds and resorts, looms ever larger until the most casual observer associates with it some of the ills of society—from divorce rate to crime and alcoholism and the alienation of youth. Outsiders view the excesses of California with a bemused tolerance; the frenzied absorption with pleasure excites relatively little attention. It deserves more.

In 1968 the Southern California Research Council completed a study of the "new leisure." To some, it showed, leisure means wealth, promise and freedom; others associate with it only boredom, hectic amusements and a feeling of worthlessness. The Council found recreation facilities inadequate, especially parks —and estimated that two billion dollars was needed to make them adequate. It found that fewer than one in twenty Southern Californians regularly attended performing arts activities, and urged more governmental subsidy for music and theater. Libraries, it reported, needed twice the existing number of volumes. Only two percent of Southern California's educational outlay was for continuing adult education, and fewer than seven percent of the adult population participated in such programs.

"Unless expanding leisure is accompanied by a profound change in our attitudes toward leisure and by marked improvements in our ability to use it wisely," the report concluded, "the diminished work week, lengthier vacations and longer retirements will be decidedly mixed blessings."

Statistics tend to conceal the high level of enthusiasm with which Californians combine their leisure time with learning. The do-it-yourself mania is not restricted to basic manual activities in the garden and home. California abounds in weekend artists and sculptors, little theater performers, and musicians who play informally as an avocation. The University of California Extension abets such activity with several thousand courses—many of them light-hearted in approach—in its attempt to help Californians stay busy constructively.

To the housewife seeking distractions, or the business or professional man wanting additional training or fresh interests for his leisure hours, the Extension catalog has the wide-eyed appeal that a Montgomery Ward catalog had a few generations ago on the farm. It prods both acquisitive and inquisitive urges. For a few dollars, one can take up such studies as Sanskrit, Stitchery as a Creative Art, the Theory of Games, or karate. There are seminars and weekend retreats, and group therapy sessions conducted by behavioral scientists.

Reading, that ultimate use of leisure, would seem to suffer in popularity in a restless land where emphasis is placed on frenetic movement. But even before the state surpassed New York to become the most populous, it had begun to outrank New York in many measurements of the sale and distribution of all types of printed matter. Many major magazines show Californians at the head of their subscriber lists; as long ago as 1962, *Harper's* magazine and *The Wall Street Journal* had higher circulations in California than in New York State. The state ranks well at the top in membership in the National Geographic Society. Book publishers regard their major markets as the megalopolis between Washington and Boston in the East, and that between San Diego and San Francisco in the West—with Chicago as the major market between. While it would be ridiculous to claim any uniqueness for the California reading audience, there is evidence that the region is no longer—if it ever was—the cultural dustbin that the literary establishment popularly assumed it to be in the past. Yet a distinction must be drawn between California as a reading *audience*, and as a creative force. In the latter regard, the state does not yet swing the weight that would befit its rank as most populous.

It is not any idle coincidence that the phenomenon of Western periodical publishing is *Sunset* magazine. *Sunset* is the leisure manual of the California masses. In subject it is limited entirely to travel, cooking, home design and improvement, and gardening. It is the how-to bible of California.

Conventional gardening magazines and books are useless in California, with its year-round planting schedule and unique growing problems. A magazine edited in New York is not likely to help the Santa Barbara home owner with his fuchsias, orchids, bougainvillaea, his orange trees or ice plant. His white grub and mealybug may resist the pesticides peddled to destroy their Eastern cousins. Sunset's *Western Garden Book*, encyclopedic and expensive, has sold more than a million copies in several editions.

Sunset is unmistakably egalitarian in mood, reflecting the assumption that the good life belongs to all. It's recipes will not be attributed to a movie queen or a governor but to a housewife. The formula has proven highly commercial in California and, in the case of the Sunset book division, all across the nation. It is the contention of the publishers that the world would like to emulate the California leisure life, and there is mounting evidence to suggest that they are on the right track. It is worth noting that a volume entitled *Landscaping For Western Living* was only slightly revised and subsequently has enjoyed a lively sale throughout the nation under the title *Landscaping for Modern Living*.

If some lingering remnant of Puritan ethic mars the Californian's bliss in his absorption with diversion, there is plenty to suggest that it is his duty to stimulate fun for civic and business reasons. California builds a sound economic future by designing itself as a playground for the nation and the world. Projections of California tourism in the years ahead pour out with such awesome multiples that they grow meaningless. Cities become entrepreneurs of pleasure. Fortunes are built at games.

One survey in 1965 showed that only the city of San Francisco exceeded Disneyland as the most-visited destination in the Western United States. Even Las Vegas followed Disneyland, and so did such natural wonders as Yosemite National Park.

Many have scorned and derided Disneyland. Others have sought to mimic it for their own gain. But this vast center for the ingestion of sentiment, nostalgia and plain corn soars imperturbably along. As an amusement park Disneyland is ingenious and diverting. In an effete attempt to put himself above it after a visit, John Ciardi once linked Disneyland with "the shyster in the backroom of the illusion, diluting his witch's brew with tap water, while all his gnomes worked frantically to design a gaudier and gaudier design for the mess."

It might be more apt to deplore Disneyland as a drift toward the vacuous and passive wasteland that so many Americans seem content to accept as their personal milieu. Yet Disneyland is super-American in all its technical finesse and its dedication to entertainment. I suppose it could have happened somewhere else, but Walt Disney put it in Southern California. Here it has succeeded Hollywood as the street of dreams, and there is no harm in that.

As though to squelch fears that he would lull Americans into a nation of spectators, Disney's next major development—moving forward rapidly despite his death—is a forty-million-dollar winter sports community in Mineral King, a narrow alpine valley on the edge of Sequoia National Park not far from Mt. Whitney in the southern Sierra Nevada, five hours by car from Los Angeles. By the mid-1970's there will be five thousand to seven thousand skiers a day on its superb ski runs. A new community is planned with fourteen lifts and ten restaurants, large enough to accommodate an eventual total of more than two million visitors a year. A twenty-three million-dollar highway, long opposed by Secretary of the Interior Stewart Udall because it breached wilderness areas, is scheduled to be completed from the Great Central Valley up to Mineral King in late 1973.

The prospects are that Mineral King facilities will be taxed from the start. The Californian is an activist, and the ski boom already inundates lesser slopes within weekend range of southern cities. For the skiers of northern California, hard by Squaw Valley, site of the 1960 Winter Olympics, and near a host of smaller ski resorts, the need is somewhat less critical.

The Disney projects are private enterprises. It is more remarkable, even in California, to find a city going into the recreation park business. But that is what San Diego has done with its Mission Bay, an aquatic sub-city with its own resort hotels and restaurants, marine parks, picnic beaches, marinas, campground and police force. The welcome signs call it a continuing development by the people of San Diego. It is public but unspoiled, one of the most disarming of all water playgrounds, a haven for active, healthy-minded hedonists. It has put almost everything aquatic within easy reach in a seven-square-mile area of blue salt water and reclaimed beaches that, until a few years ago, were no more than ill-smelling muck.

On a summer weekend about 2500 pleasure boats pass through the channels of Mission Bay; its shorelines and its new islands, created by dredging, may hold twenty thousand persons without any great sense of crowding. The park, carefully designed by city planners, has proved itself spacious enough to accommodate simultaneous races of power boats and sailboats without interfering with water-skiers, bathers or fishermen whose use of the water is carefully zoned to prevent congestion. The design is brilliant in the way it allots beach and water for specific use, and in the contour of the man-made shoreline. The shape of island and lagoon is so irregular, like the final piece of a jigsaw puzzle, that at no point do you get the impression of the bay's scope; the eye is always greeted by cozy inlets or seemingly lost islands. Developed with combined federal, state, local and private funds at a cost that will exceed $100 million, Mission Bay has become a model of urban recreational planning, a vision of the kind of facilities that more American cities will need to provide before the urban scene grows much grimmer.

Just north of Mission Bay the city of San Diego has bulldozed a canyon to provide parking areas and dressing rooms at Tourmaline Surfing Park, which is off-limits except to surfers. As a civic surfing park it is unique. San Diego beaches are zoned so that swimmers and surfers don't collide. The city trains men with the civil service job description of Aquatic Specialist/Surfing to work with surfers in classes and clubs toward safety and citizenship. About half a million California youths regard themselves as surfers; because of such work as this in San Diego, the early hoodlum image has largely been erased from surfing. As a sport it has grown organized. When a western surfing championship was held recently in San Diego, the program for Sunday morning read as follows: "6:00 A.M.: Short religious service on beach north of Crystal Pier, Pacific Beach. 6:05 A.M.: Resume surfing championships."

Despite some advanced efforts at control by their elders, California youth seem to be running away with the leisure race. Their spendable income continues to be the marvel of their parents' generation, which provides it. Their ingenuity in finding new ways to have fun commands the respect—however sullen it may sometimes be—of parents who have themselves given the matter vast time and attention.

The intellectual and the wealthy often exhibit distinctiveness in the way they join the fun. Scientists and academicians like to explore barren deserts or climb mountains. They find challenge away from the crowds. There are engaging exceptions, of course, like the Little League baseball team in La Jolla coached and managed exclusively by Ph.D.s.

The wealthy enjoy a wider spectrum of pleasures than the more conservative social establishment of other regions of America. They have second homes at desert golf clubs and third homes in northern California ski basins. If they are boat people, they may have a yawl at a California yacht club and a fast marlin boat docked far to the south in Mexican waters, accessible only by private plane.

The resorts they seek out are seldom old or traditional; such tradition as exists in California is more likely found in the city club, of which the Pacific Union and Bohemian of San Francisco are the most elite. Cruise ships are chartered for overnight parties, or a formation of private aircraft may descend on a ranch airstrip for a weekend. A San Diego couple mailed invitations to California friends for cocktails and dinner at their second home in Acapulco, almost two thousand miles away, and more than half of the invited guests managed to attend.

In Los Angeles and San Francisco especially—and their wealthier suburbs—there is a core of beautiful people who are at least the equal of any in the Eastern social establishment in their obsessive refusal to stay put. Californians turn up in undue proportion in London drawing rooms, on the slopes of Gstaad and St. Moritz, or along the Dalmatian coast. One of my favorite jetsetters is a La Jolla woman who belongs to the Century Club—all of whose members have visited one hundred or more countries. After flying a square 28-minute course around the North Pole ("We had to turn our clocks back one hour every 72 seconds," she said), she set off to conquer Antarctica. She was ninety years old at the time.

In an era where overseas travel is not uncommon among American teenagers, many California youths simply consider it obligatory. California far outstrips other states in the number of Peace Corps volunteers. Stanford University alone has five overseas campuses, and a majority of undergraduates spend two quarters in foreign study and travel.

For me it is one thing to know that Californians buy passports at a rate more than half again greater than the national average. It is another to keep meeting them wherever I travel. I try to detach myself from California idiosyncracies while I describe them, but there are frequent reminders that I behave like a Californian too. Even at home in La Jolla, living what I regard as a relatively conservative life for a Californian, I am brought up short by my own rationalizations. Once my wife and I dressed— she in a long dress and I in black-tie—for a formal summer ball that was preceded by a round of parties. As we left our house, we congratulated ourselves that none of our Eastern friends was at hand. We were carrying a bag with our swim clothes, to be ready for an after-ball beach party. Because the late August sun was still blindingly bright, we drove away wearing dark glasses. It seemed marvelously reasonable to us. Yet it is the kind of

California dementia that leaves New Yorkers shaking their heads in despair.

The attraction of oceanfront living in such communities has escalated prices of beach property, one traditional sanctum of the wealthy, to a point where the remaining building sites on the sea in communities like La Jolla and Santa Barbara—when offered—go at prices well up in six figures. Fresh water swimming pools may be found cut into the rock cliffs above the sea at waterfront estates; some of them are on cliffs so steep that there is no access to the sea, and others have beach elevators. Much of the oceanfront of Southern California is owned by city, county and state as parkland—and an eighteen-mile strip between Los Angeles and San Diego is part of a Marine Corps training base. What remains is virtually built to capacity.

Yet the urge to face the sea—for leisure as well as esthetics— seems to grow. "People are like lemmings," says George Sampson, one of the developers of Huntington Harbour, a marina home community near Los Angeles. Eighteen miles of water frontage have been created by dredging where none existed before. "Once they come West, they want to go all the way to the water." So real estate developers are busy trying to break up nature's generally straight coastline in Southern California by carving inlets and bays and building marinas where home-owners can garage their boats as well as their automobiles.

The largest public project is Marina del Rey near Los Angeles, once a waste marsh, that now offers about five thousand boat slips and fifteen hundred apartments. Part of its cost—now approaching eighty million dollars—was underwritten with a bond issue floated by Los Angeles County. Subdivisions on San Francisco Bay and the Sacramento River offer homes with boat slips as well as garages. Newport Harbor docks eight thousand pleasure boats; homesites on its Lido Isle sell for a thousand dollars per waterfront foot.

The oceanographer Roger Revelle has proposed doubling the coastline by building artificial offshore islands and sandbars as well as inlets. Recognizing the coast as one of California's great assets, he notes that by the year 2000 population will have swelled until there are ten Californians for every foot of shoreline. It would seem to be the dream of many Californians to live along the sea, especially in the less stormy south. Yet recreational lakes are also proliferating rapidly. Economics is involved. It can become frightfully expensive to go down to the sea for leisure. In 1966 the California Department of Parks and Recreation sought to buy less than four acres adjacent to a beach at Santa Monica so that it could set up a parking lot. The park people couldn't pay the price: three million dollars.

Boating traditions as well as weather differ sharply from north to south. In the view of a third-generation San Francisco yachtsman, nothing could more clearly define the distinction between northern California and Southern California than the annual Tinsley Island Stag Cruise and Rendezvous—staged to an elegant perfection by the St. Francis Yacht Club of San Francisco—and the annual Newport-to-Ensenada weekend race off Southern California, the largest and almost certainly the most democratic ocean sailing race in the world.

Yachting implies tradition. In San Francisco, boating is the word used for the flotillas in Southern California waters on weekends, many owned by *nouveaux riches* to whom a power cruiser or a motor sailor is no more than a seagoing Ford or Cadillac.

The northern California yachtsman must be a reasonably dedicated type. Even the waters of San Francisco Bay, tugged by strong currents and racked by wind, are no place for an amateur sailor. The seas off San Francisco often seem mountainous for sailing craft, and some of the most treacherous coastal waters of North America are those off the Monterey Peninsula and Big Sur. The San Franciscan does not get in as much year-round sailing as the Southern Californian, whose winds and currents are usually mild.

There is sharp contrast too in where to go. In the south, boat people sail to the offshore island of Catalina or to Mexican harbors. San Franciscans are blessed with the fascinating delta country of the San Joaquin and Sacramento Rivers. Tinsley Island, the destination of the annual autumn sail of the St. Francis Yacht Club, is in the San Joaquin River.

In the fall of 1966, that cruise involved 577 members and guests on 112 yachts and 24 houseboats—which are a favored family vehicle on inland waterways and lakes. The fleet was augmented at Tinsley Island with a twenty-piece orchestra and fifty cooks, waiters and bartenders. The cruise began Thursday at San Francisco and ended back there on Sunday. The events at Tinsley Island, aside from the largesse of food and drink (not a cash register was heard) included two days of races among thirteen-foot dinghies sailed by some of America's best-known yachtsmen. For the less dedicated, a two-day domino tournament brought fifty two-man teams together to vie for a $7,000 Calcutta pool. There was volleyball and pool swimming—even boccie, that game of bowls that the Italians brought to San Francisco. Boats paraded up and down the river, lying heavy in the water from their burden of servants. In all the weekend festivity, there was no casualty more distressing than swamped dinghies and throbbing hangovers.

A flotilla more than three times as large departs each May from Newport Harbor south of Los Angeles on the annual race to the little Mexican harbor of Ensenada. The scene from the jetty off the West Coast Newport is a blur of glittering sails. The jockeying of boats at the starting line seems more chaotic than Dunkirk.

It is an overnight, downwind run in which the frailest of sailboats competes with the stateliest schooners and yawls. But the race has developed a reputation as a weekend of *la dolce vita* for the wild and the willing. In 1961 a record 425 boats joined the race, but the gravest danger at Ensenada Harbor was not in dragging anchor, going aground or drifting with the wind into a collision, but the tequila of the Mexican *cantinas* ashore. Four policemen stood guard that year outside Hussong's saloon, an old plank-walled relic that is the unofficial finish line for the race. Inside, drunken gringos—most of them, it turned out, non-sailors who had seized the weekend of the race as an occasion to drive south into Mexico—stomped atop the bar. Ensenada mothers kept their daughters indoors. The race became an international embarrassment. In succeeding years order has been restored, but it will never be Tinsley Island.

Another traditional outing for Southern California sailors is the Labor Day weekend at Catalina Island, the resort developed by the Wrigley interests seventeen miles across San Pedro Channel from Long Beach. The channel becomes an aquatic freeway. Californians often drive cars with more skill than boats. In a state with a boat for every dozen families, one still doesn't need a license to drive one.

Every sheltered cove on Catalina has been jammed with moorings. At Cherry Cove, where I was a guest on a recent Labor Day weekend, we had just tied on to our moorings when two sailboats that have done nobly in coastal races became inexplicably engaged in fending each other off at the entrance to the cove. Several hundred thousand dollars worth of gleaming hardware was involved in a traffic argument. With that settled, a Los Angeles sportsman rammed his power cruiser into the port bow of a beautiful sloop. Two crewmen dived overboard at the impact.

"I told you," came a voice from two boats over. "I told you he'd make a fool of himself again this year."

Helicopters and amphibious planes buzzed overhead, ferrying those from the mainland who had missed boats or couldn't find weekend crewing assignments. The aircraft banked in over the narrow Isthmus of Catalina and weaved in and out among the masts to seek landing room in Catalina Harbor.

In the water among the boats were the children—skiing, aquaplaning, lolling on rafts, piloting speedboats, some of them even swimming. One group arched a rubber basketball into a hoop supported by a life preserver. The climax of the children's weekend came in a dinghy parade; aboard the winning dinghy, a pretty girl lay prostrate under a white sheet while a teenage physician administered tomato juice that looked like blood from a half-gallon gin bottle.

There was a major crisis of crowding ashore. The three pay telephones attracted standing room only and the thatch-walled *cantina* did such a thriving business that one could have been misled into thinking that liquor was not allowed on boats. The automatic laundries on shore worked, but the driers had broken down; the sleekest yachts had their rails lined with sheets and towels flapping in the breeze.

On shore too was a summer Boy Scout camp, and its troops came roaring out in canoes twice each day with war whoops not unlike those raised by their elders from the boat salons after dark when—after a few cocktail parties from boat to boat—their din descended into a stubborn quiet before midnight. It was not the sort of place that a San Francisco yachtsman regards as paradise; it was floating suburbia.

Those who ski and sail find their own leisure patterns drawn by snow and water. Surfers go to the long breaking waves, climbers to the mountains, and those who take to the air in gliders seek the thermal updrafts of steep ocean cliffs. California has its place for all these and more. The environment is as diverse as the inventiveness of the people who use it.

But there are resorts of curious, almost universal interest to which Californians are lured at least once and which often become a necessary setting of their own diversion. The rugged Mexican peninsula of Baja California, with its geographical and anthropological conundrums, draws me. So do other quiet places: the oaken hills above the Santa Ynez Valley of central California, a good place for a man and a horse; the brawny north coast, or almost any of the high mountains and open seas and lonely beaches. I am not one of the wilderness people, nor do I feel compelled to escape my fellow-man; but to me, going away means going back or going on in time or place, or going inside another people or myself. I live in the midst of California each day, and it is no pleasure for me to follow the restless migratory patterns to the weekend spas. So I am not a fan of Palm Springs or Las Vegas. But they are part of our story. It is my impression—and I have been back more times than I cared to—that they are both places at which the transient and the entrepreneur stay quite busy exploiting each other—at golf or gambling tables, at conversation and at sex.

Palm Springs, and the resorts that tail away southeastward from it, represent the most conspicuous outcropping of all that is vulgar and futile in the obsession with leisure. This is the Miami Beach of California. Its ghettos are both Jewish and gentile, cluttered with walled half-million dollar houses, garnished with Cadillacs and Lincoln Continentals, inhabited spuriously and erratically by women in tight slacks and spike heels, and men whose conversation seems curiously truncated at the level of the dollar.

There is water beneath the beige dryness of the Palm Springs desert. It is pumped up to about four thousand swimming pools and two dozen golf courses, each of which requires about a million gallons of water a day to keep it green. (The job is done with overhead sprinklers during the night.) Around the pools of its four hundred hotels and motels (a word banned by civic statute), the transients rotate toward the sun like birds on a spit. When they leave poolside it is to eat or take the mineral baths or to gawk at a house where Elizabeth Taylor spent one or another of her honeymoons, or the hardware store that Alan Ladd owned, or to lurk hopefully in bars that Frank Sinatra has been known to favor. It is considered good form to indulge in date milkshakes or the specialty of a restaurant that features "Tarzan's favorite African banana pancakes." All of the ridicule that was once heaped on the eccentricities of Los Angeles finds justification today in Palm Springs.

Golf almost redeems Palm Springs. It has been a large factor in the evolution of the desert as a resort. It is the major industry, partly because it offers restless men a reason for being in Palm Springs, along with the opportunity for real estate speculation in homesites and houses along the suddenly green freeways. The man most responsible for the golf boom is Johnny Dawson, a realtor and former golf professional who set out in 1949 to make Palm Springs the golf capital of the world on the strength of its seemingly infinite sunshine.

Financiers scoffed. They regarded the desert soil and heat as incompatible with golf courses. Dawson ordered soil analyses and studied the underground water supply, which is made up of seeping snow and rain from the nearby San Jacinto Mountains and dammed beneath the surface by a geologic fault. Paying nine thousand dollars down, Dawson took an option on a 270-acre dude ranch that later become the Thunderbird Country Club. It opened in 1954 and soon had almost a thousand members from thirty-seven states and Mexico, all of whom had been granted options on adjacent homesites. To make playing more comfortable beneath the hot desert sun, Dawson introduced the electric golf carts that have themselves become a major industry in America.

Today the most famed of the clubs that Dawson helped to build is the Eldorado, where former President Eisenhower bought a home. The annual membership fee is $10,000, and greens fees range up to $17. Its clubhouse is an immaculate white building with columns and a massive wide stairway entrance behind a cool fountain. Below the clubhouse, in an area resembling a miniature subway station, a fleet of a hundred white golf carts is parked, their fringed canvas roofs making a rainbow from above. This is one of the courses on which the Bob Hope Desert Classic tournament is played each winter, raising about $200,000 for local charities. Recently Eldorado and nearby Indian Wells Country Club have become part of a new community—Indian Wells, one of California's smallest and wealthiest cities. Its several hundred residents have an annual per-capita income in excess of $14,000. Golf is the only industry and the only business.

Those who seek the hot dry climate of this lowland Colorado Desert without the gaudiness of Palm Springs go farther south. Palm Desert, fifteen miles below Palm Springs, is closer by Indian Wells. The resorts southward from there tend to become less flamboyant and more relaxing. La Quinta is a favorite of aristocratic regulars from the East. One of the most charming of all is Borrego Springs, a placid and sophisticated resort with a spectacular view of the steep desert escarpment around a spur of the Santa Rosa Mountains from Palm Springs.

For many Californians, as for others from all over the world, the ultimate leisure escape is Las Vegas, across the Mojave Desert from Southern California in Nevada—which is sparsely populated and serves as a California fun annex, a kind of extra back yard. In a typical weekend showroom crowd at Las Vegas, at least three of every four visitors is from Southern California. (San Franciscans more traditionally visit Reno for gambling.) Las Vegas offers the closest tourist accommodations to Hoover Dam and Lake Mead on the Colorado River. They are the Western Hemisphere's biggest dam and largest man-made reservoir, but it is hard to find a Las Vegas visitor who can tell you in which direction they lie. The Las Vegas package is mass-produced gambling, glossy prostitution and an asylum of entertainers enveloped in an incomparable cynicism that even in this tuned-in, turned-on era makes Las Vegas seem like some venal Gomorrah, a molten overflow of the American passion for excess.

Las Vegas has been a haven for ex-cons and racketeers ever since the Depression, when the return of legalized gambling in Nevada and the national repeal of Prohibition brought in the mob. Their gradual withdrawal began when Internal Revenue Service investigators launched a probe of casino "skim-offs" of unreported profits. Under Nevada Governor Paul Laxalt, beginning in 1967, some effort at reform began to take place. As Howard Hughes began buying Las Vegas hotels and casinos in that same year, some of the least savory owners seemed ready to pick up their chips and fade away.

As a convention city, Las Vegas has generated gaudy high-rise hotels and waiters and casino personnel more surly than anywhere else in the usually genial West. Dreariest of all are the jaded, listless faces of thousands of guests swept up in the coldness of the world's gambling capital. It is possible to win at Las Vegas, as I have, and still leave town depressed.

In the showrooms are the toughest audiences on earth. They watch the big revues with the same glassy-eyed stares they turn toward television, daring entertainers to amuse them. Now that nudity no longer shocks, producers of the Las Vegas spectaculars have fallen back on condensed Broadway shows and the staging of disasters. Not long ago in the Lido show, a train was crashing into a stalled car onstage every night. Across the street in another revue, the Hindenburg was exploding. Audiences applauded perfunctorily.

Marriages now outnumber divorces in Nevada by about five-to-one, and the bride gets a free corsage with every $15 ceremony at one Las Vegas wedding chapel, open 24 hours a day. Others vie for trade by advertising candlelight, free transportation to and from hotels, dressing rooms, or phonograph records of the wedding. Not everyone chooses to be married behind a sign that proclaims SINCERE AND DIGNIFIED SINCE 1954, but there are enough who do to give Las Vegas more than twenty wedding chapels.

Most of the business at the chapels, as everywhere in Las Vegas, is from Southern California. Nevada demands no premarital blood tests nor any waiting period before or after issuance of a license. During one evening, that of August 26, 1965, a date made remarkable only because it was the last day during which marriage downgraded an American's draft eligibility, a single justice of the peace in Las Vegas performed sixty-seven marriages. "I got it down from five to three minutes," he explained.

Nearby at a crap table, a loser flung down his last $25 chip and said, "All I want is cab fare."

The house man raked the dice back in front of the gambler and gazed past him with Las Vegas eyes, the dull hurt in them like a machine that has forgotten how to turn itself off.

"How far you going?" he asked.

. 12 .

IMPLACABLE GREEN GIANT

I can tell Modesto from Merced, but I have visited there, gone to dances there; besides, there is over the main street of Modesto an arched sign which reads: "Water—Wealth. Contentment—Health." There is no such sign in Merced.

—JOAN DIDION.

Whatever else California may be, it is above all an agricultural state, and at the heart of its richness is the Great Central Valley with its interminable flat fields, its silent flowing canals, its monotonous towns. The valley is so enormous that the Appalachian mountain range of the East might drop neatly into it; it is larger than the total area of Denmark. "A man will plough

209

but a single furrow a day on his farm," wrote W. H. Bishop when he visited the valley in 1872, "but this may be twenty miles long." Now one senses a land subjugated by machinery, nature bent to man's will. The valley is an assembly line which spews out a dazzling variety of all those things which can come from the soil.

Much of the destiny of California has been shaped in this trough-like depression that extends for about 450 miles up the length of the state, only thirty to sixty miles wide between coastal mountains and the foothills of the Sierra Nevada. On a topographical map, upthrust mountain ranges and desert fissures give the western United States the look of an impenetrable maze. On such a map the Great Central Valley becomes the West's dominant feature, the largest level area. From Red Bluff at the north to Bakersfield at the south the horizon is broken only once, by the Sutter Buttes, an area of volcanic remains in the upper Valley.

Because the landscape deadens the gaze and there is little in its towns to hold the visitor, the Great Central Valley remains unknown to tourists and most Californians. It would be too much to call it a mystery, for there are only a few who have paused to wonder. Yet the valley has provided both the impetus and the setting for wondrous combat between man and the elements, and between man and man. In it farming became an industry. It is a laboratory of agricultural mechanization. It was the focal point for the violence and suffering of the migrant workers and later, in the 1960's, for the first breakthroughs of farm workers' unions.

Beneath the skies of this natural hothouse, humanists come to dwell on man's subjugation, while agronomists seek ways to minimize the need for man. Far up toward the northern end of the valley, beneath the gold-domed capitol in the bustling city of Sacramento, such balances of power are forever debated; but in the end little is done that might sap the agricultural might of the Great Central Valley, for in it lies much of the strength of California.

This is where California pays the piper. Life in the cities and along the glamorous coast can seem too good to be true. The coast is the front side, the onstage scene of California. The valley is the workshop, the production room, the warehouse; here is where the stuff is grown to feed California and help make it rich. Rarely in its hundreds of miles does one find any excess of amenities or any overwhelming reason to be there except the soil. State college educators complain of the brain drain to the coastal cities. "Even clergymen assigned to towns up and down the valley," insists a Sacramento State College sociologist, "are likely to be cast-offs." That is not true in Sacramento, which like many state capitals attracts those of intelligence and sophistication. Sacramento is the largest of the valley communities, and the collision of old and new is nowhere more dramatic than here.

As gold mining declined in the nearby Mother Lode, Sacramento citizens sensed their city's destiny as an administrative center and a hub of rail, river and highway traffic for the rich farmlands to the north and south. Years passed and its elm-shaded avenues grew thick with automobile traffic. The old iron-front and brick buildings of the Sacramento River front lost the period charm of the Gold Rush and became a scabrous wound of saloons and warehouses, cheap hotels and rooming houses.

In the population surge that followed World War II, hundreds of state architects labored in dreary Sacramento offices to bring forth the generally cheerless public buildings up and down California. Closer to home, civic leaders brought in architects Richard Neutra and Robert Alexander to chart a civic redevelopment plan. Urban renewal took hold and Sacramento became prideful. Where flophouses once festered (including one where Mark Twain lived) is a mall that provides a green-fringed approach to the Capitol. Garden apartments and new business buildings help replace the blight between river and Capitol. Among the impressive structures is the handsome contemporary home of the *Sacramento Union*, California's oldest daily newspaper, now rejuvenated as a member of the Copley newspaper group. In all, sixty blocks between Capitol and river are to be revamped in a $220 million project that includes restoration of a Chinatown district around a new Confucian temple; it is projected as a West Coast Williamsburg. For Sacramento the future seems bright. The city places high in all population growth projections for California. Its sense of being out of the mainstream since the

Gold Rush has been dispelled by an invasion of space-age industry.

North of Sacramento on the Feather River, the $123 million Oroville Dam was dedicated in 1968, a key unit of the multibillion-dollar California Water Project that began delivering water far down the valley in early 1968, with delivery to Los Angeles scheduled for 1971 in time to replenish dwindling Southern California water supplies. In addition to providing water and power, such dams as Oroville help control the fearsome flooding of northern California rivers.

Elsewhere in the Great Central Valley one finds a regional inferiority complex. Highway 99, the unending band of concrete that cleaves the valley, is the locus for its life. The towns tick off as one drives south from Redding through Chico, Sacramento, Stockton, Modesto, Merced, Madera, Fresno (distinguished by its own downtown beautification program in the 1960's), and on to Bakersfield.

For the visitors the names and places run together. Most towns are jumbles of two- or three-story business buildings occupied by J. C. Penney and State Farm Insurance, by farm equipment agencies and pancake houses, by the Bank of America and the Baptist Church. There is still a "wrong" side to every town. When the Mexicans or Orientals or the descendants of the Okies have prospered enough to leave the desperate ranks of the migrant worker, they often settle in on the edge of town so that some semblance of family life can go on while the man travels to the fields. They are the more fortunate ones. The others are in the labor camps beside the fields.

"An implacable insularity suffuses these towns," wrote Joan Didion, who grew up in the valley. "They think alike and they look alike." Even the transitions of geography within the valley are vague. Northbound, somewhere between Fresno and Bakersfield, one begins to see more newspapers from San Francisco than Los Angeles. The Tehachapi mountain range closes off the valley from Los Angeles, and the delta country opens a funnel-shaped route to San Francisco. Most valley people seem happy to regard their vast homeland in small perspective, within their own fifty-mile radius, where most of their needs can be filled.

Today the valley may be developing a dual track. Paralleling the towns and ranches of Highway 99, a West Side Freeway is being built. It is to become a major arterial between Los Angeles and San Francisco by the mid-1970's. The California Aqueduct, 444 miles long from the delta country to Perris Reservoir southeast of Los Angeles, cuts down this same west side of the valley. Near it is the San Luis Dam, another unit of the vast Central Valley Project which presages irrigation of millions of acres in the western valley, and new towns to serve the farms.

Along the new freeway, much of which follows an old two-lane highway, the heartland of the state is laid bare and one feels its lonely immensity. The route skirts quiet, dusty farm towns like Crows Landing, Gustine, Los Banos, Dos Palos, Mendota, Coalinga, and leads on south through the oil fields of McKittrick and Taft to the foot of the Tehachapi range that separates north from south in California. On valley freeways one finds the usual crush of trucks and cars; but on the smaller highways and the arrow-straight access roads, the car surrenders its right-of-way to the monsters of field machinery being moved from farm to farm, or oil drilling rigs en route to new fields.

The north end of the Great Central Valley is drained by the Sacramento River, and the south end by the San Joaquin before the two rivers meet in the delta lands and flow finally into San Francisco Bay and out the Golden Gate, the only aperture to the sea for the entire length of the valley. As long ago as the Civil War, huge grain ranches prospered in the Sacramento Valley at the north. In 1890 the harvest of wheat was three times more valuable than California's output of gold.

The San Joaquin in the south, developed with the help of the Southern Pacific Railroad, was at first cattle and sheep rangeland dominated by land barons like Henry Miller, who bought up homestead land until he could travel for two days on horseback without leaving his property. With the gradual development of irrigation systems, new and smaller ranches in the south blossomed in fruit and nut trees, in vineyards, citrus groves and vegetable crops, and more recently in cotton, rice and sugar beets.

One distinction between north and south now greets the eye. The north was settled more intensively, and the landscape is still warmed by tall, heroic wooden farmhouses at the ends of tree-lined roads; they were often built up high to escape the flood waters of the Sacramento. In the south, the stucco bungalow ranch house with its air conditioner is more common, usually dating back no earlier than 1920.

A typical large fruit ranch of six thousand acres in the southern valley employs up to twenty-five hundred men and women at the peak of the harvest in orchards and vineyards and packing sheds, shipping twenty to thirty railroad carloads of grapes, plums or peaches. Its labor force drops to six or seven hundred in mid-winter. The permanent staff includes the ranch manager and his assistants, an office staff, physician, electrician, and cooks. The rolling stock includes fifteen tractors, forty or fifty trucks and trailers, and fifty company cars whose drivers run up prodigious daily mileage in overseeing ranch operations. At the center of the ranch is a cluster of bungalows and a street with modest gardens leading abruptly to schoolhouse and store, labor camps, packing shed, refrigeration plant and railroad siding.

Despite their contrasting histories, the northern and southern valleys merge almost indistinguishably into one expanse, criss-crossed by irrigation canals of the Central Valley Project bringing water to more than a million acres of farmland and providing power, wildlife and fish refuges, and flood and salinity control. The soil of the valley is rich and the sun hot, providing growing seasons for nine to ten months of the year, about four months longer than the average elsewhere in America. But rainfall is scant and evaporation is prodigious. Without the waters of the Sacramento River, diverted to the more arid south, the valley's productivity would be spotty and limited largely to the north. Water demands are enormous. To produce a crop on one acre of desert land, it takes more than five acre-feet of water, the equivalent of covering an acre with water five feet in depth. Agriculture accounts for about nine-tenths of the California water consumption.

California has ranked as the most productive state since 1947, and its supremacy rests on this Central Valley Project. Plans for the CVP were first devised in 1930, and three years later Californians voted a $170 million bond issue to launch it. But the

Depression overwhelmed such planning; the bonds were never sold. The federal government then undertook to develop the system, and so far about one billion dollars of federal and state funds have gone into it. The present labyrinth of dams, canals and power and pumping plants is only a beginning. By the end of the century, engineers estimate that almost four billion dollars more will have been invested to bring under cultivation the three million acres of irrigable farmland that still is untouched by water in the Great Central Valley. Much of the choicest farmland now under cultivation lies adjacent to California cities and is being absorbed by urbanization. Growers predict that about one-third of California farmland will have been taken out of cultivation by the year 2000; a great reserve to replace it lies in the Great Central Valley, but it is useless without irrigation.

With water, it is golden. The three most productive farm counties in the United States are Fresno, Kern and Tulare, all in the lower valley. About half of California's annual cash farm receipts —which are now in excess of four billion dollars—can be traced to the valley.

From California come about one-third of America's canned and frozen vegetables and fruits, including almost all of the commercial supply of pears, plums, prunes, grapes and apricots, and most of the asparagus, broccoli, carrots, lettuce and celery. Most of America's figs, nectarines, olives, almonds, artichokes, dates, lemons and walnuts come from California. The state ranks first in production of tomatoes, strawberries, beet sugar, beef cattle and turkeys. It is second in cotton and third in milk. Of all California crops, cotton ranks first in value, followed strangely by hay, and then grapes and tomatoes.

The value of the state's farm products exceeds that of its production of aircraft and transportation equipment, the next largest industry. It is more than four times that of California petroleum production. Another two-and-a-half billion dollars of the California economy comes from food processing, canning and packing, much of it for overseas export. The ultimate figure to encompass agriculture and all related industries in California now approaches fifteen billion dollars, a sum that dwarfs the total gross product of many states.

From the start California agriculture grew more as a branch of commerce than a way of life. The family farmer could not underwrite the huge sums necessary to exploit the land, bring in water, and ship his harvest over long distances. Even now the state ranks far down among the list of states in the number of farms because many of them are so large. More than two-thirds of the California farm income is accounted for by fewer than fifteen percent of the farms. California farmers have been successful in stabilizing market prices through their own cooperative marketing associations, so that federal price control and farm support are less familiar than in many other states, although federal controls have been a significant factor in California cotton.

The valuation of each farm is extraordinarily high. Corporations operate many of them, since the high capitalization necessary to exploit farm mechanization has tended to squeeze out the small farmer. Since 1940 Californians have moved away from farms to cities in such numbers that the percentage of farm population has dropped from about ten to two percent. Yet the income of families remaining on California farms is twice the national average.

California guards this agribusiness against pest and parasite as fiercely as a military base is guarded against sabotage. For many years, until traffic jams became formidable, all incoming cars and trucks were stopped at the state's borders and searched for fruit or other produce that might be diseased. With the help of university entomologists, farmers fight more than a hundred species of insects and mites, fungi and viruses. Yet the chemical warfare—often conducted from airplanes—often makes the valley an inhospitable place for man, just as the increasing pollutants from man's motor vehicles have damaged truck crops, alfalfa, cotton and grapes, helping to drive many such farmers away from urban areas.

The extent of agricultural innovation is suggested in the career of one man among hundreds who have made this their life work. When William Vere Cruess, a University of California food scientist, died in 1968 at the age of 82, obituaries reported that during his 61-year tenure at Berkeley he had invented fruit cocktail and pioneered in commercial development of canned applesauce, raisin bread, frozen fruits, and fruit-flavored ice cream and candy. During World War I, his research led to the artificial dehydration of prunes, peaches, apricots and other fruits that had been traditionally sundried. Later he learned how to control spoilage of olives and introduced the packaged Spanish green olive. He achieved another distinction early in his career; until interrupted by Prohibition, he had served as a University specialist in fermentation and wine-making.

There is a degree of specialization in California agriculture that is unknown elsewhere. About three hundred agricultural products are grown, from artichokes to zucchini, reflecting the diverse climates and soils of the state. By experimentation and often by failure, and usually with the vast assistance of the University of California and its agricultural experts at the Davis campus in the Great Central Valley, farmers have learned the eccentricities of the land. Reversing the normal pattern, they have found, fruit ripens sooner in the north than in the south. Almonds, once planted throughout much of California, are now grown largely north of Sacramento. Cotton and forage crops prosper in the south near Fresno. Figs and grapes are favored in the south, and in the wet delta lands farmers plant asparagus, tomatoes, rice, safflower and sugar beets.

Within a single county, growers have found that the California Smyrna fig, raised for drying, grows best in some areas, and the Kadota fig, used for canning, in others. Varieties of peaches and apricots or grapes used for the fresh produce market will thrive best in separate areas from fruit used in canning or for wine. A further type of specialization results from the variable climates; table grapes can be harvested in May and June in the southernmost areas of the state, in the Central Valley from July to September, and in northernmost areas until October. Thus corporate growers maintain a continuous market by plantings that may range over six or seven hundred miles of California.

A cornerstone of the agricultural variety of the valley and the entire state was the experimentation of the Franciscan fathers on the mission farms in the early nineteenth century. Coming from Spain and Mexico, they introduced olives, wine grapes, avocados and tomatoes. Those of many other lands who settled California have been eager to grow the crops of their homelands. Japanese-Americans have been inventive in diverse types of truck farming. The Chinese helped to develop celery, which has become a year-round California crop. Viticulturists from France and Hungary introduced grape stock that prospered in the California valleys. Slavonians became apple growers, Armenians grew figs and raisin grapes, and the Dutch and Portuguese have figured prominently in dairy farming. A Pakistani at Yuba City is the nation's fourth largest rice grower. In the diverse climates of the Great Central Valley or elsewhere in the state grow dates from Algeria and Egypt, flax from India, alfalfa and walnuts from Chile, milo from Japan, and rice from China. California supplies most of the flower seed of the world, largely from its coastal valleys. Until about 1930, even Californians assumed that winter tomatoes could be produced only in hothouses. But after volunteer tomato vines were seen prospering in midwinter in an irrigation ditch of the Imperial Valley, farmers undertook to grow them commercially, with great success. From such spontaneous enterprise the California cornucopia has evolved.

It has been fostered by a state university agricultural research program that is intimately involved with the producers and their problems. In 1968 University of California scientists proudly closed a gap; they introduced a new variety of strawberry called Sequoia which ripens in January; until then, California growers had been able to harvest strawberries for only eleven months of the year.

About the same time, university scientists were testing the effect of gibberellic acid, a Japanese plant hormone, on table grapes. Sales had been declining around the nation, and grocers reported that customers complained grapes were flat and tasteless. Scientists found that many growers were treating vines with the acid, which reacted on the grapes much like silicone injections on the topless dancers of nearby San Francisco, increasing their size by as much as sixty per cent. But research also showed that such swollen grapes lacked flavor. So growers set about self-regulatory procedures to improve the quality of their product.

South of the Great Central Valley at Riverside, the University of California established a citrus experimentation station in 1907.

Not long ago I went there to visit Alfred M. Boyce, a respected entomologist who was the dean of the college of agriculture and had served as consultant on agriculture to the Rockefeller Foundation and to the President's science advisers. His scientific bent is for insects, but he could pass at any Grange convention for a wheat farmer. He put his feet up on his desk and answered my questions as leisurely as though we were standing the all-night watch at a tobacco curing barn.

"We've been here in the middle of the citrus industry at Riverside from almost the start. Where we sit now was the nursery. The Letters and Science College is built on the old experimental walnut and citrus orchard. A lot of the new men on the faculty used to think we were tractor drivers and milk cow milkers. Yet we have a job here. Agriculture is our biggest industry in California and always will be, despite urbanization, which only makes it tougher on us to learn how to grow increasing quantities on poorer land.

"You drive around and you don't see orchards any more. People think citrus groves have given way to subdivisions. But acreage in groves is the highest ever here in Riverside County. Statewide it's on the rise after hitting a low in 1957. New plantings exceed removals now. And each acre going in produces close to twice as much citrus because of improved varieties."

I asked him about the great war waged by entomologists during the 1940's against a blight that caused orange trees to die mysteriously in summer, their fruit and foliage still hanging on. For several years it threatened to destroy the citrus industry in California.

"We got a fund to study it here," he recalled. "We didn't know what it was so we named it 'quick decline,' which it certainly was. It took two years to solve it. We found a virus, tristeza, transmitted by an aphid. It's a killer.

"Then we started looking for a variety of citrus that was resistant. Had a devil of a time. I finally remembered a couple of old trees on the back lot. Come on and I'll show them to you."

We drove to the back side of the Riverside university campus and he showed me two orange trees that didn't look worth the trip.

"These are Troyer citranges. Not worth a damn," he said. "They're a cross between the Navel orange and Poncirus, an ornamental tree that's related to the orange, and grows around Maryland and also in the north islands of Japan. These are the only two in the world, so far as we know. The only reason they are here at all is that a man named Troyer with the Department of Agriculture in Washington knew a man in Alabama, where it gets cold, and he wanted to grow oranges down there.

"One of our men made the cross of the Navel with the Poncirus to impart coldheartedness to the top of the plant. He did, only the fruit was useless: a great abundance of seed, and a laughable amount of pulp and juice. So the citrus industry never developed in Alabama, and we had these two no-good trees on the back lot named for a USDA man in Washington.

"They'd been here at least fifteen years when the 'quick decline' crisis hit California. We were ready to try anything. We finally grafted rootstock from one of these Troyer citranges and that did it. The rootstock is not only resistant to cold weather, but it's impervious to the virus tristeza.

"Almost every orange tree planted in the past ten years has been Troyer citrange rootstock. About two-thirds of the two million citrus trees propagated each year are offspring of these two no-good trees."

Californians are not prone to be braggarts when they talk of their citrus crops; Florida grows more oranges. The vineyards of the Golden State are another matter; they are more significant than its groves. About half of California's grapes are crushed to provide three of every four bottles of wine drunk in America. Wine is a $700,000,000-a-year industry. The finest American wines come from California, and the state has become the world center of enological research. Innovations developed at the Department of Viticulture and Enology at the University of California at Davis now are studied and often adopted by French vintners. In 1966, with a faculty of fourteen offering a three-year series of courses in winemaking, the state-operated school at Davis was larger than the renowned enological station at France's University of Bordeaux. To the occasional grumbling taxpayer,

Dr. Maynard Amerine, who founded the school in 1935, simply tells the truth: "The wine industry is part of the agricultural interests of California, and our responsibility is to serve those interests."

His classrooms are unordinary. In one of them is a row of gray booths, each with a small stainless steel sink washed by a steady swirl of water. Student wine tasters sit in these booths to train their palates and take their examinations, spitting out wine after tasting. On a nearby wall are cabinets filled with labeled empty wine bottles of varied hues and shapes and sizes. Close by is a small still used to teach the principles of distillation.

Downstairs is the cellar, much like any other wine cellar except that its barrels hold five or ten gallons of wine rather than fifty or a hundred. Along its walls are almost fifty thousand bottles of California wine. This is, in effect, the library of the school of enology. Its vintages go back to 1934, just before the school was opened, and include almost every vintage of every California varietal wine made since.

But none of this wine is drunk; by some estimates, up to twenty thousand gallons of wine each year are poured down the drains here. It is the only winery in Yolo County, but not a drop is sold. Each summer technicians from the California wine industry come to the Davis campus to acquaint themselves with the university's latest research. There are about three hundred wine technicians at California wineries, forty of them at the huge Gallo winery in the Great Central Valley town of Modesto. With the aid of the state university, they have thrown off the enslavement to European wine standards and are producing new types of wine with refinements that already have allowed some California wines to assume a kind of separate but equal status with the French.

Yet it is trite and futile to compare French and California wines. The Cabernet Sauvignon, usually regarded as the prince of California red wines and compared frequently with the Bordeaux wines, has a higher alcoholic content and a unique taste. The Pinot Noirs of California are similar to Burgundy, but not so overpowering. Among the whites, Pinot Chardonnay, made from the same grape as the white Burgundy, is an engaging companion wine. These are the dry table wines that Californians drink twice as much of as the sweet dessert wines that still are the favorites of a majority of Americans who drink wine; the Californian has developed a more sophisticated taste and his wine consumption, not unexpectedly, is sharply higher than in most of the rest of the nation—even though still far below the European rate. The urban Californian has become conscious of California wines, and unlike some premium California fruits, which are exported, his best wines are near at hand and readily available.

A day in the wine country during the autumn crush of the grapes is something close to a tradition in rootless California. The vineyards of the choicer inner valleys—Napa, Sonoma, Santa Clara or Livermore, all within easy drive of San Francisco—lie bronzed and golden and the heavy sweet aroma of the grape seems wedded to the soil. There are ivied stone walls of wineries built in the European tradition, little changed in the past sixty or seventy years; inside are massive redwood and white-oak aging tanks, and cool deep caves where the bottles of champagne, still unlabeled, are turned each day by hand to push the sediment into the bottle neck. The hospitality of the wineries is legendary, and the visitor who manages to tour three or four of them in an afternoon drives out of the valley under the spell of the grape.

But land taxes and technology are slowly making this scene obsolete. Steel tanks, often glass-lined, are now favored over wood casks for the aging process. Intruding subdivisions have set off rounds of property tax increases that are driving wineries to more distant valleys and new, utilitarian plants. The process of wine-making has adapted even to California's pernicious inventory tax; because winemakers must pay taxes on wine as it ages, they have learned how to accelerate the mellowing process by filtering wine under nitrogen pressure. The harshness is removed more rapidly and the product is ready for market sooner. Such techniques have originated in the school of enology at Davis, and the sites for new vineyards away from the cities have been chosen with the aid of Davis viticulturists. But one phase of the wine-maker's evolution over which the campus has had no control is the corporate absorption of small wineries, often owned by gentlemen vintners like the late industrialist and diplomat J. D.

Zellerbach or the newsman Frank Bartholomew. Major distillers own all or a major part of four of the top ten premium wineries of California. The giants among native son vintners, Gallo and Italian Swiss Colony, have remained successfully independent. Both have major establishments in the Great Central Valley, which is the center for production of dessert wines and lower-priced wines.

The California wine industry thrives, despite such threats. It has, after all, a resilient and obstinate tradition. It has already survived two devastations. Fathered in the 1860's by Count Agoston Haraszthy, an Hungarian exile who brought to California cuttings of 164 European grape varieties, the industry was almost erased in the 1870's by phylloxera, a small greenish pest that destroys the vines. Its blight spread across the Atlantic to French vineyards and was halted only by a joint effort: the grafting of European vines on native American rootstock that was resilient to phylloxera.

Recovering from that disaster, California vintners were struck down in the 1920's by Prohibition. Although some growers subsisted by producing sacramental and medicinal wines, others plowed up aristocratic vineyards and grew higher-yield varieties for the fresh produce market and juice, and for raisins. Even after Repeal, discriminatory state laws persisted that still impede the easy distribution of California wine to other states. It is no wonder that Europeans still drink thirty to forty times as much wine as Americans. The miracle is that the wine industry has prospered, setting consistently higher marks for both quality and quantity. The young farmer-scientists who dominate the industry today are third- and fourth-generation descendants of French, Swiss, German or Italian winegrowers. They are not unaware of tradition, even in California. They bear out the prediction of Robert Louis Stevenson, who observed early winegrowers as he honeymooned in 1880 on the slope of Mount Saint Helena in Napa Valley and wrote: "The smack of California earth shall linger on the palate of your grandson."

In its progress through technology and its response to the obstacles posed by nature and by law, the wine industry is a microcosm of the massive overall agribusiness of California.

Labor is a basic issue. Despite a stunning degree of farm mechanization, workers are still vital to bring in much of the harvest.
It is a mismatch that was dramatized by John Steinbeck in 1939
in *The Grapes of Wrath* and documented by Carey McWilliams
in the same year in his book, *Factories in the Field.* The Great
Central Valley is farmed by giants like Schenley Industries, the
Di Giorgio Corporation, and Kern County Land Company. Facing them, in season, are illiterate migrant workers whose average
annual incomes are below two thousand dollars, the lowest wage
in the American economy. Over their heads hangs the frenzied
race toward the mechanized harvest of more and more crops; in
their behalf come the first small successes in the unionization of
agricultural workers.

When Steinbeck narrated the miseries of the Joad family in the
Great Central Valley in *The Grapes of Wrath,* his book was
banned from all public schools and libraries that were under the
jurisdiction of the Kern County board of supervisors. A powerful
agricultural cooperative, Associated Farmers, sought without success to extend the ban. The novel, with its devastating appeal
to the national conscience, had a prodigious sale and won for
Steinbeck the Pulitzer Prize. Before the film version was undertaken by Twentieth Century-Fox, Darryl Zanuck sent private
detectives into the Great Central Valley to confirm Steinbeck's impressions of poverty, hunger and oppression; they brought back a
report that conditions were worse than those described in the
novel.

In his book, McWilliams, who was then chief of the state
division of immigration and housing but later became editor of
The Nation, charged growers with "farm fascism" in the exploitation of labor. The Associated Farmers responded with a resolution
labeling McWilliams as "California's Agricultural Pest Number
One, outranking pear blight and the boll weevil."

Relief for the farm workers came with the easy job opportunities of World War II in shipyards and aircraft factories.
Growers then faced a critical shortage of farm labor, and Congress responded with an agreement with Mexico launching the
program for importing Mexican farm laborers known as *braceros*

(the strong-armed ones). Growers regard the Mexican as a harder worker than the available Anglo farm laborer. In the peak year, 1957, almost two hundred thousand braceros crossed the border, four out of five of them going to the corporate farms of the Great Central Valley. Others entered illegally and worked until deported. They were known as *wetbacks,* a word that derived from the practice of swimming or wading across the Rio Grande into the United States; more often they walked or rode across the international boundary in the Southern California desert. In 1954, more than a million wetbacks were deported. The bracero remained the major source of California farm labor until the program was terminated in 1964; Mexican laborers since have been admitted only in specific instances where federal authorities are satisfied that there is not enough available labor to harvest crops.

After the departure of the bracero, labor organizers began to make their first gains in their long efforts to unionize farm workers. In 1962, a former migrant farm laborer, César Chávez, left a $7,200-a-year job as director of a Mexican-American workers service society in Los Angeles and went to the Great Central Valley farm town of Delano, where his wife's family lived, and where he had been arrested in a movie theater in 1943 when he insisted on sitting in a section reserved for "white only." Working in the fields beside his wife, often with their eight children in sight, Chávez began talking to farm workers and signing them up at $3.50 a month as members of a group he called the National Farm Workers Association.

Small, mild in manner and then not yet forty, he succeeded where the monolithic AFL-CIO had failed. Chávez described his NFWA as a labor organization guaranteeing employers a stable skilled work force with a no-strike pledge. But when the AFL-CIO's Agricultural Workers Organizing Committee called a strike in the late summer of 1965 against thirty-three grape growers around Delano, Chávez and his NFWA joined in. The growers imported strikebreakers and brought in the largest grape harvest in their history. But Chávez, articulate and determined, attracted widespread attention from white sympathizers in the civil rights

movement. He led a 250-mile march up the valley from Delano
to Sacramento which ended with a rally of eight thousand people
on the steps of the Capitol on Easter Sunday of 1966.

Chávez became the overall leader of the strike and the target
of verbal abuse by growers. Nationwide boycotts were beginning
to prove effective and on April 6, 1966, Schenley Industries announced that it would recognize Chávez's NFWA as bargaining
representative for its vineyard workers. It was the first time a
major California grower had recognized a union. Later in 1966
the powerful Di Giorgio Corporation also accepted the NFWA.
Chávez's efforts helped to bring the workers' wage up to $1.60
an hour, and elicited the angry charge from a Delano grower
that "Chávez will remain in history as the man who broke the
back of agriculture."

There are progressively fewer migrants among California farm
workers. A report by the Governor's Advisory Commission on
Housing Problems in 1963 showed that 88 percent of the farm
worker population live in the county where they work and 73
percent have been residents there for five years. Of the remaining
12 percent who follow the harvests there are some professional
pickers, packers and loaders who make quite respectable wages. It
is among the one in ten farm workers who remain that conditions
are worst; usually with sub-standard skills and education, they
are the last to be hired, and many of them drift off to the cities in
search of work or welfare. The machine takes their place on the
farm; their crisis merges into the urban crisis.

Yet there are labor camps near Linden and Gridley where the
sense of deprivation among workers seems as great today as ever.
Nutrition and sanitation are somewhat better than in the time of
the Joads, but schooling is hit-and-miss. Most camps have running
water now, and some growers, sensing that better housing attracts
better workers, provide simple, clean dormitories. State inspec-
tors have padlocked the worst camps.

Despite their own problems, large growers seem likely to find
continuing prosperity through technological progress. Satisfactory
profit becomes steadily more difficult for the small farmer. Most
crops are now machine harvested, at least in part. University of
California agricultural engineers have developed a mechanical

tomato picker so gentle it will not even break an egg that is run through its mechanism. At the same time they have perfected strains of tomatoes that produce fruit of almost identical size, ripening almost simultaneously, to facilitate the work of the picker. An automated lettuce harvester feels the head of lettuce and determines if it is ready for picking; if it is, the machine activates a blade that cuts the lettuce's stem and moves it onto an assembly line where it is sealed in plastic film and boxed before it leaves the field. Citrus is harvested by men lofted in the cages of scissor-extender booms and wielding suction tubes so that three men can pick seven times as much fruit as three hand workers. A cucumber picker carries workers prostrate on their stomachs just above the vines. Pneumatic tree-shakers harvest nuts and olives. There is farming from the skies. Low-flying aircraft sow rice, distribute fertilizers and weed and pest killers, drop chemicals to control shrimp, and herd wild ducks out of rice fields in fall. Automatic harvesters have been devised to harvest peaches at the speed of two minutes per tree, and of prunes at one minute per tree. Nine-tenths of California's cotton was picked mechanically before the proportion reached one-tenth in the Southern United States.

Other specters hang over the California agribusiness. One of long standing is the archaic 160-acre limitation on single-owner farms receiving water from federally-sponsored irrigation projects. Enacted more than sixty years ago as a gesture of subsidy to the family farmer, this statute is unrealistic in the Great Central Valley where farm units average almost one thousand acres. Nonetheless the Department of Interior continues to press the limitation because of the federal role in valley irrigation projects. In 1964 the Bureau of Reclamation conducted a sale of Di Giorgio Corporation farmland under the regulation, dividing a farm into thirty-one parcels of 160 acres each. The sale was a fiasco. Only one bid was made. Years of litigation lie ahead if the federal government continues to seek compliance.

The ultimate crisis for California agriculture is the disappearing land. Major food processors, including some with large farm holdings in California, have set up pilot farms and processing plants in Mexico, where labor is cheaper and more readily available and land is easily leased. In California, orange groves are toppled these days for shopping centers, and cotton and tomato fields become airports and freeways and subdivisions. By 1975, in the opinion of Emil M. Mrak, former chancellor of the University of California at Davis, California will face a serious shortage of agricultural land. About 1.3 million more acres of land will be required than are available today despite projected technological advances. Yet the trend is in the opposite direction; at the present rate, about 1.2 million acres of present farmland will be taken out of production by 1975. "We need a new land ethic," writes the conservationist Richard G. Lillard. "It must become illegal to destroy beauty, violate ecology, smash history —to extinguish the natural things that give value to human life."

Such dreams still seem foreign to the Great Central Valley, where only the first tentative steps are being taken toward bettering the plight of many human beings. Californians devote more imagination to the development of mechanized prune pickers than to the cause of preserving their environment. In the momentum of an almost incredible century of agricultural development, the dynasties that it has created seldom pause to consider ethics of the land. But California produced Steinbeck and Chávez to underline the ethics of man's relation to man; it is not beyond hope that from this same soil will rise a man to plead its cause so eloquently that it will not be lost.

. 13 .

LOS ANGELES

You May Be Too Much for Memphis, Baby, but
You're Not Enough for L.A.

—TITLE OF SONG BY PAUL HAMPTON.

It has been called Moronia, and also the ultimate city, a
plastic jungle, and the first city to say the hell with it. Kenneth
Tynan speaks predictably of Los Angeles in terms of prestige-
ridden insecurity. Westbrook Pegler was among the very first to
call Los Angeles a slobbering civic idiot, back in 1934, and
Jimmy Breslin writes about little worms of light, reflected from
Los Angeles swimming pools against the walls of houses, finally
wriggling their way inside the heads of its people. But then Los

229

Angeles is also the chosen home of the urbane Clifton Fadiman, who refers to it as a city in the vanguard of social development, and of Will and Ariel Durant, whose specialty is civilization.

Los Angeles is, among other things, the great American off-ramp, the most rapidly growing metropolis in history.

Or is it a metropolis? Two decades ago Carey McWilliams wrote that "just as Southern California is the least rural of all regions of America, so, paradoxically, Los Angeles is the least citified of all the cities of America." But then what is a city? Many urbanists now regard Los Angeles as the prototype of decentralization, of the sprawling cellular metropolises that they see in the future.

Los Angeles is the center of gravity in the American West, a place seething with change, bulging with muscle. Its strength is in the diversity of its people, their hunger for innovation, and the high state of technology that they have achieved. Their overwhelming challenge is to learn to live with growth, sprawl and movement. But in a place where technological change and the pursuit of leisure are twin gods, a new catalog of human stresses comes into view. People are made obsolete and cast aside, or they withdraw. An unprecedented jumble of archaic governmental units clanks and groans and begins to totter. Los Angeles is hailed as the forerunner of tomorrow, and yet its more thoughtful citizens wince at the look of the dawn. "Why must Los Angeles become a super-city?" one of them has inquired wistfully. "Why can't it just remain a warm, agreeable place in which to live? Why must it always be leading in something? Why can't it aim for second place or third, and get the prophets off its back?"

The answer comes back like the beat of a metronome in the several hundred people who migrate each day to Los Angeles County. Their pace has slowed from the frenetic 1950s and the early 1960's, but it still seems compulsive and inevitable. Los Angeles no longer appears to have very much to do with it. The late Harold Wright, as manager of the Los Angeles Chamber of Commerce, made a statement in 1960 that was virtually heretical in his profession. "There is no merit to any more people coming out here," he said. It has been echoed many times. No merit, perhaps, for Los Angeles; but the urge to wester is not yet dormant, and the American has always been restless and anxious for a look at tomorrow. He may feel alienated in tomorrow, lonely and a little frightened, but he comes, and he does not go back to yesterday. Within a sixty-mile radius of Los Angeles City Hall live more than half of all the wage-earners of California.

"Here in Los Angeles is the pathway of the future," said Dr. Lee DuBridge, formerly president of the California Institute of Technology. "Here are opportunities for improving, for building up a better community, a better world. It is not yet built. There is still a chance for changing things." That is the sound of the Western dream, and nowhere are the dreamers more on the make than in Los Angeles. A spark of nationalism ignites the place. Every city has its robust, explosive phase, but in Los Angeles, the thing goes on and on. Optimism marches in cadence with materialism.

No other city has been so shaped by image makers, and at the same time so misrepresented. You can say what you want about Los Angeles and find something to prove it. But it is harder to tell it the way it is at any moment. At the core of the nature of Los Angeles is the predictability of vast change. The city has had many images over the years, and those images have lagged behind the fact.

The cow town of rough saloons and shoddy promoters? Go back only as far as the 1870s, when criminals banished from the mining camps of northern California found refuge in Los Angeles, and there was a saloon for every fifty persons. The city's first boom came in the 1880s with the arrival of the transcontinental railroads and the success of groves that followed the introduction of two seedless orange trees from Brazil in 1873. The historic compulsion of the city to apologize to the world was already evident in the 1880s when the *Los Angeles Times* felt obliged to announce: "Los Angeles people do not carry arms, Indians are a curiosity, the G-string is not a common article of apparel here, and Los Angeles has three good hotels, twenty-seven churches, and three hundred and fifty telephone subscribers." During 1887 there were real estate transactions in Los Angeles County totaling one hundred million dollars; but in 1888 the bubble burst, banks restricted their loans to downtown property, and chaparral grew up around the speculators' stakes in the empty suburban cities.

Another image emerged at the turn of the century when tourism and oil discovery spurred growth once again and Los Angeles became the most ballyhooed city of America. Promoters lured God-fearing Midwesterners with special trains and brass bands, subsidized novels and magazines, and newspaper advertisements that made claims so outrageous that it was half a century before history could fulfill them. Los Angeles passed the hundred thousand mark in population in the 1900 census and for the next fifty years came close to doubling its population with each decade. After an abundant water supply from the Owens Valley was assured in 1913 and its unnatural harbor was completed, Los Angeles rapidly outgrew San Francisco. The sick and the aged came in response to exaggerated claims for the healthfulness of the climate. Speculators continued to come to deal in land. Iowans sold corn fields and came to set out groves of citrus. With the 1920's and 1930's the new image of Los Angeles was spiced with the glamour of Hollywood. Then drought and the Depression drove thousands out of Texas and Arkansas and Oklahoma toward the coast. This was an influx not anticipated by the boosters; for a time Los Angeles police were stationed near the state line to warn the Okie tide that no jobs and no dole awaited them.

World War II brought hundreds of thousands of new Californians to work in aircraft plants and shipyards. Peace set off the mightiest surge of all with the veteran who had first seen California while he was in uniform and was determined to have a piece of its future. That migration changed in nature with the emergence in the 1950's of the electronics and areospace industries; Los Angeles began to draw a highly-skilled, well-educated wave of newcomers. Universities handily recruited faculties from campuses in the East and Midwest. Think tanks and research laboratories were set up in Los Angeles when scientists decided the benign climate would provide a pleasant environment for their families and themselves. Then in the 1960's came an accelerated influx of Negroes from Southern farms and Northern slums, jobless and unskilled, unwanted in Los Angeles—just as unwanted as where they had been.

Each of these new waves of migrants transformed the city and gave it new orientation, drowning much of what had come before. The submerging strata of each of those societies are visible in Los Angeles like the earth layers of an exposed canyon wall. Almost everything of importance about Los Angeles is involved with newness and bigness, with the overpowering force of the newest migrants in collision with the most recent establishment, melding, interlocking, forcing change, taking over.

With each wave have come new movers and doers. Among those who arrived at the end of World War II was Dr. Simon Ramo, who got his doctorate at Caltech and spent the war years with General Electric in the East. "I felt a technological industry could be created here," he said in describing the attraction of California for migrants as a kind of "California-itis" which brings capable people who themselves attract good projects that in turn bring more good people. Working with Hughes Aircraft Company after the war, Ramo hired more than four hundred Ph.D.s. Later with Dean Wooldridge, a Caltech classmate, he set up a systems engineering company that became pivotal in the Air Force program for the intercontinental ballistic missile.

A symbol of the later professorial migration was Franklin Murphy, who came to UCLA in 1960 as chancellor and almost immediately became involved in the vigorous efforts that brought forth an eruption of museums, music halls and theaters appropriate to the city's sudden metropolitan status. Allied closely in those efforts with Mrs. Norman Chandler, matriarch of the *Los Angeles Times*, Murphy left the university in 1968 to become chairman of the board of the powerful Times Mirror Company. Thus another recent migrant sank new roots within the establishment.

It has seemed easiest over the years to express the changing nature of Los Angeles in terms of such infusion into the power structure; recently political leaders have emerged from the growing black minority that has been so spectacular a part of recent migration. Yet it is not practical to explain Los Angeles with symbols. *Time* editors chose in 1966 to do a cover story on Los Angeles in terms of its mayor Sam Yorty, who was described as "in many ways the personification of the city he heads. He is a maverick in a land of mavericks, a scrapper who is part political opportunist and part high-minded booster . . . He is defensive about California's virtues and suspicious of condescending Easterners. Like Los Angeles itself, which has long put up with the patronizing attitude of northern neighbor San Francisco, he seems to take pleasure in playing the underdog even when he knows that he is top dog." Such parallels, so far as they went, were almost but not quite as apt as they were convenient.

It is harder, of course, to encapsulate the nature of the more mundane Los Angeles resident. In an area of fluctuating and mobile settlement, surprisingly few attempts are made even among the social scientists. But the Bureau of Census has turned up some clues. It has found the typical Los Angeles married couple to be two or three years younger than the national average, and to have been married about two years younger. Both have had 12.1 years of schooling, slightly above the norm. Their family income is substantially higher. The husband is likely to be performing a highly-skilled professional job. Fewer Los Angeles wives work. Their family is distinctly smaller—with an average of 1.2 children as compared with a national average of 2.4 children. They have 1.5 cars, half a car more than the national average, and they travel vastly more, both within the United States and outside its borders. They are less likely than other Americans to own their own home, but they live in more material comfort— with a sharply higher inventory of household appliances: clothes dryers, freezers, color televisions and air conditioning. Los Angeles had its aged Townsend Plan boosters, its Ham-and-Eggers, and it still has its flagrant obsession with Forest Lawn. But its median age is down below the national average, and its people do not even grow as old as others; contrary to the traditional image, the life span of Los Angeles men and women is about two years shorter than the national average. It is a young city with an almost indecent exuberance still akin to the frontier. It talks of tomorrow but it is living for today.

Direct commuter flights between San Francisco and San Diego pass over Los Angeles at altitudes of about twenty thousand feet, setting off a variety of impressions among passengers. Remembering slow dreary hours in Los Angeles traffic, I always feel an elation in crossing this congested metropolis at five or six hundred miles an hour. It is seventy miles from north to south across the Los Angeles metropolitan area as it is described by the Census Bureau. At ground level this is a bewildering expanse of coastal plain with mile after mile of squat skyline rising no higher than the long rows of palm trees that line many of its streets. There are ugly patches of derricks and rocker pumps, some of them covered over and soundproofed, some landscaped but many of them blatantly creating an oilscape. Factories and subdivisions, equally faceless, sprout up from pastures and bean fields and orange groves. The location of the city is improbable. In a setting with inadequate water, it is insulated from the interior by high mountains. Unlike San Francisco, it is without a natural harbor or a fertile back country.

Yet looking down from twenty thousand feet, especially if it is night and offshore breezes have cleared the air of smog and given this vast seaside saucer a chance to look its electric best, I am always stunned at the appearance of orderliness. Within sight are a hundred or more separate municipalities run together in an almost unbroken grid of lights. Great hunks of the city are drab and others are ugly, but darkness and altitude mask these flaws. What one sees is the most expansive urban area of America, spilling over into five counties and nine thousand square miles at elevations ranging from sea level up to more than ten thousand feet. The brightly lighted freeways circle and bisect the metropolis in a plausible pattern. Los Angeles spreads along a coastal plain in a southerly arc that begins where the Santa Monica Mountains rise out of the sea. After twenty miles or so the coast turns almost due east and Los Angeles turns with it, past its man-made harbor, on beyond Long Beach and the coast of Orange County, where the dazzle of lights begins to fade into a dimmer patchwork of coastal towns. Off to the north as the jet crosses the center of Los Angeles is the dark strip that marks the ridge of the Santa Monica Mountains, setting apart the million people who live on the other side in San Fernando Valley, the geographical center of California population. To the north and east, beyond other mountains, lie the deserts. I am content when I fly high over Los Angeles at such moments, for I feel I can give up worrying about it. When I am poking around at ground level by day, I am always eager to get where I am going and be off the streets. The air may be acrid with smog or not, but there is still not much to see. Los Angeles does not communicate the physical sense of excitement that many cities do. I have immense respect for Los Angeles, more than a little concern, and sometimes even a trace of affection; but the affection always passes quickly, for I can seldom define it—only, perhaps, at twenty thousand feet, from where Los Angeles seems to be all one place.

The shape of the city is in fact ragged and grotesque; as seen on a map, it most nearly resembles the chess piece called the knight, except with a single skinny leg, or perhaps a sea horse reeling back on one leg. The leg, in either case, is a twenty-mile corridor annexed by the city, when it was land-locked, as an outlet to the sea at San Pedro. From the sea at the south to the northernmost city limits in the desert foothills beyond San Fernando Valley is a distance of about forty miles, strangely lacking in identifiable landmarks. Along the western flank of the city is a strand of fine beaches, almost unbroken for more than twenty miles, mostly public. Los Angeles is short of parkland, but its beaches provide open spaces that are usable throughout the year.

Both to the north and south of the mountains, the map of the metropolitan Los Angeles area is dotted with separate municipalities, incorporated islands within the great urban sea of the city. Many cities were absorbed into Los Angeles between 1910 and 1927 as the city pushed its limits outward, swapping its water for territory. Gilt-edged Beverly Hills and Pasadena and San Marino are among other cities that militantly maintained their independence so that now there is an encircling ring of sturdy municipalities. There are yet other islands, unincorporated communities surrounded by the city, under jurisdiction only of the highly efficient administrative behemoth of Los Angeles County.

Under the Lakewood Plan, county government effectively provides many municipal services to such communities by contract; as a result, annexation has become less prevalent. Yet the confusion inherent in all these units is compounded by makeshift arrangements in services, as when one little city may provide its neighbors with school facilities but decline to cooperate in traffic enforcement. The juxtaposition of urban units is so diverse that many citizens do not seem to know or care where one ends and the other begins; if it were not for postal addresses, many would go on for months without identifying themselves as residents of little Vernon, for instance, rather than of adjacent Commerce. The repetitiveness of tiny urban cores seems one of the drearier aspects of the Los Angeles environment. One drives into a town, passes through its downtown, swings out into its suburbs, crosses an invisible boundary at some intersection and begins the whole process again with a rising fear of infinity. On the freeways, at least, one literally soars above such impediments in a speedier kind of sameness, looking down on the tops of the rows of palms and the pastel roofs of tract houses or older expanses of red tile-roofed stucco homes in the neo-Spanish tradition that swept Los Angeles in the 1920s, a revival set off by the restoration of California missions and the exposition architecture of Bertram Goodhue.

Even on raised freeways, the barnyard smell of several Los Angeles cities penetrates to the speeding motorist. Urbanization has not yet moved out all of a dairy belt that originally included a trio of odd cities incorporated by dairy owners more as protective societies for their cows and barns and pastures than for conventional municipal functions. Cows outnumbered humans for a time in one of them, Dairyland, which was incorporated to protect dairies against intrusion of housing subdivisions. But megalopolis conquers all; in 1965 Dairyland became La Palma and builders began transforming its pastures into tracts.

The diversity of these communities and cities within the Los Angeles basin is nearly incredible: from the harbor city of San Pedro to the shaded estates of Chatsworth in the desert, from the sordid hippie haunts along the Venice waterfront to the old Victorian mansions that abut Pasadena on the east. Downtown Los

Angeles seems small for the area of the city and its population. It is a tiring sector of about two hundred city blocks that has become largely a place to work. It is the center of old-line business: banking, finance, oil, insurance, and publishing; but the loyalties of its people are to the suburbs where they live. There is increasing downtown rejuvenation, with the construction of its Music Center, new high-rise office buildings, and the beginnings of a five-hundred-million-dollar renewal project in the Bunker Hill area. It is a reasonably pleasant place where one can shop well and eat well and find amiable bookstores and clubs and attend concerts and plays. It gapes with open spaces where buildings have been torn down to make parking room for cars, but what has been razed was seldom good architecture and is no esthetic loss.

Downtown Los Angeles would seem large if set down in San Francisco or Manhattan, but the immense scale of the Los Angeles coastal plain dwarfs its center into insignificance. The new linear downtown is more exciting: a fifteen-mile stretch of Wilshire Boulevard that runs from the city's center to the Pacific at Santa Monica. It is lined with high-rise apartments and skyscraper offices, the smartest shopping centers and the beautiful County Museum of Art. Its route passes the suburbs of Beverly Hills, Alcoa's new Century City, Brentwood, Bel Air, Westwood and Pacific Palisades, one of the most sumptuous urban corridors of the world. Other tangents of the city's growth follow in other directions from downtown Los Angeles along most major freeways to include well over twenty thousand factories that provide employment for more than a million industrial workers. Everything is decentralized. There are more than two hundred newspapers and over five hundred banks and uncounted shopping centers with as many as fifty or a hundred stores in each. Yet with all its sprawl, there is a curious parallel between Los Angeles and ancient Pompeii, which has been so long admired for its organization around courtyards and pools, all with views of surrounding mountains. Los Angeles is built around its shopping centers and backyard pools, with the mountains as backdrop.

The Pacific coast hooks around so that from central Los Angeles one goes either west or south to reach the sea. Beyond a range of hills in the desert to the east is another metropolitan area centering on San Bernardino and Riverside. Along the coast to the southeast, on the way to San Diego, is the new sub-metropolis of Orange County, which grew in fifteen years from fewer than two hundred thousand people to more than a million, picking up the appellative, along the way, of hypersuburbia—and a clinging reputation as the stronghold of political reactionaries. In part because of Disneyland, the annual number of visitors from outside California outnumber the residents of Orange County by about five to one. Orange County has, quite suddenly, its own major league baseball team, the California Angels; one also finds the Garden Grove Community Church, notorious both because it is actually a drive-in church and because of its 252-foot fluorescent cruciform. The people of Orange County are a moderately affluent collection of homeowners, heavily native-born Americans with few blacks, deeply enmeshed in federal aerospace contracts and real estate development. There is a vocal core of prominent right-wing activists, but the weight of civic and elective strength is dedicated to maintaining the status quo of society while moving ahead with such basic essentials as roads and schools and services. In this Orange County is arch-typical of American suburbia. The minority of radical reactionaries continues to uphold the Orange County reputation as right-wing because the churning majority, rapidly moving in and out as their aerospace jobs change, do not pause to become entrenched citizens of the political community.

The population of the city of Los Angeles itself is nearing three million, and that of the county has passed seven million; but these other millions begin to hem it in. Few open spaces remain to delineate urban borders and one forgets that Long Beach, the second largest city of Los Angeles County, is a city in its own right of four hundred thousand people. Long Beach knows it is Long Beach, all right, but to most Americans it is all part of Los Angeles. It *looks* the same, whether at high noon on the Pacific Coast Highway or from four miles in the sky at midnight.

In the sea of motley gray funk there are new islands of cultural significance. Sixty per cent of all pornography distributed in the

United States is produced in Los Angeles County and nude model studios do a thriving trade with perverts who never held a camera. But it takes a troupe of fifty-eight guides to conduct the tours that file through the cultural temples of the Music Center, which are the pyramids of Los Angeles: the stunning 3200-seat Dorothy Chandler Pavilion, the more intimate Mark Taper Forum with its resident theatrical company, and the adjacent Ahmanson Theater.

The self-obsession of Southern California produced a subconscious blunder in a Los Angeles magazine not long ago: "Knotts Berry Farm has improved its early California atmosphere by putting in a replica of Independence Hall and the Liberty Bell." But the outdoor sculpture courts at the Los Angeles County Art Museum and UCLA reflect a participation of private enterprise in the arts that is not approached in San Francisco; private contributions for the Music Center totaled more than eleven million dollars, and an even greater sum from private sources went into construction of the County Art Museum. The taxpayers do not complain excessively when the county budgets two million dollars annually to the operating budgets of such art and music centers.

These days there is about as heavy a pedestrian count in and out of the art galleries of La Cienega as through the park of the dead at Forest Lawn, with its laborious copies of Michelangelo's David, Moses and the Pieta. When a new painting was unveiled in 1965 at Forest Lawn, the pageantry included music by the Roger Wagner Chorale and an inspirational message by Norman Vincent Peale, along with a summary of the fifty-year history of Forest Lawn by its chairman, Hubert Eaton, who referred to himself as The Builder (up to two million tourists and five thousand funerals each year). The more serious art world of Southern California is being bolstered by active collectors and by strong art staffs and historians at universities and galleries, creating a ferment so contagious that, as a New York art critic wrote not long ago, "one begins to picture Europe as the Renaissance, New York as the avant garde and L.A. as the 'orgiastic future' that year by year becomes more actual and immediate, replete with an art already actual and immediate." There are few who begrudge Los Angeles ranking stature in athletics and aerospace and brain factories, but now the city demands attention for its leaders in architecture, art and music.

Hollywood has been a literary dead end for a host of writers, and now the movie industry itself seems enveloped in a haze of geographical nostalgia, as if no one around Los Angeles can recall where it has gone. "I remember Doris Day before she became a virgin," wrote Oscar Levant, himself a rare but jagged bit of flotsam set adrift in the shipwreck of Hollywood. Much of the film industry has gone abroad, of course, and television has moved in behind it, crisp and workmanlike. The thing called Hollywood is usually a disappointment to those who go in search of it. It is dispersed, past its prime, and slightly shoddy. Hollywood is a post office address, but otherwise it is not much different from a hundred other slurbs in the Los Angeles basin. It has always been the euphemism for movie lots and studios from Culver City to Burbank, and even for companies on location five thousand miles distant. The film industry came first to Los Angeles for its clear skies and photogenic backgrounds. For a time there was something Californian about the industry. As the director and producer John Houseman once said, California supplied "the solvent, the atmosphere of unbounded self-confidence" through which Hollywood films mirrored the euphoria of space and self-discovery that were so much a part of California in the 1920's and 1930's. By the 1940's, close to four hundred movies a year were being made in and around Los Angeles, and box-office revenue reached its peak of $1.5 billion a year. Since then there has been erratic decline, not only in volume and income but in spirit.

Occasionally one finds some of the old Hollywood in a new role as civic cultural custodian. There is Gregory Peck, on a summer day in 1968, rich-voiced and irresistible, standing in the lofty hilltop living room of Mrs. Simon Ramo, the wife of the aerospace genius. He is chatting with the woman of the new Los Angeles about what they must do to insure that the performing arts within the newly-built pyramids of the city live up to the architecture. Poised with their coffee cups around the room are Mrs. Kirk Douglas, Mrs. Mervyn LeRoy and Mrs. Frederick Brisson, along with the wives of scientists and educators and industrialists. Peck is discussing the new Performing Arts Academy, just launched with seventeen students and two masters: Gregor Piatigorsky and Jascha Heifetz. "Come to Southern California and look at the future," Peck is saying. "This is still the one place in the United States unrooted enough to be able to create and innovate. We can build, through the arts, toward the twenty-first century for all, in this megalopolis of different races and creeds and colors that is Los Angeles." It is the old California cry of *Why not?* It is a different vision from that of Gloria Swanson and *Sunset Strip*.

The image of Los Angeles as a bastion of the white Anglo-Saxon Protestant has been overdrawn. Its ethnic mix is rich and complex and it has fluctuated wildly. On his northward march from San Diego in search of Monterey in 1769, the Spaniard Portolá camped near an Indian village called Yang-na, close to the Los Angeles and San Gabriel rivers. Today the rivers and the Indians all seem to have been displaced. Portolá renamed the site Nuestra Senora la Reina de Los Angeles—Our Lady Queen of the Angels. The first colonists, twelve years later, were forty-four peons from Mexican Sinaloa. Twelve were Negroes and the rest were Indians, some with a trace of Spanish ancestry. Los Angeles had its beginnings as a melting pot and so it remains. During the brief rule of Mexico, the pueblo of Los Angeles served as capital of California under the governor Pio Pico. It came under American occupation in 1846 but it did not get its start as a city until the migratory surges of the twentieth century.

Much of this migration was indeed made up of Anglo-Saxons coming overland from previously settled regions of the United States. But there were minority movements from all over the world. Today about ten percent of Los Angeles residents are Jewish, many of them in the entertainment business. Beverly Hills is a heavily Jewish community. Some came as refugees from Hitler's Germany and a large number came from Russia. (The American Jewish Committee estimated in 1968 that one in five Los Angeles college students was Jewish.) There are about thirty thousand Chinese. But the Japanese, twice as numerous, make Los Angeles the center of the Japanese-American world. Detained and placed in relocation camps during World War II, the Japanese-Americans have returned in greater numbers. Meanwhile the Negroes, who numbered only about seventy-five thousand in 1940, have migrated to Los Angeles at such a rate that they now approach and may soon surpass the size of the huge Mexican-American community, close to a million persons.

The social problems of this divergent mixture are legion. There are nearly one hundred thousand people from twenty-five different nations who speak no English. As in other large cities, there are districts of Los Angeles where most of the signs are in Japanese or Chinese, Spanish, Yiddish or Russian. The largest non-English speaking minority is Mexican, a fact attested to by prospering Spanish-language radio and television stations and by crash schooling programs in English in the Mexican-American communities of east Los Angeles. For many of the foreign-born, a main key to the almost inscrutable mysteries of Los Angeles has been a young school teacher, Ginger Cory, whose assignment was to teach elementary English on a Spanish television station—but who, in fact, has become a patient counselor and correspondent with hundreds of Spanish-speaking Los Angelenos who are seeking jobs, transportation or citizenship.

The barrier facing the Mexican-American—who is often shy and withdrawn into a family that maintains, rather than adapts its language and traditions—is an especially formidable one, overshadowed by the black revolution. For me, its poignancy recurs in the image of a tiny boy selling newspapers on a street corner in Boyle Heights. As I stood waiting for a bus I greeted him in Spanish. He stared at me for a long time and then asked in a soft voice if I would help him pronounce the headline of the afternoon newspaper. Before my bus came he was calling out some catchy headline from the 1968 presidential campaign, and his business seemed to have improved.

Although black leaders have been more voluble and their militancy has brought them greater attention, the plight of the Mexican-American is in some ways more desperate. It is a classic instance of the collision of cultures. Written off around the turn of the century as a vanquished element in California, the Mexican was soon returning in large numbers as an imported laborer.

Railroads brought peons from northwest Mexico at the rate of two or three carloads a week to work on railroads and farms and in mines, factories and cement plants. In 1900 there were only about eight thousand native-born Mexicans in California. The number grew steadily with the expansion of California agriculture and during the dark years of the Mexican Revolution. Today fewer than one in ten California workers are farm laborers, but two-fifths of the Mexican-Americans work on farms. They still find it hard to penetrate the skilled crafts and professions. The American pace and intensity seem foreign to their nature. In Los Angeles they tend to keep to themselves in east side settlements like Happy Valley, Clover, Custer, Rose Hill and Bunker Hill. The corn *tortillas* and *frijoles* that are the staple of their homeland remain basic to their diet in Los Angeles, where the fads of specialty foods, sometimes bizarre, are pervasive; Mexican food has become, in fact, a staple of the Anglo-Saxon menu.

More than half of those older than fourteen have not been schooled beyond the eighth grade—two years less than the blacks of Los Angeles. The typical Mexican family does not stress achievement outside the home, and in the *barrios* of Los Angeles young Mexicans find scant incentive. Edward R. Roybal, who was the first Mexican-American to be elected to Congress from Los Angeles, was counseled during his ninth school year to become an electrician. Julian Nava, a youthful state college professor with a Ph.D. in history from Harvard, was urged by his high school counselor to take body and fender repair courses, and did so. The presumption has too often been that the Mexican-American could neither afford nor complete a college education, and that no appropriate job would be open to him if he did. In general the Mexican-American has a lower income than the black, and in areas where blacks move up or out to better housing, the Mexican-American is likely to come in behind. Under the federal Economic Opportunity Program, funds have been designated for the Mexican-Americans of Los Angeles—to divert delinquent teenagers into useful pursuits, to serve impoverished families through neighborhood centers, to provide day care for children of mothers who enroll in adult educational programs, and to reduce the number of school dropouts. But the war on their poverty remains only a skirmish.

Some militant leaders have begun to emerge from the community, although militancy is alien to their basic nature. "Our people are being ignored in favor of rioters," one of them complained in 1968. The political weight of Mexican-Americans is beginning to be felt at the polls for the first time, yet surveys show that the real income among Mexican-Americans in Los Angeles has been in decline. In 1968 a modestly-financed federal program began to help launch Mexican-Americans in professional careers. There was in 1968 only one bank in Los Angeles operated by Mexican-Americans, and one savings-and-loan association; there are far fewer really prosperous Mexican-Americans in Los Angeles than Negroes. Part of the problem is that in the past some successful Mexican-Americans have changed their names and become Anglos. Now they are more conscious of their identity and are staying to help lift others. Students are organizing in heavily Mexican-American high schools. Yet the Mexican-American is amiable and anxious to please, and he has seemingly inexhaustible patience. "I would be embarrassed to file a discrimination complaint," said Philip Montez, director of the Foundation for Mexican-American Studies in Los Angeles. "It's this great thing called pride. I'm proud to be a Mexican."

Such a Mexican-American lives quietly within a city that took its name from his language, and the names of its valleys and mountain ranges and rivers and many of the streets of its new subdivisions. He is not the target of prejudice in the same way as the black, but instead is in limbo—neither within or without the California society. Discrimination against the Mexican-American is more economic than personal, less active and more a matter of default. It is the Mexican-American who has most effectively segregated himself, and it will not be easy to bring him soon into the Anglo society.

The sorriest chapter of California racial affairs—graver in its feverish prejudice than the unconcern for the blacks—was the deportation of Japanese-Americans from the West Coast at the start of World War II. It was an act of official bigotry, founded on public fear of sabotage or collusion with invaders. There were about 93,000 Japanese-Americans in California; about sixty percent were Nisei, American-born citizens, and most of the remainder were Issei, older adults who had come from Japan before Congress halted such immigration in 1924. The Issei had never been eligible for naturalization and thus were classed at the outbreak of war as enemy aliens. During the spring of 1942, under Army supervision, nearly all Japanese-Americans were confined in makeshift quarters at racetracks, fairgrounds or exhibition halls. In the summer and fall, long after the danger of Japanese invasion or air raids had been mitigated by American victories at Coral Sea and Midway, families were moved to ten camps in bleak and isolated parts of the nation, where they were guarded by soldiers and surrounded by barbed wire fences. Among them were many second- and third-generation Americans, but few voices were raised in protest. Earl Warren, later governor of California and chief justice of the United States Supreme Court, was outspoken in favor of their relocation, as was columnist Walter Lippmann. By contrast, the more numerous Japanese-Americans of the Hawaiian Islands continued to live in freedom, many of them working at United States military and naval installations.

Most of the internees remained in the camps until 1945. Then many of them began the slow trip back to the areas of their former homes, their journeys made more tragic by the widespread loss of their property. Many had sold out in haste and at heavy loss. The property of others was sold for taxes or storage fees during their internment. Eventually the United States government reimbursed about 26,000 claimants at an average of about thirty cents to the dollar of valuation. But their old communities were overrun. Some eighty-five percent of the Japanese had been farmers; their fields were gone. Fishing fleets were lost to the Italians, Portuguese and Yugoslavs. Some became gardeners, but typically the Japanese-American of California is now involved in business or the professions. With infinite patience he has rebuilt and gained heightened prestige and respect. Little Tokyo still exists in Los Angeles, but only as a center for daytime business; the Japanese live today virtually wherever they wish in Los Angeles, and few areas of employment are closed to them. The third generation of Japanese-Americans, the Sansei, now typically of college age, are emerging as a highly-trained and skilled group who are much sought in technological fields. Many have sensitive positions in aerospace industries. Other Sansei may be among those presented in the annual Japan America Society debutante ball, which in 1968 was in its fifth year. Having won the respect of a conscience-stricken community, the Japanese-Americans of Los Angeles have reached a plateau which, in the opinion of a UCLA sociologist, ranks them as the one ethnic minority which has "made it."

In the central and south central districts of Los Angeles, where most of its blacks live, no such happy prospect is in sight. From 1940 to 1960 the proportion of blacks rose from 4.24 per cent of the city's total population to 13.5 percent. Projections for 1985 raise this to about 40 percent. The pattern now becoming evident in New York and other cities seems imminent in Los Angeles: steady movement of industry and retailing out of the central city, and massive requirements for public services and facilities of every kind within a city that begins to tax itself to a point of no return.

Yet in the first half of this century—long before the Watts rioting of 1965—Los Angeles developed a reputation as a good town for Negroes. It has helpful precedents in the current black crisis. It was one of the first cities in America to employ Negro police and firemen. By the early 1940's there were Los Angeles Negroes in the state legislature and on the judicial bench. Its ghettos are not typical multi-story tenements but are more often single frame houses on lots of thirty- to fifty-foot width that, with better upkeep and landscaping, could be attractive. The sorrow of Watts, as of every other black community, is in under-education, under-employment, and poverty. The youngness of Los Angeles may help toward solutions. There is less political corruption in Los Angeles than in most older cities, and public facilities are not so dilapidated nor housing so decayed.

Los Angeles businessmen, aroused by violence in Watts, have made earnest and fruitful efforts to boost job training and employment for blacks. A 1968 study by the Federal Reserve

System showed that minority group employment by California banks was considerably higher than the national average for Mexican-Americans and Orientals, and slightly higher for blacks. A similar pattern appears in other segments of the economy. But in Los Angeles, as elsewhere, both blacks and whites committed to bettering the opportunities of minorities are reminded often that the simple solution is ephemeral, and that no single answer is without its qualifiers. For example, the lack of public transport in the Watts area was regarded as the prime bottleneck for black residents seeking to commute to jobs in other areas of Los Angeles. Yet when some bus service was established, patronage was so sparse that buses often rolled with only two or three passengers.

But the Southern California euphoria prevails even in the stubborn and complex problem of minority opportunity. Victor H. Palmieri, who left a private development firm in Los Angeles to become deputy executive director of the National Advisory Commission on Civil Disorders in 1967, believes Los Angeles has "the resources, the youth, the mobility and the growing room to cope with its problems of human development, as the community has coped with its problems of physical development."

There are many ways to see a city. The most elemental is the superficial view, with eyes alone. In that view, Los Angeles is a mess. Sprawled across its face are interminable areas of ragtag housing and sun-faded commercial buildings that are as expendable as the shacks of old mining towns. Architects and planners —and Los Angeles has a surprisingly generous share of both— profess to see some virtue in this structural rubbish; they establish on the basis of past performance that only a small part of it will outlive the mortgages, and there will be scant resistance to replacing it—at least sometimes with something better.

Los Angeles merits more respect when it is seen as a machine. Already more bound up in contemporary technology than any other city, it is sophisticated in such matters as its water supply and distribution system, its police force, its freeways, and in fire and flood control techniques that have made metropolitan life feasible in so unlikely a setting. Research into smog and underground water pollution is advanced. Although the battle is far from won, Los Angeles has led in the nation's most stringent smog control and it can at least be said that matters are not growing worse. Disposal of human and industrial waste is becoming refined, though inordinately complicated by the jumble of administrative authorities throughout the Los Angeles Basin: a host of cities, county-administered areas and separate tax districts including several hundred cemetery districts, library districts, garbage districts, school districts, lighting districts, debris districts, hospital districts, and more. If a breakthrough eventually comes toward the growing inevitability of some type of metropolitan government, it should come in Los Angeles County on that day when the interests of all these conflicting districts reach a crescendo of chaos that will lead them all to surrender a measure of autonomy for the good of the whole.

Communities like the Irvine Ranch are meanwhile employing technological advances to build toward the planners' dream of coordinated environment. Less than forty minutes from the Civic Center, the Irvine Ranch is three times the area of San Francisco and more than six times that of Manhattan; it is the largest singly-owned parcel of metropolitan area land under development anywhere, and among the most valuable. Ranging 138 square miles from ocean to mountains, it is in the path of the southward expansion of Los Angeles—and is itself an area where half a million people may eventually live. Until the early 1960's the ranch was almost unchanged from the era of Spanish settlement. Then under the stubborn leadership of Joan Irvine Burt, an attractive young heiress, its diversified development began under a master plan that may serve as an example for future urbanists trying to untangle the Southern California jungle.

Yet to view Los Angeles merely as melting pot, ugly sprawl, or technological test tube is to overlook the core of the phenomenon. What matters about Los Angeles is that despite its appearance of chaos, it functions well enough to be the center of attention for many who work to involve the drawing board and the textbook in planning the directions that urban America will take. Los Angeles may not be "super city," as so many boosters and journalists insist, and its bigness alone is not enough to attract attention in a world already frantic with urban crowding. What counts is that Los Angeles has grown large and continues to work while having been, from its inception, a consciously different kind of city.

In the early twentieth century those who were already beginning to give Los Angeles form and thrust rebelled against the nature of the nineteenth-century city and sought to build a cellular city whose smaller communities would more readily allow for the amenities of family and community relationships as opposed to the overpowering concentration of life in the largest cities of that era.

Los Angeles was the prototype of a concept of urban development in which the vitality of the city was not concentrated at the center but spun out into the periphery. The dream of Los Angeles —and it is not yet destroyed—has been that of the native American middle classes: their aspirations in regard to setting, community affairs, and political organization. In some ways Los Angeles is succeeding, most spectacularly with the help of a leisure-class leadership, and in those ways it has grown to be a model; in other ways it is failing, and its future hinges on the innovative and persuasive powers of a leadership element that emerges less readily in Los Angeles because of the nature of the city: loose and scattered political responsibility, small and diversified government, and the social fragmentation that has resulted from the philosophy of suburbanization.

So the significance of Los Angeles is not in its size but in how it copes with size. If the conventional American city is doomed, as many have begun to believe, America will look to Los Angeles to see if the fragmented metropolis can work any better. With a rush now on toward the suburbs in older American cities, the urban planner studies Los Angeles to see how those other cities may evolve. For better or worse, as the historian Robert M. Fogelson points out, since World War II, "most American metropolises have duplicated, to a remarkable degree, the patterns of Los Angeles' landscape, transportation, community, politics, and planning."

Los Angeles has stood accused of defying all laws of municipal gravity. The truth is that, in the California tradition, Los Angeles has been writing laws of its own almost from the start. The city may be regarded as an ill-formed and shapeless mass, "spreading over the fertile plains like an oozing Camembert," as one critic has written, but as early as 1909 the city pioneered in urban planning by establishing zoning systems for industry and restricting the height of office buildings. It is not unique to Los Angeles that its efforts in civic planning have been frustrated and abused by its politicians and real estate exploiters, or that its citizens have been usually too absorbed with civic development to accept adequate restriction on private enterprise. Even now, elected and appointed officials of Los Angeles stand charged with subverting public planning for private gain. But that is true in most cities, and it will remain true until more people care. There are indications that the citizens of Los Angeles are becoming at least as aroused over such civic abortions as are any other Americans.

With its propensity for extremism, Los Angeles has much of the worst as well as the best of the new, but its newness is not in doubt. "It might still seem a collection of suburbs in search of a city," the historian Earl Pomeroy wrote. ". . . It had stopped looking; it had built Long Island (though in more interesting style than most of the Eastern tract suburbs) without bothering to build Manhattan."

The vision of the great American middle class city may have come much closer to fulfillment in Los Angeles than is apparent. The Los Angeles family, retreating into its suburban ranch house with its walled patio and built-in swimming pool, its two-car garage and its electronic kitchen, is made vaguely uneasy by some sense of personal isolation; it feels no kinship with any metropolitan mainstream, nor with any nearby forest or field or river. But is that not the apprehension that the people of other American cities more and more often sense? Less infatuated with the Los Angeles Philharmonic than with one of sixty community symphony orchestras of which he may be a part, is the Los Angeles man not virtually a textbook example of metropolitan cultural fragmentation? Speeding over his freeways to pursue his spectacular avocations anywhere within a range of two or three hundred miles, does he not do much to explain the demise of the church, the bowling alley and pool hall, and even the neighborhood bar? Is it any wonder that in Los Angeles a major share of good architecture has been put there by private rather than public interests? Is it any surprise that the pursuit of good design seems now more concentrated within the home than in some community monument?

Those who have founded and guided Los Angeles have preached a gospel of equality and homogeneity, progressivism and innovation. They have not seemed to suspect that fragmentation would surely result and lead toward a vagrant society that seeks to abdicate traditional civic and social responsibilities.

Los Angeles is unified economically; its people are spirited and imaginative, possessed of a raw excitement yet unstirred by any civic or regional vision. By the year 2000, there may be twenty million of them. In the opinion of the urban critic Allan Temko there is room for that many and more, if existing modern communities and islands of development are cohesively linked and gray areas like Watts are renewed so that "an urban civilization of unprecedented force and graciousness would appear," and if present open spaces like the Santa Monica Mountains are preserved as parklands.

That is the physical prognosis. A deeper and more pivotal question is whether a cellular city can overcome the spiritual handicaps of its fragmentation to cope with social problems; and whether strong regional leadership can emerge to arouse a citizenry that is increasingly prone to aloofness. "We won't become a great city until our local officials develop a little more sophistication," said publisher Otis Chandler of the *Los Angeles Times*. "It's silly to think of Los Angeles as a city, or of all these little urban areas around it, each with their own mayors and city councils," said Franklin Murphy, an advocate of regional government. "Local governments in the old sense are outmoded."

Los Angeles remains an inquisitive city. There is the sense of emancipation, the awareness that new patterns in science and education, business, industry and in the art of living, are constantly being made here on this Pacific shore. This is a symbol of vitality, an embodiment of American drive. To dismiss Los Angeles would be to dismiss the future of America.

. 14 .

THE SIXTH NATION

Positions Available—Male: "PRESIDENT for newly approved Republic National Bank of San Diego, California. Opening date will be in approximately four months. President to pick own staff of executive officers and operating personnel."

—ADVERTISEMENT IN THE *Wall Street Journal.*

When the founders of a San Diego bank resorted to the classified ads to employ a bank president in 1964, there was no flurry of surprise. This, after all, is the state where a young produce dealer named Amadeo P. Giannini designed a bank to act as a money store for wage-earners, and helped to build his resultant Bank of America into the largest in the world. It is also

253

the state where, at about the same time that the San Diego bank president was being sought, the vice president of a bank in San Francisco grew tired of banking and opened a restaurant to the south in La Jolla, serving as chef. Nobody seemed startled by that, either.

The financial lords and industrial princes of California have often been mavericks. They have chosen the unconventional approaches, violating the traditions of the older American establishment. So the economic history of California has been turbulent. For most of a century, California was scoffed at as an outpost of almost colonial nature. Its economy was widely presumed to be shaky, based on weather, and prone to instant collapse. In the 1930's, it was traditional in some circles in the East to warn a California migrant against taking with him anything that he couldn't handily bring back on the old Super Chief.

Somehow California has continued to evade economic disaster. Now the strange ways of California business are being copied and adapted around the world. Success is the ultimate argument. The willingness of the Californian to experiment is a magnet.

"Whenever we have had anything new to try out," a New York businessman told a Los Angeles audience, "I have always asked our people to send it out here because I knew you would try it. I knew that you would not think of all the reasons that old established communities can think of why it wouldn't be successful, but that you would take it and say: 'Let's try it.' After you have tried it and made a success of it then the old established cities accept it."

The innovative capacity of the Californian is only part of his success formula. Despite pockets of poverty, the overriding impressions in California are of prosperity and abundance. The populace that the journalist T George Harris has called "the first mass aristocracy" now has its solid roots in a proliferating economy that is not going to blow away with the next Santa Ana, but instead continues to build up a bewildering array of superlatives. More than half of California's six-and-a-half million families have incomes in excess of ten thousand dollars, well over the national average and substantially above that of the second state, New York. At the end of 1968 about ten percent more persons lived in California than in the state of New York. They earned fifteen percent more and spent twenty-one percent more than the New Yorkers. Almost eight million Californians were holding jobs and unemployment was below five percent. Californians ranked far ahead of Americans from any region in air travel, including foreign travel, in use of credit cards and travelers checks, and in the valuation of their automobiles. Typically they lagged behind other Americans in purchase of U.S. savings bonds and low-priced cars.

Migration to California has begun to level off, but it continues to be far greater than that to any other state. With twenty million residents early in 1969, California was showing monthly business gains with monotonous regularity. Demographers predict that close to four million more people will have migrated to California by 1975 (with about half that number leaving the state), and personal income will have soared to $110 billion, compared with $76 billion in 1968. California has led all other states since 1960 in actual dollar gain in personal income. The greatest economic growth in the nation in the years until 1975 is projected for the Far West and Southwest, with California in the lead. In 1968 the California economy was outpacing the national growth rate substantially in every measurable way. It was more than double the national rate in population growth, triple in employment growth, five to six percent higher in growth of personal income, and double in housing construction. The California job increase of 300,000 in 1968 represented about one-fifth of all new jobs in the United States.

The unhealthy dependence of Los Angeles, in particular, on the defense dollar, which long made it a kind of federal city, is being minimized by diversified industrialization. California is importing less of its working capital. As income levels rise and prosperous migrants bring their own savings to California, the financial institutions of Los Angeles and San Francisco grow stronger and provide a larger proportion of expansion capital. Its aggressive savings and loan associations are attracting capital at a record rate. Californians have grown rich enough to become a breed of minor capitalists. They have astonishing rates of participation in stock and mutual fund ownership, in real estate ventures and land investment syndicates. One-fifth of all U.S. mutual fund shares are held by Californians, and private investment club meetings have become a standard feature of many housewives' schedules. Most California cities have small financial centers adjacent to major shopping centers—mini-Wall Streets that house banks, savings and loan, and brokerage firms, with insurance and related business firms occupying upstairs office space. Such a financial center is part of the Irvine Ranch master plan. Already at Anaheim, in Orange County, another is included in a two-hundred-acre, $300 million development called "The City," in which apartments, theaters, medical offices and a commercial center also are included—virtually superimposing a planned modern city atop a slightly older city.

Along with their ebullience and innovative capacity, Californians go further than older societies in linking education, science and industry with both public and private business. Education, after all, ranks with agriculture as the state's largest industry: the total outlay for learning approaches four billion dollars a year. Fewer than sixty percent of the nation's high school graduates go on to college, but in California the number is close to eighty-five percent. Many of these students attend two-year colleges; in terms of four-year college graduates, California ranks below the national average. Yet the average educational level in California is that of a college freshman.

Nowhere is continuing adult education more closely tied to the profit motive. In 1968 University Extension was offering a course in mergers and acquisitions, bringing together for a layman audience a cast of characters that included professors of law and business administration, officers of stock brokerage houses, corporate attorneys, an assistant chief of the Department of Justice antitrust division, and businessmen including the senior vice-president of Whittaker Corporation, a Los Angeles-based firm that was the rage of the financial world at that moment as it went about acquisition of companies all over the United States.

Californians have been quick to recognize the increasingly complex web between science and industry and the amenities. Industry places heavy emphasis on the laboratory, and the demarcation between laboratory and factory is harder to detect than in other regions. In the mid-fifties California began to assume leadership in exotic industries: electronics, aerospace and oceanography. Certain sections of Los Angeles, the Palo Alto-San Jose complex and, increasingly, La Jolla, rank along with the Harvard area as centers where science and industry merge. As vast aerospace manufacturers make the laborious transition from military to peacetime research and development, there is promise of continued acceleration in economic growth. The gadgetry of the mass aristocracy is being shaped on the drawing boards of Lockheed and North American Rockwell, Hewlett-Packard and TRW, Aerojet General and Gulf General Atomic. The youth market crowds in to buy. If the social problems of the cities and the minorities are to be solved, the future-oriented planners of California laboratories will be involved.

The scope of the California economy is commonly described by relating it to that of nations. In 1967 the California "gross product" amounted to more than $88 billion, a total exceeded only by that of the United States, the Soviet Union, West Germany, France and Japan. It was eight per cent greater than the gross national product of Great Britain. By 1975 the California figure is expected to reach $138 billion, and by 1980, $182 billion. The per capita income of California exceeds that of any country, including the United States. There is a Japan-California Association to foster mutual trade. An East Coast manufacturer led a research team to California recently and admitted that statistics had led his firm to reappraise California. "We had a division office and subsidiary for Colombia and a couple other countries," he said. "We kept thinking of California merely as a state. We treated it as a mere segment of the United States when, in fact, it represented more business and more potential than a dozen Colombias. So we have regrouped and organized our structure as though California were a separate nation." Publishers in the *Kiplinger Newsletter* reacted similarly. In 1965 they dispatched investigators to California. Such a bullish report resulted that a full issue of the newsletter was devoted to the state and a new all-California newsletter was added to the service. Yet at about the same time the California State Chamber of Commerce adopted the slogan: "Nothing we have done in the past will ever be good enough again."

Why California? Why such an extraordinary dynamism here and not in adjacent Oregon or Nevada or Arizona? At the start of the westward trek of the 1840's, it was Oregon more than California that lured the settler. By many measurements, the Comstock Lode of Nevada brought as big a boom in the 1870's as California's Mother Lode had set off among the Forty-Niners.

The explanations are both physical and mystical: the unusual meeting of unique people with extraordinary environment, their ingenious mastery of its resources, and the momentum of the innovative society that has resulted. Sift out the overkill of romance and prophecy, and California history remains almost a melodrama of destiny. Whatever has happened to the American West between the Rockies and the Pacific has happened in large part because of what has gone on in California. For much of its first century, the American West was in almost a colonial status; just a tier down the ladder, other Western states were, in varying degrees, like colonial outposts of rich and populous California, even while the state supported little more than a basic mining economy. Yet there were brash portents of what lay ahead. Until the arrival of the first transcontinental railroad in 1869, the region was isolated; entrepreneurs appeared on the frontier to launch primitive industries to supply the miners. Mining machinery represented the first innovation in production. By 1866 there were thirty-six iron foundries in California and thirty machine shops in San Francisco alone. California mines became proving grounds for new techniques that later spread around the world, and local manufacturers were launched in their first native industry. Expensive mining equipment imported from the East and from England was junked in favor of more practical machinery designed in California. More diverse methods of mining came to be employed in California than anywhere else, and each required unique equipment. Here was an early tie between research and industry. In 1851, it was noted in the journal *Alta California* that "the miners are beginning to discover that they are engaged in a science and a profession and not in a mere adventure."

To produce the vast number of wooden sluices and flumes used in placer and hydraulic mining, and the timbers for underground mines, sawmills rose beside northern California forests. Flour mills appeared near the wheat fields of the Great Central Valley. Newcomers began operating steamboat and stage lines that thrived from the mobility, even then, of the Californian. Gradually, among the thousands who arrived in California, there began to be more and more who were uninterested in mining and eager to establish roots. They were attracted by the early success of California industry and by the novelty of the environment. As population grew, they prospered. Much Eastern and foreign capital flowed into the mines, but from the profits of the miners investments were funneled off into fisheries and factories, into farming and sawmills. Isolated but with growing stability, Californians were discovering the economic self-reliance that so rapidly grew to distinguish the state and its people. The California spiral had begun.

Four of the early entrepreneurs were catapulted into wealth with a tremendous assist from a man who has been too often overlooked in American history, a brilliant engineer named Theodore D. Judah. Californians longed to overcome their isolation with a transcontinental railroad, and Judah was fanatically committed to a central route over the Sierra Nevada, which towered in its path for most of the length of the state. For financial support of his plan, Judah turned in 1860 to four Sacramento merchants, Charles Crocker, Mark Hopkins, Collis P. Huntington and Leland Stanford. Their venture company was launched with less than sixteen thousand dollars in cash; the combined personal assets of the Big Four in 1860 were only about one hundred thousand dollars. Their ultimate profit from construction of the railroad alone was to exceed two hundred million dollars; yet Judah, frustrated and angered by the profiteering schemes of the Big Four, died in 1863, unrewarded and unacclaimed, six years before completion of the railroad.

Its route was blasted over and through the Sierra Nevada with the labors of more than ten thousand Chinese imported for the task. Working at little more than survival wages, they sometimes hung suspended over Sierra chasms in wicker baskets as they chipped out roadbeds from sheer granite cliffs. Their coming was the origin of San Francisco's Chinatown, and it made possible the beginning of a long period of domination of California by its railroad barons. As a subsidy, the United States government awarded the Big Four close to twelve million acres of land adjacent to their right-of-way. Later federal investigations indicated that the Big Four may have received twice as much in cash and land subsidies as they paid out for construction of the railroad.

On May 10, 1869, at Promontory, Utah, the Chinese coolies of the Central Pacific ended their race to meet the Irish-American crews with which the Union Pacific had been building its roadbed westward across America. Driving of the final spike in America's first transcontinental railroad occasioned tumultuous celebrations all across the young nation. It came exactly one hundred years after the first settlement of California at San Diego by the Franciscan priest Junípero Serra.

Instead of the expected surge of prosperity, the completion of the railroad set off a decade of depression. The new manufacturers and merchants of California were now vulnerable to competition from the East. Land prices that had soared in expectation of the railroad boom fell dismally. But for the Big Four, this was only a threshold to greater fortunes. They gained control of the waterfronts of San Francisco and Oakland through devious means, including a network of local rail lines, and set out to lock up the rest of California with new railroads, new land grants, and control of river commerce. The Southern Pacific, completed in 1882 from New Orleans to Los Angeles, seemed to compete; but it too was controlled by the Big Four, and they came to be known as "The Octopus." They made or broke towns through routing of their rail lines with an eye only to personal profit. With virtually no competition, they established discriminatory freight rates in agriculture, mining and manufacturing to reward their friends and punish their enemies.

The Big Four kept rival railroads out of California until the Atchison, Topeka and Santa Fe reached Los Angeles in 1887. They maintained their monopoly eastward from San Francisco until 1910 and northward until 1931. The railroad barons captured majorities of the legislature and corrupted power at every level until the reforms instituted by Hiram Johnson as governor in 1911–13 began to break their grip.

The Big Four were not the only ones vulnerable to charges of land grabbing. Henry Miller came to San Francisco as a butcher's helper and was soon buying cattle and pasturage in the Great Central Valley. Before he was through he owned land on both sides of the San Joaquin River for a distance of more than one hundred miles, from near Modesto to Madera. With an Alsatian named Charles Lux, Miller eventually owned more than a million acres in three states and controlled vastly more through a tight grip on water rights. He boasted that he could ride from the Mexican border to Oregon and spend each night at a ranch house of his own. The Miller and Lux empire laid the basis for the massive scope of California's factories in the field.

Despite appalling abuses of power, California moved into the twentieth century with what was rapidly becoming a balanced (although not a self-sufficient) economy. The railroads brought entrepreneurs to the West and opened Eastern markets for wheat, cattle and citrus fruits. Agriculture supplanted mining in importance. At the turn of the century vast petroleum discoveries were opening riches greater than those of gold and silver. Tourism and transportation began to prosper. At the core of the economy in 1900, as now, was the pyramiding of wave after wave of migrants to California. The growth of San Francisco was remarkable in the early years of the twentieth century; that of Los Angeles became phenomenal.

With big business came unionization. Labor unions thrived in San Francisco and by 1900 the closed shop was as much accepted there as anywhere in America. In contrast, Los Angeles became virulently anti-labor, with low wages and open shop conditions leading to bloody union warfare from 1907 to 1910. The *Los Angeles Times* was under virtually incessant strike between 1890 and 1910, when its building was dynamited and twenty-one men died. Clarence Darrow led the defense of two union officials and a dynamiter charged with the tragedy. Samuel Gompers staked the emerging prestige of the labor movement on their innocence. Tension was strong as the three men went to trial in 1911, and during the six weeks of courtroom bickering that passed

without the completion of jury selection. Meanwhile the dynamiter turned prosecution witness. Suddenly the nation was
stunned by a plea of guilty from Darrow's two remaining clients,
the brothers John J. and James B. McNamara. Both Darrow and
labor were discredited. In Los Angeles, for thirty more years, the
open shop prevailed.

Upton Sinclair moved to Southern California in 1916 and was
not impressed by its economic potential. "The country has been
settled by retired elderly people, whose health has broken down,
and who have come here to live on their income," he wrote four
years later in calling the area "a parasite upon the great industrial
centers of other parts of America," a view that was widely accepted for years to come. But by 1923 more tonnage was passing
through the manmade Los Angeles Harbor than through San
Francisco, and there were more factory workers in Los Angeles
than in the northern city.

Still the image of Los Angeles was more the fluttering, giddy
one associated with its most prominent industry, motion pictures.
In that year a film called *The Covered Wagon* set an industry
mark for consecutive showings; *The Birth of a Nation* was already
a hardy perennial of eight years' standing. Samuel Goldwyn, Ce-
cil B. DeMille and Jesse L. Lasky were the ranking tyros of the
new Hollywood, and their infant industry was on the march
toward its ultimate pinnacle in the mid-1940's, when box-office
revenue reached its peak at $1.5 billion and almost four hundred
movies a year were produced in Los Angeles.

Throughout the booming 1920's, California speculators were
winning and losing fortunes in the film industry and in oil and
real estate. But economic pioneers were launching dynasties that
have provided cornerstones for the growth of modern California.
Today in Los Angeles about thirty thousand people have jobs in
the film industry, about one per cent of the metropolitan area
employment. The Bank of America now has more employees than
the entire movie industry. The evolution of the bank, moreover,
provides greater insight into the peculiar dynamism of the state.

Born in California to immigrant parents, Amadeo P. Giannini
was a 34-year-old produce dealer when he opened a one-room

neighborhood bank in a remodeled tavern in San Francisco's North Beach. He called it the Bank of Italy. On the first day of business in 1904, he received twenty-eight accounts totaling less than nine thousand dollars. It was not an auspicious beginning, and Giannini's timing was less than fortuitous; the date was only eighteen months prior to the earthquake and fire, and less than three years before the bank panic of 1907. But Giannini proposed shrewdly to capitalize on frontier egalitarianism. Banking in those days was a tool of the wealthy; Giannini believed a bank could serve as a money store for those of little means. He was derided by established bankers for his small personal loans to wage-earners. Even in days just after the earthquake and fire, he was dispensing loans over a plank-and-barrel counter at the waterfront, at a time when no other San Francisco bank had reopened. Soon he began to exploit the relatively new concept of branch banking. In 1915 he expanded to Los Angeles, a move which his distractors regarded as his ultimate folly; Southern Californians, then as now, were on the whole not as good credit risks as northern Californians. But Los Angeles was on the threshold of tremendous growth and Giannini's little bank grew with it. After a series of mergers, it became known as the Bank of America, but even that name seems inadequate in view of its present rank as the largest non-governmental banking institution in the world, with close to one hundred overseas branches or offices. Giannini had sensed the potential of branch banking from his knowledge of the produce business: California agriculture is highly specialized, and the failure of a Great Central Valley grape crop in one season might bring farmers of an entire county to the edge of bankruptcy, and carry with them any regional bank. Bank losses might be offset, however, by a bumper crop of potatoes in the same season in an adjacent county, if it were financed by another branch of the same banking system.

It has worked just as Giannini believed it would, and today Bank of America loans make up about one-half of all those that sustain the four-billion-dollar agricultural industry of the state. At the start of 1968, there were 939 domestic branches. From its inception the bank has been a peculiarly California institution. Giannini, sixty years old and ill, relinquished control in 1930 to Elisha Walker, a young New York banker who set out to modify policies in conformity with Eastern banking traditions. But the results were disastrous. Less than two years later Walker convened his executive committee and proposed salvaging bank assets through contraction and liquidation.

Giannini, convalescing in Germany, was outraged. He returned to California and barnstormed up and down the state soliciting proxies. At a special stockholders' meeting in 1932, he resumed leadership and recharted a vigorous course which saved the bank and made it a dominant factor in California's recovery from the Depression. Giannini died in 1949, but a succession of strong managements has continued his innovative policies. The Bank of America led the nation's banks into the electronic age with the industry's first fully automated electronic accounting system. A fleet of small aircraft flies checks and records by night from remote branches into central data processing offices. The bank has led in credit card development and in methods of international expansion.

Like the Bank of America, the Pacific Gas & Electric Company was completing a high-rise corporate headquarters building in San Francisco in 1969. PG&E is both the West's oldest and the nation's largest gas and electric utility. With roots in predecessor companies dating back to 1852, four years after the discovery of gold in California, PG&E in 1968 had eighty thousand miles of power lines serving 4.3 million customers throughout northern and central California, a service area about equal in size to New York State and Pennsylvania combined. It has joined the list of American corporations with billion dollar gross annual incomes. Its projections for 1985 suggest the future economic expansion of California: an electric load more than three times that of 1967, with nearly seventy per cent coming from plants not in existence in that year.

Shipping has been a bulwark of the California economy from the start. Ship clearances have declined in recent decades, but tonnage has increased despite the soaring role of air and land cargo shipment. The harbors of Los Angeles and Long Beach combined rank second in tonnage to the collective ports of San Francisco Bay, although Los Angeles is the individual leader. Petroleum, both inbound and outbound, accounts for almost three-quarters of the tonnage of the southern ports. Lumber and other building materials are a major import from the Pacific Northwest. Minerals and farm products lead the list of exports. The port of San Francisco, more compact than that of Los Angeles, has terminals for lumber and cotton, fresh fruits and produce. Its major exports are machinery and vehicles, cotton fibers, chemicals, metals and grains. Incoming ships bring bananas and coffee from Latin America, copra, crude petroleum, metals, wood and paper and foreign automobiles. The share of San Francisco shipping has declined sharply since World War I. State ownership of its waterfront has been a handicap. Maritime union discord allowed expansion of the harbors of Oakland and Stockton and the southern harbors, including that of San Diego. Oakland has more than twenty miles of waterfront, two-thirds of it now owned by the city government. The nearby Richmond harbor is a leading port in petroleum traffic. But shipping through California harbors is small when measured against its potential as the nation's front yard facing the rich and emerging markets of the Pacific Rim. Even now American trade with Pacific nations far exceeds that with Europe. California trade with the Pacific constitutes about three-quarters of the state's exports and a slightly higher volume of its imports. More than five billion dollars of the state's personal income and one in every eighteen jobs are related to foreign trade. California's share of U.S. world trade doubled in the 1957–67 decade to more than eight percent, with an annual volume valued at close to five billion dollars. The California foreign trade projection for 1980 is fourteen billion dollars, almost triple the present figure. Rich prospects lie ahead in the maritime Pacific, factors that may push the economic center of the nation farther toward the Pacific gateway.

The top ten California corporations as ranked in 1968 reflect the technical orientation of the state's industry: aerospace, electronics, computers, oil and gas. The perennial leader is Standard Oil Company of California, which built its first refinery on San Francisco Bay in 1902; its sales neared four billion dollars in

1967. North American Rockwell ranked next; it is a diversified firm involved in electronics, aerospace, and vehicle component manufacture. Next came Lockheed Aircraft and Litton Industries, another diversified international company manufacturing electronic systems and components, business machines, materials handling equipment and ships; its services extend as far afield as its twelve-year economic analysis contract with the government of Greece. Then came Foremost-McKesson, whose varied units and subsidiaries are involved in dairy products, chemicals, drugs and liquor. Ranking sixth and seventh were two oil firms, Union and Signal. FMC Corporation, a diversified manufacturer with headquarters in San Jose, ranked eighth. Getty Oil was ninth. Carnation Company, a producer of dairy and food products, stood tenth.

Of the top ten, only two—Standard Oil and Foremost-McKesson —are based in San Francisco (although the northern city retains many corporate headquarters). Seven are in the Los Angeles area. Their scope has overwhelmed the old Los Angeles of film studios, luxury kennels and funeral chapels. Yet neither Los Angeles nor the San Francisco Bay area comes close to ranking with major industrial cities of the Midwest and East in the proportion of its labor force engaged in manufacturing; service industries are unusually strong; tourism is a major economic factor, and real estate development and building construction continue to provide tremendous impetus to the economy as in-migration continues.

The state population growth was averaging half a million persons per year in the late 1960's, and the seeming inevitability of rising land costs was drawing investment capital from throughout the nation. Firms such as Los Angeles' Property Research Corporation were packaging land speculations for public participation with expectations of appreciation of fifty percent or more during each three-to-five year period. By 1968 there were few major U.S. manufacturers that had not established branches or divisions in California. The projection of a population that would double from twenty million to forty million by the year 2000 seemed a compelling lure to almost every type of growth company.

Home construction in California has been characterized by spurts of over-building and periods of digestion; a building recession during 1963–66 was followed by a period of gradual recovery, financed in large part by the California savings and loan industry, whose thirty billion dollars of assets in 1968 made up almost one-fifth of the total assets of the national savings and loan industry. The trend throughout California was away from the single-family dwelling and into apartment house construction, suggesting at least a slowing of the urban sprawl that has devoured so much of the California landscape. Prodigious sums were going into educational construction. At the University of California at San Diego, one of nine campuses in the state university system, construction was proceeding in 1968 at a cost rate of $218.75 a minute. Among the many fortunes made in California real estate since World War II is that of S. Mark Taper, an English builder who came to California to retire on the eve of the war but later built more than thirty-five thousand houses. As he donated $1.5 million for construction of a theater in the Los Angeles Music Center complex, he communicated an understandable if overblown sense of enthusiasm: "This West Coast is the greatest center of civilization in modern times," he said, "not only as far as the United States is concerned, but for the world."

Countless other new fortunes were drawn for the ongoing California boom. When Howard Ahmanson died in 1968, he was the sole ruler of a $3 billion Southern California combine in banking, insurance and savings and loan that had earned a personal fortune of at least three hundred million dollars. Ahmanson had been one of those who moved to California as a youth during the Depression; he got his start selling fire insurance. Another fortune was amassed by Norton Simon, who had been an unspectacular high school classmate of a former California governor, Edmund G. Brown, in San Francisco, but who went on to become chairman of Hunt Foods and Industries and a factor in at least half a dozen other major corporations—as well as a University of California regent and one of the world's most renowned art collectors. Terrell Drinkwater, a former tire salesman, sold the spare tires off his airliners to meet his payroll when he became president of Western Air Lines in 1947, but built a fortune with the spectacular growth of air traffic in the West over the next two decades.

Entertainers have parlayed their earnings through California investments into huge fortunes. There is the Gene Autry empire of hotels, radio and television stations, real estate, film studios, athletic teams and music businesses. Art Linkletter is the epitome of the California legend: a man who has made it big by his wits alone. In 1967 he figured as president, chairman or board member in more than twenty-five corporations, ranging from frozen pizza to real estate. ("Get in on the ground floor in a medium-small company with a large stock option," he urged. "That's how you make money. You don't learn by investing five thousand dollars and having some other guy do all the work.") California has seemed to be a paradise for less ambitious entrepreneurs like George Millay, a former restaurateur who launched San Diego's Sea World marine amusement park; and Jack Hanson, who built his fortune in the Los Angeles sportswear industry with his Jax line of snug-fitting women's slacks, launching a vogue of the 1960's. Bruce Brown, a youthful surfer, gambled fifty thousand dollars on a film called *The Endless Summer,* which he produced, directed, photographed and spliced without professional help; it went on to make Brown a profit of about three million dollars and launch him as the beach bums' tycoon. There have been big losers, too, like the flamboyant savings and loan entrepreneur Bart Lytton, who made and lost a fifteen-million-dollar fortune in the upswing and downswing of Los Angeles real estate during the 1960's. Typical of a growing number of newly-arrived California businessmen is Ed Taylor, who stepped away from a hundred-thousand-dollar vice presidency of Motorola Inc. in Chicago to take over a Chevrolet dealership in San Diego and relax—but found his business opportunities expanding so rapidly that he was quickly drawing a larger income than before, while spending much of his time at a seaside home in La Jolla and a desert house beside a golf course at nearby Borrego Springs. There are countless more new anonymous fortunes. At Laguna Beach in 1967, twenty-one men gave a dinner for their stockbroker; over a brief number of years, they indicated in their toasts, his counsel had made millionaires of each of them.

The climatic and scenic advantages of California draw new residents and fresh capital, and also an ever-growing surge of visitors, making tourism a major economic factor. Tourist officials estimate that one in five California jobs is involved in tourist-related services. Out-of-state visitors in 1966 totaled more than fourteen million; an annual total of thirty-seven million is expected by 1975.

The growth in California personal income has naturally created a parallel climb in spending among residents. While national department store sales increased fifty-eight percent in the ten-year period through 1965, those in Southern California increased eighty-nine percent. The newness of California and the existence of a certain glamour are quickly confirmed in its retail stores. They are spacious and colorful, well-lighted and of contemporary design. Sales people are generally gracious. When the Pasadena branch of Bullocks' department store opened, the magazine *Architectural Forum* reported it had the appearance of a "rather expensive club." Architects design stores to blend with community styles and traditions. Merchants display the work of local artists and stage community parties. Their private dining rooms are the site of service club and community meetings. Shopping centers provide stores and services of infinite variety in tree-shaded parks that often may include the finest restaurants and night clubs in the community. The results of such merchandising are impressive, with retail sales in the five-county area of metropolitan Los Angeles exceeding those in forty-seven of the fifty states.

Like others across the nation, California retailers are focusing on the youth market. Nowhere will that market soar in such proportions as here. Between 1967 and 1980, the number of Californians under the age of 25 is expected to increase about ninety percent, compared to national projections of fifty-nine percent. The vitality of Southern California as a fashion-setter for American youth was confirmed in a 1966 survey of businessmen across the United States. Metropolitan Los Angeles was regarded as

primary trend-setter for the under-25 generation by thirty-six percent of those polled, and was followed distantly by New York,
Chicago, San Francisco-Oakland and Houston. Trends originate
in the Los Angeles sportswear industry, among its surfers and
divers, in garages where youths customize their cars, and in re-
cording and film studios. The year-round outdoor life may not
be practical in much of the rest of America, but it is widely
simulated.

The most optimistic predictions for the California economy
have been consistently exceeded. But despite the avalanche of
bullish projections, pitfalls line the course of the California economy. Expansion and prosperity are not synonymous; for each
new California family, the cost of providing streets, schools,
water and other services is estimated at about fifteen thousand
dollars. There are unbalances. In 1968 an estimated ten thousand factories in Southern California alone served the aerospace
industry in some way. California led the nation by far in military
contracts, and had many more federal workers than any other
state, a number about equal to that of the metropolitan area that
encompasses the District of Columbia. Despite a steady decline
in recent years, California received about eighteen percent of
prime military contracts in the fiscal year 1967—close to seven
billion dollars—almost twice as great a sum as that awarded to
the second-ranking state, Texas. The state has a unique heritage
of natural endowments, and it has had prudential direction. It
has achieved leadership in urban and industrial development.
But it remains highly sensitive to national policies.

A 1968 study by the University of Maryland ranked the Los
Angeles-Long Beach metropolitan area as second only to that of
Detroit in potential problems of unemployment by 1975. The
area would have to lose more than half a million people by that
year, the survey showed, to maintain its unemployment rate at
four percent or less. At the same time, three other California
metropolitan areas—San Jose, Anaheim-Santa Ana in Orange
County, and San Bernardino—ranked among the top four metropolitan areas in job availability projections for 1975. Such statistics indicate the accentuation of the suburban development

pattern already under way, but they also point up the potential crisis of ongoing boom.

"The great industrial development that lies ahead, while it will make a few Californians richer, also threatens to blight the esthetic living values for the great majority of California residents," a Stanford University economist testified before a legislative committee in 1966. "The idea that we must stimulate new growth is a holdover from the days when California was, in fact, underdeveloped. Today, as the nation's largest state, with a decade of tremendous industrial growth ahead, the problem is to direct that growth to optimize the welfare of the state's people."

Thus the California emphasis moves from quantity to quality. There is already the affinity for experimentation which can be a continually regenerating factor in the economy. The state has led the way into space-age industry and it is not so vulnerable to obsolescence as are those regions of more established industry. Its prosperity and high productivity, the novelty of its setting and its benign climate seem to guarantee growth; the challenge to its economic and political leaders will be to channel that growth qualitatively. Otherwise Californians may destroy the virtues of the innovative society that they have so ebulliently created.

. 15 .

THE COAST

You must remember, my dear, that we are three
thousand miles from the ocean.

—AN ELDERLY VISITOR FROM BOSTON AS SHE AND HER HUSBAND
DROVE FOR THE FIRST TIME INTO LOS ANGELES.

It was one of those mornings of sapphire and gold when the
California coast seemed dressed for a party. The sun gleamed
out from behind the snowy peaks of the coastal range and across
the populous plains. Whitecaps sparkled in its glow. It was
still too early for the sun to brighten the ocean side of the sheer
sea cliffs, and they cast weaving shadows over sand and rock.

But it was not too early for the surfers, and as we skimmed
northward in a light plane just a few hundred feet above South-

273

ern California, they made artful patterns like little clumps of tadpoles bobbing on the waves, their formations changing as abruptly as iron filings trapped in magnetic fields.

My excuse for being off to look again at California—any flimsy pretense will always do—was to show California to a New York editor. He was Manhattan-born and Ivy League-bred. He was coming to see California only because he and I agreed that he should; he was skeptical of some of the things I had been writing. Until now, his California had lain between Los Angeles Airport and the Beverly Wilshire Hotel, and between San Francisco Airport and the Clift Hotel. So I was the zealous missionary and he was the atheist.

"Don't go to any trouble," he had said. "I'll just rent a car and drive up the coast for a couple of days."

Someday I may learn to let Eastern visitors handle their own affairs in California, but until now I have been ready to intrude. I keep telling myself the state is grown up and we can stop explaining ourselves. But when we do, California too often swallows up visitors and they fly away home in a daze.

"Nonsense," I had told him. "You won't last two days on California highways." No one can sample all the Californias in two days by land, not even if he knows where to go. So we had chartered a plane and pilot.

There are over twelve hundred miles of California coastline. For millions of years the currents that begin at New Zealand and off Japan have slapped away at this incredible flank, nibbling jagged inlets, piling up thick sandy beaches in summer and eroding them in winter, chewing away at soft sandstone cliffs so that every year a little more of California disappears.

Settlement is concentrated within a few miles of this coastline. But the contrasts along the oceanfront belt are awesome, in climate and geography as well as in density of population. The gilded south, thick with the paraphernalia of leisure and the guts of industry, gives way to the treacherous seas and barren, rolling hills of central California. Then the Santa Lucia Mountains drop off into the Pacific with the sheer thousand-foot cliffs of Big Sur. The gnarled cypresses and sea-carved stone relics of the Paleozoic age mark the Monterey Peninsula, and then there are flat rich valleys that ease gently down to the sea. North of the Golden Gate the coast is a wilderness world set apart with a unique ecology; even the insect life is different from that a hundred miles to the south. Soon the redwood forests march down to the raging sea, and the tentative little settlements are heavy with the smoke of sawmills and the odor of fish. This northern coast, making up more than one-third the length of California, is known to few. It is not a part of the frenetic California, but a quiet land of forest temples and surf so wild and cold even in summer that one does not come here to frolic; it is the great California reserve where conservationists still can win their battles with the spoilers, a balm to the soul of a state where the urgent priorities of destiny seem elsewhere irrevocable.

To see what we could of all this, we flew from San Diego in the early morning over the almost unbroken settlement of the Southern California coast. Coastal towns shimmered and winked up at us. Housing tracts swept crazily up over the foothills to the horizon. The eight-lane coastal freeway unwound like ribbon candy spewed by some giant sugar machine. In the ocean at our left, almost devoid of traffic, offshore islands etched low silhouettes against the sky. Ahead, the patches of open land began to disappear. The boats of Newport Harbor bobbed like a pygmy armada; as we passed over the Irvine Ranch, the Matterhorn of Disneyland came into sight, dwarfed by black aprons of parking areas. We rounded the corner of the Los Angeles coastline, the gray basin brightened only by a horde of backyard swimming pools. At Santa Monica we skirted the cliffs of Pacific Palisades, seeing the scars of slides which each year tumble more houses toward the sea.

The Santa Monica Mountains that rise up from the sea at Los Angeles emerge again offshore as the northern Channel Islands. From Malibu we flew west over the ocean toward these islands, brown warts on the blue sea. A land area totaling more than 132,000 acres, they are hardly changed since the landing there of the explorer Juan Rodríguez Cabrillo in 1543. The National Park Service has called these Channel Islands "the most important underdeveloped portion [with] the greatest recreational potentialities and scientific values on the Pacific Coast." Elephant seals doze by the hundreds on the stony beaches, and sea birds nest by the thousands. First in our line of sight was long, narrow Anacapa, now a national monument—but clearly one that does not draw many visitors. Its lighthouse stood atop sheer cliffs, and a helicopter pad at the top of the island showed more evidence of use than the finger pier in the crashing surf below. Close by was larger Santa Cruz Island, oyster-shaped, sheltering a ranch retreat in a hidden valley. Even here, on an island so unsettled and remote that it seemed a century ago in time, there was the sparkle of a swimming pool at the Santa Cruz ranch. It was a reminder that back over our shoulders lived the twelve million people of the Southern California megalopolis.

Across the Santa Cruz Channel was Santa Rosa Island, one great privately owned ranch, where deer and wild goats outnumber cattle and sheep. Just beyond was little San Miguel, the island which is thought to hold the grave of Cabrillo, the first European to step ashore in California.

From the Channel Islands we flew north across the Santa Barbara Channel to skim beside much higher-priced real estate along the coast at the foot of the beautiful Santa Ynez Mountains. Santa Barbara is a rich and gracious little city whose courthouse resembles the palace of some Spanish prelate and whose railroad station was built to look like a bullring. This is the architectural center of the romanticized, pseudo-Spanish tradition of California; its Old Spanish Days each August is a fiesta of parades, music, horsemanship and dancing. The restored Santa Barbara mission, one of four still occupied by the Franciscan order which founded the California mission chain, has come to be a tourist's symbol of California much as the Eiffel Tower is of Paris. Lacking a seaport and averse to industry, the wealthy settlers of Santa Barbara have surrounded the city with estates, many of them lemon plantations lined with the stately tall eucalyptus trees that serve as windbreakers against the prevailing ocean breezes. Offshore floats the kelp, making the sea rust-colored, rising and falling with the swells. Southern California ends not far north of Santa Barbara, where the coastal highway tunnels under wind-racked Gaviota Pass. By road, one emerges in a different land of rolling hills dotted with groves of oak; the desert is at last behind.

As we flew low above the coast, the Santa Barbara control tower was calling: "You'll be approaching Vandenberg Air Force Base shortly. Check in with Frontier Control after you turn the corner at Point Conception." Then the coastal corner was below us, and we turned at a right angle, due north into central California. Our New York guest had been wondrously rapt. Finally he broke his silence. "When you California people talk about turning a corner," he said, "you're talking about a lot of real estate."

The coastal rangelands of central California are both cattle and missile. Eight of the restored Franciscan missions form a chain along the coast in the company of the major West coast missile bases of both the Navy and the Air Force: at Point Mugu, Point Arguello and Vandenberg Air Force Base. Yet the central coast is a kind of no-man's land, not yet changed strikingly by the California boom. Between Santa Barbara and San Simeon, the only sizable coastal towns are Pismo Beach and Morro Bay, where an immense offshore rock—known to local residents as "the Gibraltar of the Pacific"—rises 576 feet above a shallow lagoon that is enclosed by sand dunes.

At Morro Bay, the more adventurous highway travelers take to the rising coastal cliffs along which State Highway One makes its tortuous way north to Big Sur and the Monterey Peninsula. From the air, the spires of William Randolph Hearst's San Simeon castle can be seen from many miles away. Perched in isolated and somewhat moldy grandeur atop a knoll of the Santa Lucia Mountains, the castle is an irresistible lure to those who travel by private plane. We banked and circled above it. Painted on the roof of a service building in the rear was a warning to aircraft to maintain fifteen hundred feet altitude. Nearby was a landing strip Hearst had bulldozed out of open range, and where he had installed the first private-field instrument landing system in the world; he and his visitors were not inclined to allow coastal fogs to interfere with their going and coming. The Hearst estate once stretched for fifty miles along this coast and about ten miles inland. Much of it had been bought by his father, Senator George Hearst, for sixty or seventy cents an acre. Today San Simeon is a state park, and the ranch is idle; the state conducts tours through La Cuesta Encantada, as Hearst called his castle, and maintains the immediate gardens.

Hearst spent more than thirty million dollars just in furnishing this strange castle that he began building in 1922. By the time he left it, moving to Beverly Hills four years before his death in 1951, it had grown to more than one hundred rooms. It had its private stables and zoo, a garage with twenty-five limousines, and a staff of up to sixty persons. More than half a million visitors a year trudge now through La Cuesta Encantada, pausing longest beside the 104-foot Neptune Pool, which Hearst surrounded by Etruscan-style colonnades, and backed by a Greco-Roman temple. Inside is the eighty-three foot long assembly hall with its sixteenth century Italian carved walnut ceiling and a French stone mantelpiece of similar vintage for which Hearst outbid John D. Rockefeller.

Away from the area seen by most tourists, the castle is filled with reminders of the anomalies of its creator. In the massive kitchen can still be found some of the red, white and blue monogrammed paper napkins that were used instead of linen in the cavernous refectory with its choir stall walls. Cheap chintz seat covers are seen on many of the couches and chairs, their patterns clashing grotesquely with tapestries and Persian rugs.

In the hallway between Hearst's upstairs apartment and his personal elevator stand the newspaper racks—one for each newspaper then in the Hearst chain—into which copies of the papers were dropped each day for the publisher's inspection. The racks have been unchanged since his death in 1951, but the Hearst newspaper empire has not been so fortunate; scanning the mastheads on the various racks brings on a mood of requiem. An upstairs bedroom suite presents a minor problem for State of California guides. The south room was Hearst's; the north room, with pink alabaster lamps, belonged to Marion Davies, the former chorus girl who played hostess at San Simeon. "So much has been said about her and so much is on the record," a state historical guide has said, "that it would be ridiculous to try to ignore her existence." So like the castles of Europe, La Cuesta Encantada unfolds for tourists replete with evidence of the vagaries of its creator.

We flew from San Simeon north above the coastal highway that coils upward until it is perched on cliffs eight hundred feet above the surf and the giant broken rocks. Much convict labor went into the eighteen-year project of building this highway, first opened in 1937. Its ledge along the sinewy shoulder of the Santa Lucias bridges chasms where streams gush in season down through redwoods and eucalyptus to their sudden final fall. The weather—just as noticeably as the terrain—changes at Big Sur. It was a sunny day as we flew beside its cliffs; but fogs hung moodily over the Santa Lucias, and cloud shadows swung smoothly up and over their soft green domes. About seven hundred bohemians live hidden on the green mountainsides or sea cliffs in everything from rough board cottages to the towering A-frame "Wild Bird," the home of Margaret and Nathaniel Owings, who is the founding partner of the architecture firm of Skidmore, Owings & Merrill. The Owingses have led in efforts to preserve, by ordinance, the unspoiled wildness of the Big Sur, which has always attracted artists and escapists. The poet Robinson Jeffers worked nearby in a study of gray granite boulders at his home, Tor House. The author Henry Miller lived at Big Sur for nineteen years, describing the area once as "a region where one is always conscious of weather, of space, of grandeur and of eloquent silence." Now that Jeffers and Miller are gone, Big Sur finds its way into the public consciousness most often as the site of the Esalen Institute, where behavioral scientists and psychologists probe the human potential with year-round programs: lectures, group exercises and baths designed to expand sensual awareness.

Here the California coast becomes perpetually windblown and chilly. Cypress and pine dig into rocky crevices and defy the shear of wind; bracken and purple lupine and the flaccid sprawling ice plant hug the ground. In the more sheltered valleys are laurels and live oaks. The Big Sur eases off into a less dramatic series of coastal cliffs but the surf grows even more fierce, as opposing tides meet and swirl. Near the rocky promonotory of Point Lobos State Park we saw from overhead the southernmost outpost of the Monterey cypress. Just ahead was Carmel Bay and the rolling wooded peninsula of Monterey.

Carmel, founded in 1904, began to take root when Mary Austin and a group of other writers and artists built cabins among the trees. Today it retains a studied quaintness as though it had been built in a Disney forest. Its founders fought to keep out paved streets and utilities; these have come now, but still Carmel has no house numbers, and it is illegal to cut down a tree without a police permit. Neon signs and jukeboxes are off-limits. So are billboards and street lights, and sidewalks are prohibited except along the major business streets. One wanders among art galleries, thatched roofs and protecting pines. Carmel has the air of an English village, but its original settlement was around the Mission of San Carlos, founded in 1770 by Junípero Serra. The mission, handsomely restored, is the resting place for Serra's remains.

On the Monterey Peninsula the privately-owned Seventeen-Mile Drive winds through wooded hills, along the golf courses of Cypress Grove and Pebble Beach, and among some of the more fashionable estates of California. This is the southern anchor of San Francisco society, the domain of the developer Samuel F. B. Morse. Nearby is the town of Monterey, where the flags of four eras fly: Spanish, Mexican, the California Bear flag of the interim pre-statehood period, and the United States flag. As California's first capital, Monterey has preserved more than forty adobe structures built before 1850—qualifying them as antiquities in this new state.

Monterey Bay, twenty-two miles across, washes up against Steinbeck country. But the fishing fleets and sardine canneries of Monterey are gone, and so are the old saloons and gambling halls, bagnios and tattoo parlors that made up *Cannery Row*. Purse seiners brave the heavy seas; from here northward the California coastal waters are treacherous. Along the inward sweep of Monterey Bay, coastal fields, often shrouded by fog, provide the center of the artichoke industry. Past Santa Cruz, a town that once was a kind of Atlantic City of California, lies the quiet coastal side of the San Francisco peninsula. Old farm houses stand weathered along beaches and gentle mountainsides. Less than ten percent of the land has been developed, but promoters are moving their monotonous tracts southward across Skyline Ridge and the Pacifica slope, and already the conservationists are raising a cry to preserve some of this open space.

We flew our Eastern visitor on past Half Moon Bay until San Francisco came into view, and then the arches of the Golden Gate. We banked in over the bridge and flew around the haunting skyline of downtown San Francisco. Ahead of us a storm front was moving in over the lonely northern coast. It was not a difficult decision to land for the night at San Francisco.

In 1579 the doughty English explorer, Sir Francis Drake, anchored his *Golden Hinde* north of San Francisco at a bay later named for him. He was pausing to repair his ship and to await trade winds for a historic Pacific crossing. He wrote in his journal of the "most vile, thicke and stinking fogges." The Portuguese navigator Juan Rodríguez Cabrillo had been the first white man to land on California shores in 1542; but powerful northwesterly winds beat back his two small ships and held them south of Point Conception until after his death in January of 1543. His crews continued northward, finally reaching the southern coast of Oregon before turning back south, half-starved and racked with scurvy. They had sought an inland passage and rich treasure and found neither. But they had been the first explorers of the northern California coast.

Drake's visit was incidental. On a three-year voyage to harass Spanish ships and to open up English trade, Drake remained ashore for five weeks. His ship was small, and already carried thirty tons of booty, mostly Spanish silver. The *Golden Hinde* was bulging at her seams, and Drake hauled her out of the water for repair. While there, he routinely claimed the countryside for England, erecting a brass plate with a chiseled inscription. A plate matching the one described in his journal was found in 1937 and placed in the Bancroft Library of the University of California at Berkeley. Scholars have argued bitterly over its authenticity, but the weight of evidence supports those who hold that the plaque is the one erected by Drake.

The English made no effort at colonization, and the next ex-

plorer to sail the California coast—the Portuguese Sebastián Rod-
riguez Cermeño—sailed past the Golden Gate without leaving any
evidence that he had noticed it. The Spaniards' interest in the
California coast was to establish a satisfactory port of call to ease
the rigors of the long Pacific voyages of the galleons from Manila
to Acapulco as they followed the trade winds homeward from
the Orient to the northern California coast and then ran downwind along the coast. Sebastián Vizcaíno charted the bay of
Monterey in 1602, but the galleons never paused there as the
Spaniards regarded the California coast as treacherous and barren. The southward-bound galleons were pushed along so swiftly
by the wind that they simply finished the run home without
halting; these same winds made the beat northward from Mexico
so painstakingly slow that such voyages seemed useless. Monterey
remained unsettled until 1770, when the supposed threat of Russian landings brought Portolá and Serra northward.

In 1812 the Russian American Fur Company erected a fortified village, Fort Ross, north of San Francisco near Bodega Bay.
The Russians proposed to use Fort Ross as a base for sea otter
hunting, for trade with the Spanish Californians, and to grow
food for their Alaskan operations. The Spaniards lacked the force
to repel the Russian settlement; their San Francisco garrison
was so ill-supplied that its men once borrowed powder from a
visiting Russian ship in order to fire a salute. Yet Fort Ross
never fulfilled Russian hopes. Diplomatic pressures built up
against the Russian outpost. In 1841 the Russians withdrew,
selling the fort, its arsenal and furnishings and even a 20-ton
schooner to John A. Sutter, the Swiss settler who gave his name
to Sutter's Mill, where gold was discovered seven years later.
Fort Ross has been partially restored in recent years; otherwise
the intrusion of the Russians on American soil leaves little mark
except for the name of the Russian River, which swings through a
broad valley to the sea eleven miles south of the fort.

The sea otter and fur seal began to diminish in California
waters long before the Russians departed. Maritime commerce
turned to tallow and cowhides, transported to Boston on sailing
ships that brought manufactured goods to California in its Mexican colonial period. That is the era depicted by Richard Henry

Dana in *Two Years Before the Mast*, a chronicle that gives a somber picture of the California coast. Dana described the coastal plateau of Southern California now known as Dana Point as "the only romantic spot in California." Close by the Mission San Juan Capistrano, Dana Point offered a small cove where Dana and his companions heaved hides over the cliff to the beach 250 feet below. But his affection for the bleak ocean precipice that bears his name has baffled California readers through the years. The greater beauties of the coast lie to the north, at Big Sur and along the rugged and often wooded north coast.

"There is little mystery," wrote the geographer Richard Joel Russell, "as to why the Russians worked southward along the coast only as far as Fort Ross, less than seventy miles from San Francisco, or as to why the Spanish missions stopped just north of the bay. Each group had come to the end of territory to which it was accustomed and where it knew how to make a living."

When the Spaniards withdrew from the southern coast, and later Mexicans gave way to the Yankee newcomers, a unique society began to form in a climate and environment more Mediterranean than typically American. But north of the Golden Gate, Indians dominated much of the land until the Gold Rush. After the Russians, the influences were those of the British and later the New Englander. With its rolling fogs, its elevated terraces and coves and rocky shores, the north coast of California resembles rugged parts of the New England coast. The fern and sheep and windswept promontories of the area around Cape Mendocino suggest the highland shores of Scotland. In both geographic and cultural senses, the scantily populated California that lies above San Francisco is a different land. The Golden Gate, that most stunning of all breaks in the western coast, sequesters the pastoral north from the California of contemporary legend.

It is typical of the north coast that its weather did not lift in time for my Eastern friend to see that part of California from the air during his brief tour. The north coast has more rain, fog and wind than other areas of the state. Rainfall decreases in California as one moves southward and eastward. At Crescent City, on the coast near the Oregon border, almost 370 miles north of San Francisco, more than seventy inches of rain falls each year. The village of Honeydew, in the stately redwoods of Humboldt County, has received 174 inches in a single year. Fog is so intense that the military chose nearby Arcata for fog dispersal experiments in World War II. Point Reyes, on Drake's Bay close to San Francisco, has a Weather Bureau station that is both the foggiest and windiest along the Pacific Coast. One visits the north coast at ground level, and—along much of its distance—stares upward through dark forests toward a redwood canopy.

For two hundred miles north of San Francisco, Highway One, a two-lane road, braves the headlands of the coast up through the counties of Marin, Sonoma and Mendocino. It crosses countless streams and little rivers jammed with splintered logs. It climbs after each crossing to a high meadow within sight of the sea. Weathered rail fences run beside the road, and sometimes scattered redwoods or Douglas firs reach down near the sea; but the groves of redwoods do not appear until one nears the northwest corner of California. There are few billboards, and the towns are remnants of a quieter age than any that the other California has known for many years. Lumber mills blend the smells of burning chips and sawdust with the scents of the sea. An occasional fishing harbor finds its place in a sheltered cove. There are Gothic reminders of days when house builders were more inclined to spend their time shaping wood into curlicued pillars and arches. It is a land filled with ghosts: lumber towns where thousands once lived, and now only a few; abandoned lumber mills, and lumber schooners wrecked on the reefs. Among the ferns in spring the calla lily and the iris grow wild. The largest town for almost four hundred miles is Eureka, with about thirty thousand people, and one counts on his fingers all the towns with more than a thousand residents. Lumbering has moved inland, the weather and the terrain make farming marginal, and fishing is of only modest importance; more and more this north coast comes to survive on tourism, the whimsy of those who seek out an area that is apart in time and place.

Drake's Bay, with its long arc of flat sandy beach, is little changed from 1579 when Sir Francis Drake careened his *Golden Hinde* to brace it for its load of silver booty. On the bay's northern fringe, in 1962, Congress approved establishment of Point Reyes National Seashore, a relatively pristine area of beach, dune and forest, fifty-three thousand acres in size, to be maintained in its splendid isolation. The northernmost confines of the Point Reyes seashore are set apart from the mainland by Tomales Bay, through which the notorious San Andreas faultline disappears into the Pacific. Thus the national seashore moves northward at the rate of two inches a year while the mainland is stationary. Even so small a shift has caused such variations of plant and animal life that certain species cannot endure the change from Point Reyes to the mainland, a distance of only two or three miles.

Northward, Highway One leaves Tomales and Bodega bays and snakes along cliffs above roaring white water and tumbled granite. Here the Pacific reaches full frenzy, and the lazy water life of Southern California seems suddenly foreign. At Duncan's Point, behind a barbed-wire fence, a sign warns that twenty-one persons have been swept off the rocks to their deaths, each of them underestimating the soaring power of the waves below. Past the old Russian Fort Ross are recent resort developments, Timber Cove and Sea Ranch, built beside the rare crescents of sandy beach. This part of the north coast has the gloom and cragginess of Wales. The village of Mendocino, with a two-block-long downtown and a population of about one thousand, has been revived from the brink of extinction by a colony of artists; but their coming has brought division among old residents, who are against anything that might fulfill modern standards of progress.

At the town of Fort Bragg, dominated by the huge Union Lumber Company, is the western terminus of the little California Western Railroad, which makes the eighty-mile round trip inland through forests of fir and redwood to Willits by day with tourists and, in season, does the run again at night lugging logs. Known as the "Skunk," the train crosses thirty-two trestles, passes through two tunnels, and makes enough curves to bring it acclaim as the most winding railroad in America.

The Redwood Highway begins north of Fort Bragg. Narrow and slow in summer with its clog of logging trucks and tourists, the Redwood Highway skirts Cape Mendocino, the massive protrusion that is the apogee of the California coast, the westernmost point of the state. There are almost no roads in the Mendocino area, and no people. Until after World War II, this area was called the Unknown Coast. It presented the longest roadless section of coastline in the contiguous United States, a distance of about forty miles, most of it blanketed by redwood forest. In 1965 this sanctum of privacy attracted resort developers who proclaimed their intent to open the "lost coast" to public use at six thousand dollars a lot. Now an airstrip is the marvel of Shelter Cove.

Between the often flooded plains of the Van Duzen and the Elk and Eel and Mad Rivers lies the capital of the California redwood country, the old town of Eureka. It shares with San Francisco and San Diego a distinction that few Californians know: its Humboldt Bay is a fine natural harbor, fourteen miles long and up to four miles wide, sheltered by two sandbars. Yet its hinterland is so thinly settled that the harbor of Eureka has little ocean commerce; from it go lumber, fish and dairy products, and to Eureka come petroleum and machinery. But Eureka has the largest redwood mills to be found in the world, and in 1968 it was the locale of a major conservation victory. Northward from Eureka past Crescent City to the coastal corner of California grow the finest stands of redwoods that remain on earth. While lumber crews sawed away, the fight to consolidate a group of state redwood parks into a national redwood park was won. Lumbermen had opposed conservationists, who sought to spare all the redwoods possible. Land-holding federal agencies opposed each other when land swaps were discussed.

Except perhaps for Grand Canyon, no natural legacy in America has aroused such basic and widespread involvement as the redwood forests of this north coast. Conservationists have done battle in behalf of both the canyon and the redwoods, but the alarm over extinction of the virgin redwood has surpassed that over any threat to Grand Canyon. Logging began among the redwoods in 1820, when redwoods grew in a twenty-mile-wide belt that extended more than four hundred miles, from California's Big Sur country up into Oregon. The almost denuded hillsides of the southern part of this belt are presumed to be a foretaste of what might have occurred in the area of the tallest trees between Eureka and Crescent City. But conservationists beginning with John Muir have been effective enough that by 1968 there were fifty thousand acres of redwoods preserved within the California state park system. Of nearly two million acres originally covered by redwoods, there are today less than three hundred thousand acres of virgin trees.

The California coastal redwood, less commonly known as Sequoia sempervirens, is one of the tallest trees in the world. It often grows higher than a twenty-story building, and sometimes more than thirty stories high. It is relatively slender, its trunks usually from fifteen to twenty feet in diameter. The redwood is sometimes confused with the "big trees"—the Sequoia gigantea, commonly called sequoias. These bulkier trees do not form continuous forest belts like the redwoods, but grow in about thirty-five scattered groves at higher altitudes on the western slope of the Sierra Nevada. Sequoias are not significantly taller than redwoods, but their cones may be triple the size. The sequoias are among the oldest living things in the world; some were twelve hundred years old when Christ was born. But sequoias already are protected, notably in Sequoia National Park, oldest of California's four national parks, which was established in 1890 even before Yosemite, in order to preserve thirty-two groves of giant sequoias. The redwood forests of California's north coast, though they have been a subject of conservation concern equally as long, did not come under any federal protection until 1968.

The redwood is a tree of exquisite beauty. Its gently tapering trunk is usually bare of branches for a hundred feet or so above the ground. Its bark is spongy and fire-resistant, a purplish red, heavily fluted. Its foliage is feathery and delicate. One of the most exalted feelings in the world is to be deep within a virgin redwood forest as the light filters through in shafts from the furry canopy high above.

But the redwood is commercially valuable, bringing several times the price of other common woods. From one big trunk may come a thousand dollars worth of lumber. The fifty thousand acres of state redwood parks are scattered from Humboldt, about 250 miles north of San Francisco, over a 150-mile area northward to the Oregon border. The rest of the redwoods are privately owned and logging has been proceeding at the rate of ten thousand acres each year—despite some moratoriums agreed to by lumbermen during negotiations over establishment of the national redwoods park. The world's tallest tree is a 367-foot redwood in a remote part of Redwood Creek near Eureka, on privately-owned land that was expected, in early 1969, to become part of the national park.

Foreseeing eventual destruction of virgin forests, conservationists began agitation soon after the turn of the century. In 1918 the Save-the-Redwoods League was formed in San Francisco. By 1968 the league had raised more than twelve million dollars, which had been matched with state funds to buy many of the groves that had become parkland. Many of the redwoods are on inaccessible, steep mountainsides, and are mixed in among firs, hemlock and spruce. Such stands of redwood are not particularly impressive, even to the conservationist. Logging them produces as much fir as redwood. No opposition has been raised to such logging. Replanting of cut redwood areas already is enforced by state law and in the best interests of lumber companies, and so there is no fear that the redwood will become extinct.

The issue that Congress resolved in 1968 was how much virgin redwood forest should be preserved as parkland. Some held that the acreage within the four state parks should be enough to satisfy the need, even in the midst of the environmental revolution during which Americans have recently displayed increasing interest in natural conservation. But the Save-the-Redwoods League had suggested a national park that would include privately owned forests near Jedediah Smith Park, northernmost of the state parks. The Sierra Club, more militant, had held out for a ninety-thousand acre park taking in the Redwood Creek basin, which includes some of the tallest trees—among them the 367-foot monarch that ranks as tallest in the world.

The compromise park plan adopted in 1968 included some areas proposed by both groups, and created a fifty-eight thousand acre national park extending for close to forty miles along the Redwood Highway in the Crescent City area. Congress set up machinery for purchase or trading of 28,100 acres of redwoods held largely by lumber companies. Three state parks were to be incorporated in the national park. The two major units of the park were to be connected by a corridor including a thirty-three mile stretch of California ocean beach. Private land acquisition was divided among four companies and two counties, and some federal forest lands were made available as compensation for parkland.

Along the north coast, where milling is the major source of income, private citizens had grown as intense as lumbermen in protesting any change that would disrupt their economy. The solution of the redwoods issue was a classic exercise in democracy. If the 1968 rate of logging had continued, the last of the unprotected virgin redwoods would have fallen before 1986.

Yet the long debates in distant committee halls and on the floors of Congress seemed almost irrelevant within the redwood groves themselves—forest churches, as John Muir called them. Awesome and overpowering, the redwoods reach for the sky and blot out the light. Yet few visitors drive as much as a mile from the freeway to see the largest specimens like those along the nine-mile course of the Avenue of the Giants in Humboldt Redwoods State Park. For some people, a day among these giants is a demoralizing experience. Even Californians, who are accustomed to the mammoth scale, do not linger long on this north coast.

. 16 .

THE INCORRIGIBLE ELECTORATE

In California politics, I've learned never to be surprised at anything.

—JESSE UNRUH

Soon after the national census of 1970, California will take its place as the most politically powerful of the United States. The state surpassed New York as most populous in 1964. But not until Congressional reapportionment, which occurs after each decennial census, will California's political strength reflect its emerging dominance. The number of California congressmen will probably rise from 38 to about 44 as the New York quota drops from 41 to 40. The California electoral vote will jump from 40 to about 46, giving its people additional heft in the selection and election of presidential candidates.

Yet California, with its bewildering party disunity and its haphazard pattern of electioneering, its lunatic fringes and the apparent unpredictability of its voters, continues to be the despair of political scientists and practicing politicians. It has become a kind of national pop art to deplore the politics of California. When the film actor Ronald Reagan was elected governor in 1966 without having spent a day in public office, such criticism reached a crescendo.

"California voters," wrote the novelist Herbert Gold, "who can be relied upon not to do the sensible thing, can also not be relied upon to do the foolish thing. They are simply unreliable." Actually California voters are somewhat predictable, even though they behave in ways which appear to outsiders as irresponsible. They are indeed indifferent to traditional laws of politics. They cross party lines with consummate poise. They are prone to experiment with extreme swings to left or right, and to unite only against some familiar danger or behind some bland candidate.

The California voter is incorrigibly independent. He improvises but he prizes a kind of stability and is offended by roughhouse tactics or by harping criticism. The journalist Gladwin Hill wrote that in California elections the nice guy always wins, and he is the one "who manages to seize the defensive, making his opponent seem contentious and crotchety, who comes out for home, mother and highway safety, and deflects all criticism into attacks on such verities."

Californians are almost gleeful in their obstinate lack of political organization. No crisper synthesis of this trait has occurred than during a roll-call vote at a convention of the California Democratic Council in 1964. In the sing-song tones of the old-time political orator, a rural delegate rose and announced, "In the great tradition of our great state of California, and in the great tradition of our great Democratic governor, our delegation is divided!" His audience understood; they laughed and applauded.

Party politics are relatively impotent. There are none of the familiar precinct or ward bosses, and it is almost impossible to deliver any faction or bloc of votes en masse. City politics are generally uncorrupt, lacking entrenchment and organization. In a state whose people are constantly on the move, party machines simply are too difficult to organize and hold together. Civil service job examinations supplant the ward heeler's pork barrel. Yet the apathy of the shifting communities of strangers toward political affairs can be as distressing a syndrome as the over-zealousness of the political hack in more organized societies. Parties are so weak that candidates and elections more accurately reflect the state of social ferment, the aspirations and frustrations and fears of a mobile population. In that sense, at least, the California politician is plugged into his constituency.

California voters behave in ways that seem especially appalling to those from the Eastern United States, and the Westerner is sensitive to the criticism of what he regards as the "Eastern Establishment."

"California is scarcely farther from New York by jet than Hackensack is by taxi," James Phelan wrote, "but politically it is as remote and baffling as Ulan Bator." James Michener wrote that "many of my Eastern friends take pleasure in deploring the garish architecture [of the West], the John Birch Societies, the overemphasis on youth and the development of a culture which has only a parochial significance. I, on the other hand, view with envy the West's freedom, its wild joy in living, its vital experimentation in the arts, and its willingness to cultivate new industries and new ways of doing old jobs. Immediately after the census of 1970, when we witness the transfer of political power from East to West, we will all be forced to contemplate these things."

Probing with experiments in government as in all other facets of their lives, Californians are prone to causes, both good and bad, both right and left. Theirs is an individualism that is often described as conservatism. The Californian has often come West undergoing some kind of personal rebellion. He thinks he can get along all right by himself, with less central government than the voters of some other regions.

The schism between outlooks of East and West is not likely to disappear soon, and the rising tide of political strength is with the West. Yet as California has become the most populous state, it has not been quick to produce its share of the national political leadership; in California there is scant reverence for Washington, and generally less eagerness to move there.

"In my years as vice-president," Richard Nixon recalled, "I often sought Californians to fill vacancies in federal jobs. Since California had been my home state, I naturally wanted to find a fair share of Californians in federal office. But so often there would be a capable and qualified candidate in the East for the job, eager and ready for appointment, and I would be unable to turn up a Californian who was both qualified and anxious to serve. From the standpoint of influence and impact on the nation, California has hardly scratched the surface. It is still at the other end of the line. There must be more intellectual ferment, a better balance, a faster pace." A portent of that balance came with the Nixon administration that took office in 1969. Robert H. Finch, the former lieutenant governor of California, became Secretary of Health, Education and Welfare, and Cal Tech president, Lee DuBridge, was named science advisor to the President.

As the new world's own new world, California should be on the cutting edge of the nation's political evolution. With its population of young adults increasing at a rate half again as great as the national average, California produces new voters far more rapidly than any other state. As the political balance of power moves west it moves also to the young, and the youth of California may be studied for insight into the future. Despite the noisier minority of militant radicals, California young adults seem to be inching toward the right. If Los Angeles voters come closer than those of any other metropolitan area to typifying national voting patterns, as the pollster Samuel Lubell has argued, one might then assume that Americans could look to the young people of Los Angeles to see how their nation goes. At first glance, that can be horrifying. But their brashness and naiveté are tempered by a passion for the ideal society; their thing is not so unrelated, after all, to what brought their parents to California.

A Manhattan attorney, high in the Democratic Party hierarchy of his state, periodically distracts himself from local political debacles by writing letters to me in which he vents his outrage at the conduct of the California electorate. He was angry at the voters' repudiation of a fair housing law in 1964 and the election of the actor George Murphy to the United States Senate. When Ronald Reagan became governor in 1966 he charged the electorate with "immaturity bordering on political lunacy." He was shocked almost into silence when Shirley Temple Black launched her unsuccessful bid for Congress in 1967. "Every demagogic appeal appears to find a following in California," he wrote finally, "and the more clear its defiance of well-established economic law, the more certain it is to obtain political backing. Surely it must be possible to achieve a working democracy with a loyal and constructive opposition without dismissing all experience and all semblance of common sense."

I have reminded him that I do not set myself up as a critic of the New York electorate, although there are occasions when they have been an inviting target. But that, of course, is irrelevant. We in California are accustomed to ridicule. Our flamboyance invites it. Our rapid rise in national political power assures that it will continue. The underlying fear of many critics of California politics is that the aberrations of the most populous state may become national political traits. It has happened already, notably in the matter of paid professional campaign management, and in a trend toward nonpartisanship of voters. "The overriding conclusion about the political experience of California in this century," Robert L. Woodbury wrote, "is not the erratic character of its politics, but how closely it has paralleled the national experience." So the alarm of my Manhattan friend grows more personal. "Is it really too much to expect that some semblance of responsible political opinion can be developed under the hot sun of California?" he pleads. I try to calm him with history. What he regards as the idiocy of the California electorate is in large measure the result of progressive political reforms instituted in 1911–13 by Hiram Johnson as governor of California. Despite the raucous sounds of the lunatic fringes, to whom the Johnson laws insured a voice, the nuts have never gained a foothold in

Sacramento. Earl Warren, as an almost monolithic moderate, was the only California governor elected to a third term. Not even with former actors in the Senate and the State Capitol have the demagogues begun to control California. It is hard to convince my New York friend that moderation is the common denominator of politics in psychedelic California, but history establishes that it is. California has bred many extremist movements, but none has made any lasting imprint on its government or on the wide middle spectrum of moderate citizens.

At the beginning of this century, when political reform was sweeping the nation, California was a ready market. It was already a highly urban society, but with remarkably few slums and few illiterates to become the prey of political cynics. The proportion of skilled workers was high. Newspapers and colleges were abundant. Yet the railroad barons—labeled "The Octopus" by novelist Frank Norris in 1901—had established such a web of corruption that they had become the hidden rulers of California. Newspapers were subdued with subsidies or through the boycotts of Octopus-controlled advertisers. But the era of the muckrakers was at hand. Thomas Storke, who later had a long and distinguished career as a Santa Barbara newspaper publisher, wrote that he "saw the Octopus nominate and elect governors, U.S. Senators, judges, and even town constables who owed their jobs to the machine." Lincoln Steffens singled out William F. Herrin, chief attorney and political director for the Southern Pacific, as political boss of California. Legislators were bought and sold.

After Leland Stanford, as governor, had blatantly diverted state funds to the aid of the Big Four in railroad construction, fourteen successive governors under the control of Southern Pacific countenanced bribery and graft to maintain the iron grip of the railroads and their owners. William Randolph Hearst became publisher of the *San Francisco Examiner* in 1887 and launched a campaign against the Southern Pacific, loosing the eloquent talents of Ambrose Bierce in the cause. The thirty-year domination of California neared its end with the state Republican convention of 1906 at Santa Cruz. The historian George Mowry writes that "never in the history of California had the Southern

Pacific been so brazen in dominating a state convention as it was at Santa Cruz, threatening the wavering, providing for the faithful . . . In the drive to nominate [James M.] Gillett, even the higher judicial positions were traded like commodities." Flagrantly successful in electing Gillett and a controlled legislature, the ruling machine went too far. In the 1907 legislative session there were illiterate stenographers, and prostitutes serving as committee clerks.

In the same year, the San Francisco political boss Abraham Ruef was brought to trial for graft along with his puppet mayor, a violinist named Eugene Schmitz. The chief prosecutor, Francis J. Heney, was shot and almost killed in the courtroom, and his role in the trial was assumed by a 41-year-old lawyer named Hiram Warren Johnson. Ruef went on to San Quentin Prison and Johnson mounted a campaign for governor in 1910 on a pledge to "kick the Southern Pacific Railroad out of the Republican Party and out of the state government." He won, and he did it. He was elected twice as governor, and five times as United States senator before his death in 1945.

His first victory in 1910 did much to set the course of California. Described by a later colleague as "a bifurcated, peripatetic volcano, in perpetual eruption, belching fire and smoke," Johnson brought into the statutes a barrage of legislative and constitutional devices designed to make boss rule of California forever impossible. The major tools were the initiative, through which citizens could enact their own laws; the referendum, through which they could reject legislation, and the recall, with which they could oust unsatisfactory elected officials. The 1911 California legislature, dominated by Johnson, enacted a volume of reform laws which Theodore Roosevelt called "the most comprehensive legislation ever passed at a single session of any American legislature." It included establishment of the direct primary at the polls, replacing the machine-controlled party convention, and it wiped out patronage by placing state and local offices under civil service.

In ridding the state so zealously of political corruption, Johnson opened the door for every California election to become a comic free-for-all. Yet most of his measures have prevailed. They have placed political parties in conditions bordering on perpetual chaos. There always seem to be at least two Democratic and two Republican parties within California—reflecting the lack of rigid party structure and the permissiveness granted to splinter factions and volunteer political groups. They have made California the most unmanageable and unpredictable political jurisdiction in America, one where flagrantly unconstitutional initiatives can be qualified for the ballot and approved at the polls, or where some minor group of extremists or cultists can get measures passed into law largely because they are buried in a ballot so lengthy and so ponderous that few voters become familiar with every issue on which they are asked to vote. In a 1966 state election there were only six statewide offices on the ballot, but seventeen propositions that demanded answers of Yes or No. They included a law to suppress supposed obscenity, another involving prize-fighting, and others ranging from benefits for the blind to taxation of insurance companies. Sponsors of initiative propositions can put their proposals on the state ballot by securing signatures of five percent of the voters. There are firms which specialize in obtaining such signatures at a charge of twenty-five cents or more for each name; thus any well-heeled fringe group can get its measure before the voters. With enough deceptive advertising, calculated obtuseness of phrasing (the double negative is commonly employed), and some good luck in placement on the ballot, the measure may be approved; more than once, Californians have come back to the polls to undo the damage they have caused in a prior election.

It took forty-six years for Californians to erase from the statutes an insignificant sentence that found its way into law in a Johnson bill passed in 1913. "Nothing in this act contained," it read, "shall be construed to limit the right of any person to become the candidate of more than one political party for the same office . . ." This sentence laid the basis for the curious system of cross-filing under which California candidates, until 1959, were able to run in both Democratic and Republican primaries without designating their own party allegiance. Sometimes candidates assured themselves of early victory by winning the nomination of both parties in the primary elections. Cross-filing made it impossible to organize strong political parties, as candidates who had cross-filed were not the responsibility of either party. They turned not to party structures but to other sources for campaign contributions. Once elected, they owed their party nothing. This and other Johnson statutes have had the result, as Caspar Weinberger has said, of ensuring "that the party can never prevent the candidate with the most popular appeal—or at least the candidate who can secure the most votes—from being the party's nominee."

Along with political reforms in the Hiram Johnson administration came a flood of other progressive legislation. Woman suffrage was voted in 1911, eight years before it became the national law. The workday for women was lowered to eight hours. Child labor was prohibited. Free school textbooks were authorized. Funds were allotted for reclamation and flood control and to halt destruction of natural resources. Old-age pensions and employers' liability laws were passed. The railroad commission was strengthened and its jurisdiction extended over all public utilities. Liberal laws concerning housing, immigration and laborers' welfare went into the books. California led all major states in the scope of its reform.

Hiram Johnson moved on to Washington in 1917, but not with the help of the conservatives among California Republicans. The election that sent him to the Senate was also the one in which the liberal president Woodrow Wilson defeated conservative Charles Evans Hughes by a margin of only 23 electoral votes. Hughes, on the same ticket with Johnson, had snubbed Johnson during a campaign visit to California. It was a strategic error that probably cost Hughes the presidency. California voters sent Johnson to the Senate with a heavy majority, but Hughes lagged far behind his partner on the ticket and lost California by 3806 votes. The state's thirteen electoral votes went to Wilson in a late count after most of the nation had assumed Hughes to be the winner. Thus California voters helped to set the stage for American intervention in World War I. It was the first time that California had played so pivotal a role in national politics.

The momentum of Johnson's leadership helped to carry the Republican party toward a long period of domination in California affairs, with only one Democratic governor elected until

1958. Republicans learned to capitalize on the neutered political system that Johnson had created, but progressivism gave way to fundamentalism between the two world wars and California became one of the most reactionary states in the nation. Harsh prejudices erupted against religious, racial and political minorities. There were labor wars and class conflict. In 1934, a period of depression and hostility, the amiable Socialist writer Upton Sinclair won the Democratic nomination for governor and campaigned on a reckless program to "End Poverty in California." Businessmen panicked at his revolutionary proposals. Estimates of the funds raised to fight Sinclair range as high as ten million dollars, far more than has been spent on any gubernatorial campaign to this time. The incumbent Republican governor Frank Merriam was reelected in a close race, and Sinclair went back to his typewriter.

This period did most to give California its reputation as a hotbed of crackpots. Dr. Francis E. Townsend, a retired physician who had come from South Dakota, prescribed a Depression cure that would simply have given $200 monthly to all people over sixty. It might have bankrupted California, but the voting power of the aged and the poor was so great that in the closing days of his campaign against Sinclair, Governor Merriam had frantically endorsed (and later renounced) the Townsend Plan. Californians were assaulted with other movements: Technocracy, under which engineers and technicians would run the nation; the Utopian Society, which claimed half a million members and proposed a controlled society with three-hour work days; and Thirty Dollars Every Thursday (otherwise known as Ham and Eggs), which offered a $30 weekly pension for all unemployed people over fifty. His endorsement of the Ham and Eggs plan in 1938 helped elect Culbert Olson, the first Democratic governor since 1898. But he repudiated the plan after taking office. The advent of World War II ended the most perilous years in California political history.

The election of Earl Warren as governor in 1942 brought echoes of Hiram Johnson's progressivism and launched a modern and mature political era. As an almost painfully earnest young district attorney and later as state attorney general, Warren had studied the pendulum swings of the nonpartisan voters. Warren was a Republican, but Democrats had come to outnumber Republicans heavily in California and a Republican's election was no longer possible without Democratic help. Warren got it with a pledge against "partisanship of any kind," and went on to govern California longer than any other man. He paid off the state debt, improved education, launched a vast highway system and reformed prisons. Social legislation, including a fair-employment practices commission, was enacted at a brisk rate before Warren was appointed Chief Justice of the United States in 1953. He left behind an electorate so imbued in the ways of nonpartisanship that in 1966, when Democrats had a voter registration margin of more than a million, the Republican party's Ronald Reagan won a landslide victory over the incumbent Democrat, Edmund G. (Pat) Brown. Yet it was not so much a party victory as a triumph of shrewd professional campaign management.

"I'm not running against Ronald Reagan," cried Brown in 1966. "I'm running against Spencer and Roberts."

In the yellow section of the Los Angeles phone book the firm of Spencer-Roberts & Associates is listed under Public Relations. But the firm handles nothing but campaigns, a specialty that is coming to be known as Political Management. Stuart Spencer and William Roberts, two ordinary looking young businessmen in their early forties, opened their office in 1960 after meeting in volunteer Republican campaign work in Los Angeles and deciding that "there must be a more scientific way to get our men elected." Roberts had been selling television sets; Spencer, a sociology major in college, had been director of recreation for the city of Alhambra and an official at night basketball games.

But by 1967 they had masterminded forty-eight political campaigns in California, ranging from Los Angeles city council to United States president, and won all but seven of them. One of their seven losers was Nelson Rockefeller, who ran a hairbreadth second to Barry Goldwater in the California presidential primary of 1964. One of their winners was Ronald Reagan.

Spencer and Roberts were not the first nonpoliticians to exploit the peculiar vacuum of organized party activity that had been the result of the Hiram Johnson reforms more than fifty years ago. In 1933 the late Clem Whitaker, a newspaperman, and Leone Baxter, who later married him, had teamed up to represent California farm interests. They beat the omnipotent Pacific Gas & Electric Co. in a statewide referendum over water and power; PG&E responded with the supreme accolade: they put Whitaker and Baxter on a retainer. In the next twenty-two years, they ran seventy-five California campaigns and won seventy of them. "The average American," Whitaker once said, "doesn't want to be educated; he doesn't want to improve his mind; he doesn't even want to work, consciously, at being a good citizen." So he and his wife made their campaigns simple, tolerated no grays, and enshrined their clients in dazzling auras of goodness and light.

But it remained for Spencer and Roberts to lift professional political management to a pseudoscientific level. Other firms had copied the successes of Whitaker and Baxter, and among them were unscrupulous profiteers. Some advertised in classified sections of California newspapers seeking candidates to run for such offices as state legislator. But Spencer and Roberts hired a behavioral sciences firm to counsel them on how voters would react to candidates and issues. They helped to set up an allied firm, Datamatics, Inc., to provide a computerized battery of detailed information on voters. Compounding hard work and a scholarly, dignified approach, Spencer and Roberts came on the scene at a time when television had outmoded the practical primer of the old courthouse politician, and when the pressures of expanding population in a 700-mile long state had made logistic problems for candidates seem almost insurmountable.

"One of the first things we do for a client," Roberts once explained, "is to decide where our candidate goes and how he uses his time. We say where and how he should spend his dollars. We choose to whom letters should be sent, and we place precinct workers in position and tell them what to say. We don't make these decisions on hunches. We know. Nobody wins a campaign. Somebody always loses it. Our job is to see that our man doesn't make mistakes."

Even Roberts, who regarded Reagan as "one of the most cooperative candidates" his firm had handled, sometimes has seemed disturbed about the directions in which professional political management seems headed. *The New York Times* stated in an editorial in 1966 that "the cool professionalism of their operations in California politics is chilling . . ." Roberts replied that John F. Kennedy had used the services of Simulmatics, a group of MIT academicians employing similar techniques, in the course of his election as president in 1960, and added, "it's just a question of whose ox is getting gored." But Roberts admitted to a friend: "Suppose five thousand people got into this business and tried to do what we're doing? Could they form an association and, among them, simply pick a president of the United States? I don't think so, but I'm not sure."

Such professionalism, in any case, is becoming more common across America. With the impact of immediate media communication, mounting a campaign has become increasingly expensive and logistically more difficult. "These days new candidates just don't know what they're in for," Spencer said. "They need a pro to guide them. Politics is just damned hard work. This is what we do for a living."

For them it has been a good living. They work for a flat fee that may range between ten and twenty per cent of the total expenses of the campaign they handle. The cost of getting a California legislator elected ranges from $20,000 to $50,000. Even a Los Angeles city council candidate needs to raise $300,000 to pay for broadcast time, billboards, newspaper and direct mail advertising, office help—and Spencer and Roberts. It can cost between $50,000 and $100,000 to send a congressman from California to Washington. Someone running for governor or United States Senator—"depending on how much heat is raised," Roberts says—should have a campaign budget of $1,500,000 to $3,000,000.

Even politicians who have been defeated by the firm have grudgingly admitted that Spencer and Roberts operate ethically, but they decry the trend toward professionalism. If such a firm can take any candidate and put him into office, they argue, then it is simply a political whore. "Up to a point," Roberts has replied, "we don't care what a candidate believes, so long as it doesn't make him unelectable. But we put other things ahead of

making a buck. We take only Republicans because we like to
see our own party win. We have to feel something emotionally
about a client and a campaign."

Yet their feelings can change. In 1964, when they represented
Rockefeller, Spencer and Roberts included the name of Ronald
Reagan in a list of right-wing extremists. In 1966, after a cram
course of several months during which they brought in academicians and government experts to coach their client, they sold
Reagan to the voters of California as a moderate. Whether they
are "selling candidates like soap," as one critic put it, "or producing a better informed campaign," as Spencer replied, the
professional campaign managers are proliferating in California,
where candidates have no party machine to put them across to
voters, nor any prospect of a straight-ticket vote. Now most advanced in California, the system is becoming a factor in elections
all over America.

Within California, the election of 1968 made increasingly clear,
sweeping changes are taking place in the political structure. The
cleavage between north and south has always been distinct. With
population increasing more rapidly south of the Tehachapi, the
political power of Southern California is dominant. In 1960 the
north lost a bitter fight over diversion of water from its rivers
through the multi-billion-dollar California Aqueduct to the
south. In 1964 the north gave Rockefeller a clear majority but
Southern California elected Goldwater in the crucial presidential primary. In the heat of that campaign, William Brinton, a
San Francisco attorney and Rockefeller supporter, published
legal proposals to divide California into two states at the Tehachapi. Twenty-five state senators from the north, belonging to
both parties, supported abortive bills to implement a secession;
it was a proposal that has been made periodically since the 1850's.

With the reapportionment that followed the one-man, one-
vote ruling of the United States Supreme Court, the political
fortunes of northern California sustained a mortal blow. Thirteen
of forty state senate seats that had been filled by men from the
sparsely populated counties of the north were turned over to

Los Angeles County, giving the populous south practical control in state affairs.

Northern Californians have been more politically organized and usually more liberal than those in the south—reflecting the more urban style of life in San Francisco and the greater consciousness of religious and ethnic blocs. The south is in contrast. Typically Anglo-Saxon migrants with low-church Protestant affiliations, the newly prospering Southern Californian has approached politics as though he were shopping for competent property management. When he has felt his economic advancement to be in jeopardy—as in matters of open housing and soaring welfare programs or violence-in-the-streets—he has retreated into conservatism, a plea for orderliness, limited government, and old-fashioned patriotism.

The rootlessness of the Californian is presumed to explain his periodic outbreaks of extremism. He is usually less interested in community issues than in abstract political concepts that he can handily carry over from another region. Yet as the Harvard government professor James Q. Wilson has pointed out, it was during the era of most rapid growth that Southern Californians voted over and over again for Earl Warren, who was then considered the essence of moderation. The truly rootless voter is most likely to respond to the appeal of television or newspaper advertising, billboard or direct mail. Thus he is especially vulnerable to shallow distortion and to the manipulation of a candidate by a professional manager like Los Angeles' Hal Evry, who insists he can elect any man who has enough money and an I.Q. of at least 120, and who will keep his mouth shut.

The California newcomer lacks a sense of tradition, and its moderating influence; seeking an alternative, he sometimes finds a niche in the uncompromising paranoia of extremism on the left or right. Etched against the traditional and still overriding California search for moderate government, unspectacular and dependable, there is the increasing phenomena of polarization between Left and Right. Both sides seem busy trying to dismantle the political structure that Hiram Johnson built.

Ideological carpetbaggers find audiences in any fluid society.

Yet as the University of California's Paul Seabury observed, nearly all statewide political contests since World War II have found "candidates of each party struggling to capture the high terrain of 'moderation' from which to hurl aspersions on their opponents' 'extremism.'" The role of the moderate continues to be the most politically successful course for any California candidate. But those who seek to envision the nation's political future will watch Californians intently. Their concept of moderation may be changing from the moderation of past years. If California has been a valid early-warning signal, the national pendulum is swinging toward the right. In the same way the inevitable swing back in the direction of the left may someday be telegraphed in advance by the California electorate.

. 17 .

THE CALIFORNIA SYNDROME

What will happen when California is filled by fifty millions of people, and its valuation is five times what it is now, and the wealth will be so great that you will find it difficult to know what to do with it? The day will, after all, have only twenty-four hours. Each man will have only one mouth, one pair of ears, and one pair of eyes. There will be more people—as many perhaps as the country can support—and the real question will be not about making more wealth or having more people, but whether the people will then be happier or better.

—LORD JAMES BRYCE, SPEAKING AT BERKELEY IN 1909.

307

A former president of Yale once made an engaging case for what he said, in gentle scorn, would be Harvard's eternal superiority to Yale. Harvard is part of a large metropolitan area, he explained, while Yale is not. Thus there will always be more disease for Harvard's medical students, more crime for its law students, more uglinesss for its architects, and more vice for its social scientists.

Somewhat the same case could be put for, or against, California. Battered by growth and sweeping change, its people have never achieved the kind of lull that breeds complacency. The challenge of an obstinate environment was inherent in the founding of the state. "Bring me men to match my mountains," cried the early poet. The men have come, and with them an assumption that crisis is inherent in California life. The crises are eternally changing in nature, from the blizzards that brought death to the Donner Party in the Sierra Nevada on to the threatened disruption of life in the complex cities of tomorrow. California has been a frontier for problems and also for solutions. A society that is attuned to crisis may have a shorter reaction time in coping with it. A putty culture can be more swiftly reshaped, and a rootless society more easily diverted. A climate of change, the designer Henry Dreyfuss wrote, is ideal for creative design. It can be equally stimulating to those who seek to shape and preserve the quality of living.

But the climate of change tolerates mediocrity, worthlessness and ugliness. "A general sense of social irresponsibility is the average Californian's easiest failing," Josiah Royce wrote in 1886. That sense may be less prevalent today than in the frontier days after the Gold Rush that Royce knew. Californians have a curious capacity for taking mediocre materials and using them interestingly, for taking fairly good schools and squeezing out a high proportion of gifted students, or for taking tolerable public servants and somehow achieving good government. But mediocrity invites compromise, and compromise gorges itself on mediocrity. The symbols of the Californian's affluence and leisure tend to overwhelm him, and his quest for the new tomorrow seems stunted. A population of consumers may constitute an affluent society, as Archibald MacLeish wrote, but it can never compose a nation or a state in the great, the human, sense. A society that feasts on the largesse of technological advances can fester inside itself. Among California's myriad problems, the most critical may be one that has been, for many people, her most alluring trait: the absence of restraints. California has grown without consideration of its own effect. The shape of Los Angeles is a result of freedoms rather than restraints. A swelling metropolis has made its decisions, public and private, without drawing on any cultural tradition, and without any common sense of social responsibility. Throughout California there have been too few indignant bodies of citizens to serve as check and balance, and virtually no entrenched aristocracy to retard the flouting of tradition. The restraint of strong religious or patriotic ties is absent. Even the family is scattered and weakened, leaving the individual to scorn family responsibility without the censure of society. Each man is free to blight his community with his own esthetic blunders so long as they are sanitary and they are properly designed to resist an earthquake.

Another problem is the Californian's lack of commitment. He is nostalgic about his frontier past, but it is the fictitious past of the televised Western and not the sociological fact of how he came to be what he is and where he is. He is far more absorbed with the present and even with his surrealistic future. Such interest as there is in history, as Wallace Stegner has observed, is often "the activity of uprooted people fumbling for the broken threads of their continuity." The ambition of the Californian is to be the first to say what is about to be said, or to do first what is about to be done. It is a young and half-formed society still, and the sense of historical continuity is not widely felt. The gold-camp motivation can be detected. It is said commonly in Alaska, as it was in the gold fields, that most of the residents are there to make a killing and then get out. One moves to California these days to make a killing, perhaps, but without planning to get out. Yet the migrant from Kansas may go on talking about Kansas as "back home" through the rest of a lifetime in California.

Because of its absence of restraints and its lack of commitment,

California rushes at sometimes dizzying paces into a future that it does not understand and has not charted. The landscape architect Garrett Eckbo has said, "We are producing with staggering velocity and astonishing self-assurance, the most mechanical, regimented, sterile, uncultured, inhuman urban environment in the history of the world . . ." If the upward growth projections indeed come true, it is not hard to envision a California whose people stand on each other's shoulders eating seaweed because all their farmland has been paved over. Some demographers recoil from their own prophesies. Kingsley Davis and Eleanor Langlois projected that the San Francisco Bay region would be inhabited by 18.8 million people in the year 2000, and then rejected their conclusion as improbable. Yet California has made up a constantly increasing percentage of the national population, from just over five percent in 1939 to about ten percent in 1969. A recent study gave this day-by-day picture of California growth: about 1,000 babies are born each day in California, and nearly 1,000 people arrive from other states and countries. One hundred persons leave and four hundred die. At the end of the day, California has fifteen hundred more people than at the beginning.

Despite the cry of many that such growth must be halted, or will halt itself, there would be no essential evil in rapid California growth if the people of the state understood its scope and forced such growth into patterns that would not further deteriorate the climate and environment. California has about twenty million residents. England and Scotland, half the size of California, have a population of more than fifty million. So does Italy, which is about two-thirds the size of California. Japan, smaller than California, has one hundred million. Puerto Rico harbors its population on a basis that, granted certain climatological changes, would in California support a population of about 110 million people. Nor does such crowding necessarily imply economic or esthetic impoverishment. Jobs and food remain plentiful, investors appear to have no apprehension that the California economy will fail, and the existing standard of living is highest among all the states in the richest nation of the world. "If Californians really want the prize for size," wrote

George W. Mitchell as a member of the board of governors of the Federal Reserve System, "I am sure they can muster the ingenuity and determination to adopt policies that will make this not only a painless distinction but possibly a pleasurable one."

Most thoughtful Californians are less sanguine about the chance to retain the flavor of present-day California in a state with fifty million residents, a figure that may in fact be viewed quite casually by the year 2000. About one-fifth of the state's 103 million acres is barren mountains and desert; a breakthrough in water desalinization cost would very likely make such areas populable. Another one-third of California is forested and serves as watershed. Only one-sixth is cultivable. Land is about equally divided between public and private ownership. Yet in 1968 three hundred to four hundred acres each day were going under the blade to urbanization or freeway development, land lost forever to agriculture or to esthetic development as open space.

The loss of open land is precipitous and grave in itself, but it becomes more so in the absence of any integrated development planning. Neither local nor state government effectively controls the location or extent of urban growth. In 1968, after six years of discussion and an expenditure of two million dollars, the California Development Plan—supposedly a blueprint for the state's future—was finally published. Yet in a state where disruption of the environment proceeds routinely at a greater rate than in any comparable area of the world, no one is in charge of the future. The lofty dreams of the Development Plan lack the nourishment of budget or of law.

In 1963, as California became the most populous state, the University of California sponsored an imposing series of seven conferences on the challenge of growth in education, the cultural arts, science, the metropolitan future, natural resources, food production, and human stress. But the findings of those conferences have gathered dust. An increasingly shrill minority has protested the vacuum in which California growth continues to occur. In his book *How to Kill a Golden State*, William Bronson wrote that "California has led the rest of the world into the age of mass affluence and has become standing testimony to man's infinite capacity to befoul and destroy in the quest for an ever-higher standard of living."

Yet one cannot fairly state that the destruction of the earth's beauty and livability is proceeding in California at any greater rate than elsewhere in America. It is a relative matter, and in a world that is not growing any more pleasant to live in, California has not had as much time to suffer at man's hand as have more settled regions. The clutter of signs and wires and traffic need not be exaggerated by the cameraman's telephoto lens—as is often done—to bring a shudder. California has more to lose than most states.

In fact the consumption of space and facilities for recreation is much higher in California than in most of the nation. Such space is available, and so is the opportunity for leisure; those who migrate to California are exceptionally conscious of such matters. Thus there has evolved a relatively powerful minority whose concern is to preserve open space and natural amenities. Although there are bitter protests at the inadequacy of parkland, California had 783 public parks in 1968, more than double the number in any other state. It led also in the number of campgrounds and campsites. Although 150 miles of the coastline is in the state park system, thirty percent of those seeking to use such parks on an overnight basis were being turned away in 1968. Scare stories on crowding at national parks had reached such an extent in the summer of 1968 that they were cited as the cause of a significant decline in those visiting Yosemite Park.

Despite the crowding of its urban areas, California has the sea at one side and the mountains and desert at the other; most of the state's people live within twenty miles of the sea, and open space is not yet obscure enough to bring a shadow of worry across the consciousness of most of its people. The Golden State has not been killed, only constricted. "When I come back to La Jolla I am overwhelmed by the clarity of the air, the brilliance of color, the immediacy of natural elements," says Roger Revelle, who left California to head the Center for Population Studies at Harvard. "In California, you can't help but be more sensitive to your natural environment, and this has a constructive effect on society."

A more skeptical point of view was advanced by the planner Harold F. Wise, who left California in 1959 "with some reluctance" for a faculty position at the University of Pennsylvania. "I was surprised to find that in the East there is a level of political maturity and a willingness to tackle problems that surpass anything I had known in the West. Maybe things were worse in the East. Maybe in the state of California you have to wait until you are as bad off as they are in the East before real action and fundamental reform can happen. The way things are going this could take place before 1970." The designer Charles Eames expresses the challenge in other terms when he describes Los Angeles as an "esthetic nightmare," but not because the people of Los Angeles are any less sensitive than others. "It would have happened in any group freed from restraints of tradition and with no new restraints to take their place. The problem, of which Los Angeles is such a dramatic example, will soon be a universal one."

The word *slurb* was coined by a small but influential group known as *California Tomorrow* to describe "sloppy, sleazy, slovenly, slipshod semi-cities." The slurb consumes open land, tending to separate more and more people from the countryside, from access to environmental variety. The projected population increase in California by 1980 will be sufficient to duplicate the entire existing metropolitan system of the state with its core cities, suburbs and all. Unless the slurb is controlled through better urban planning, it will become a giant web of horror. Regardless of how mobile Americans become, each person still needs a *place*. More and more commonly, that place to belong may be a mobile residence—a structure that, granted, is not necessarily fixed, but to which one returns and at least *hooks on*. If citizens and government cannot arrest the spread of the slurb, there will be ever more complex means devised to escape it.

It is commonly assumed that the increasing penetration of mass communication media has diminished contrasts in regional social patterns in America. But a study published in 1967 by the sociologists Norval D. Glenn and J. L. Simmons establishes that beneath the superficial homogenization of attitudes and behavior —the so-called mass society—there persist wide and even widening differences in values and beliefs. The same television report or newsmagazine cover story is apparently interpreted quite differently by the people of separate regions, in terms of their dominant or ingrained cultural mores. The division of the vote in the 1964 and 1968 presidential elections points up continuing contrasts in attitude among regions of America, notably between the politically conservative West and the more liberal Eastern seaboard.

Californians are the people of all states, migrated in search of common quests, and thus they are the paradigm of America—but with the brash trait, as Thomas R. Edwards wrote, "of being open and insistent about things that the rest of the country has preferred not to say out loud." This thread of distinction has run throughout the course of California history. "Californians are a race of people," wrote O. Henry; "they are not merely inhabitants of a state." In 1915 Paul Elder wrote that "it seems hardly too much to say that a new type of civilization is being developed on this coast, one which is built up out of much the same cosmopolitan elements as the rest of the country, but under conditions of rare isolation and freedom, new as compared with the earlier American life along the eastern seaboard, new in contrast with later European history, but strangely like the old Greek life in its isolation, its place over against the Orient and in touch therewith, its study of problems on its own account and without precedent." There is still an intensity of feeling along this Western coast. Californians are not yet resigned or subdued. The world seems keen and fresh.

That spontaneity is demonstrated in a massive public involvement with the arts. There is considerable artistic professionalism in California, and some creativity. But most notably, it is the do-it-yourself center of the arts. Weekend painters abound. Their easels are perched beside mountain roads, on city beaches, or across some busy intersection from a tattered palm tree. There are more than sixty community symphony orchestras in the Los

Angeles area alone. Little-theater groups are beyond count. Writers' conferences are almost inescapable. After a survey of cultural affairs in 1965, the California Arts Commission concluded that the "upsurge of interest in the arts is apparent throughout the country; but nowhere . . . more so than in California." Its inventory turned up symphony orchestras from coastal cities on tour in desert ranch towns, classical Spanish dance being taught in a town adjacent to the Mexican border, and in San Francisco, such structures as stables, garages, churches, a wax factory and even a wine warehouse converted into theaters. The University of California, with a continually expanding program in the arts, piles up gate counts of hundreds of thousands of paying citizens each season for lectures, concerts, films, plays and dance recitals.

It has been easier over the years to deride this yeasty California culture than to explain it. F. Scott Fitzgerald and Budd Schulberg are among those who have effectively dismantled the Hollywood legend. In *The Loved One*, Evelyn Waugh exposed the morbidity of the old Los Angeles. Nathanael West lashed out at its barrenness in *The Day of the Locust*. The vogue continues with lesser efforts in more contemporary settings. But there is a curious vacuum of California fiction that reflects any historical continuity. The state provides a marvelous literary setting for outbursts of black humor. Those writers of the I-live-in-hell school usually go through a Los Angeles phase before moving on. A recent study of forty-six novels about Southern California revealed that none of the authors was born in the region and most had lived there only for a short time.

Even those modern writers whose work is most closely associated with the California landscape—Steinbeck and Saroyan—lost ties with the West. What has come to be expected of Western writing has not changed much since Edmund Wilson wrote in *The New Yorker* of a book by Walter Van Tilburg Clark that "like the fiction of the Pacific slope, like Steinbeck and Saroyan, this book does not quite meet the requirements of an Easterner . . . too easy going and good natured, too lacking in organization, always dissolving into an even sunshine, always circumventing by ample detours what one expects to be sharp or direct." It is the same complaint that the journalist Walter Duranty made to John Gunther two decades ago when he insisted that the effect of sunlight on in-migrants from more northern latitudes caused wackiness in Southern California. "Iowa comes here and goes crazy," Duranty said.

There are moments still that live up to that appraisal. In the book department of a large Los Angeles store, a friend asked a pretty young clerk for a copy of Bartlett's *Familiar Quotations*. He insists that she blinked her eyes and said, "Is that a mystery?" On another occasion I went to a Sears store in Southern California to see a touring exhibition of paintings that the collector Vincent Price had gathered under Sears auspices. As I stood in front of an Andrew Wyeth canvas priced at $30,000, an attendant in a white dinner jacket stepped up and handed me his card. Beneath his name were the words, Washers-Dryers. Perhaps clerks from the appliance department presided over the exhibition in Sears stores everywhere; in California we are ready to find in such a scene some general evidence of regional vulgarity.

Yet in contemporary California the cultural tide is high and rising. There is an eagerness to compensate for lost time in support of the arts. Building empirically on the experience of older regions of America, Californians seem likely to achieve within their first two centuries a level of cultural involvement that has taken far longer to reach in most parts of the world. The vogue for popularization in California—mass participation in the performing arts—cannot be dismissed as cultural nihilism when it brings so large a segment of society into touch with much that is valuable. Prosperity, leisure, and the acceptance of knowledge as the key to progress have helped to set a mood on the West Coast that many intellectuals regard as conducive to creative work. The poet Kenneth Rexroth regards the level of cultural participation in San Francisco as "incomparably richer and of higher quality *proportionately* than New York's." For some, like the painter Ed Ruscha, "the greatest thing about Southern California is that the pressure is just nonexistent." There has been a sustained creativity by West Coast architects. The contemporary wood-and-glass ranch house, now familiar in much of America, is a California contribution, descended from the redwood bungalow of turn-of-the-century days. The work of the landscape architect Thomas Church and the mass housing designs of Joseph Eichler have been landmark contributions in their fields.

Some of the cultural scene in California is embarrassing in its naive enthusiasm, but that is a symptom of the people's arts. "I don't mind if the beauty is a bit cockeyed sometimes, like the Grauman Theatre or even the wildest excesses of de Mille," wrote the late British novelist T. H. White on his last visit to California. "The point is that the money *is* being spent on culture of some sort, that it is an individual culture, and that even millionaires care about it." I remember a weekend of discussion of the arts on the hyperthyroid campus of the University of California at Los Angeles. Between sessions, the actors Dana Andrews and Lew Ayres poked about looking for seats on an old yellow university bus, and settled for a commuter's grip on the handrail as they stood. The New York critic Howard Taubman stood in a cafeteria line for ten minutes waiting for a fresh pot of coffee to brew. The poet Lawrence Lipton stubbornly managed to appear without a necktie, even at a formal reception at the chancellor's house. Carey McWilliams drew knowing smiles with his comment that "all civilizations are man-made, but California's is more man-made than most." The late Aldous Huxley, his eyesight failing, held close to his eyes the yellow pad on which he had scrawled notes for his address, and concluded with a whimsical inquiry into the literature of the nightingale.

"Some great poet someday will show us," Huxley said, "how we can render the spiritual facts of the ecstasy which the nightingale's song produces in man, but also render the physical fact which science has recently learned of why he sings in the night: His digestive system is such that he wakes up every four or five hours for more worms, and he sings to warn other birds that he is prepared to defend his territory."

In California such mysteries of the arts and the sciences are pursued with common interest and with rare unity among the varied disciplines involved. It would seem natural that this be true in California, where the cultural and academic and even the corporate worlds are less tightly structured than one has come to expect. The state has a strong appeal for inquisitive men who cross over with ease from one discipline to another: men like Jacob Bronowski, the mathematician-philosopher of Salk Institute, or Edward Teller of the University of California. The crossover in the arts is widespread. Yet no one is very surprised to find a first-rate show of paintings by an electronics specialist, or to discover the director of the University Art Museum at Berkeley earnestly describing his exhibition of "funk art" as an expression of defiance by youth who believe that "it's a groove to stick your finger down your throat and see what comes up." San Franciscans share with equal verve in their grand opera and the topless cult. The California Sound is an evolution of the rock music of youth that began with the surfing music of the beach. The executive secretary of the California Arts Commission is a respected and distinguished citizen named James L. Lyons, who was known until recently as Jimmy Lyons, the founder of the Monterey Jazz Festival.

The conglomerate teamwork of scientific studies within California "think tanks"—most notably the Rand Corporation at Santa Monica—concentrates on the future shape of the nation and world. The dominant role of California in federal research contracts tends to perpetuate the scientific migration westward, and new contracts follow the most recent migrants. In 1966 a *Fortune* survey turned up more than six hundred science-oriented firms in the Los Angeles and San Francisco areas alone. Between 1961 and 1965, 38.5 percent of federal research and development funds went to such firms and universities within California. The National Aeronautics and Space Administration has committed as much as forty-five percent of its research and development funds in California—and R&D absorbs as much as ninety percent of NASA's budget. Almost half of the Nobel laureates in America are in California. In 1962, 135 members of the National Academy of Sciences listed California as their home state; in 1968 there were 185, and the next states in line were Massachusetts, with 138, and New York with 132. California has a commanding role in the lunar program (all major components of the Apollo spacecraft were developed in the state) and in oceanographic research directed at developing underwater sources of food. The California culture is, in fact, not so much a regional culture as a futurist culture, which now begins to appear as a logical out-growth of the combination of unique people and extraordinary environment.

With the kind of self-assurance that comes to few, the Yale economist John O. Wilson undertook in 1967 to define the Ameri-can concept of "the good life" and to measure the extent to which it exists in each state. The resultant survey ranked Cali-fornia first in economic growth, technological change, agricul-ture, and in overall goals, his term for a kind of sweepstakes average of all nine fields of study covered in the survey. The state was ranked third in living conditions (Connecticut and New York were in the first two places), third in status of the individual (Massachusetts and Connecticut ranked higher), fourth in edu-cation, sixth in the status of democratic process, fourteenth in health and welfare, and seventeenth in individual equality, or the absence of discrimination. The survey was typical of the kind of numbers game for which Californians themselves have often been criticized, but it was at least as valuable as a Gallup Poll in pointing to the strengths and weaknesses of the state.

On balance, the strengths of California are immense, on the order of those needed by a people who have struck out ahead of America like a scouting party of the future. Its weightier social crises are not the more conventional ones of prejudice, poverty and oppression, but the more complex and nebulous ones involv-ing the future: the quality of aspiration and the degree of integrity. California is young, cocky and eternally hopeful; it is new and big, a sort of Texas-come-true and gone to the city. But newness and bigness are not in themselves worthy objects of search in today's society. California, letting the chips ride and coming out for another roll of the dice, might yet roll a seven and lose it all. It seems less likely all the time, as a scattering of thoughtful leaders accumulates wider and wider followings.

The late Catherine Bauer Wurster, a dedicated planner, de-fined the California goal as that of maximizing individual choice —in housing and job, in public and private recreation, in natural amenity and urbanity, in life styles, social contacts, cultural op-portunities and conveniences. To move toward the achievement of such aims entails a search by an untraditional people for new traditions. The search may in fact be for a sense of discipline and restraint—not in accomplishment, but in approach and problem structuring. Innovation has been the theme of California's advance, yet innovation which occurs without the restraints of some disciplines must suffer from the lack of seemingly obscure bits of human knowledge that, carefully nurtured and remembered, become the stepping stones to golden eras. It is not enough to face a doubling of population in California in the next twenty years by redoubling the expenditure of energy, imagination and political leadership. Those commitments must take ingenious new forms. The innovative genius of the Californian must be etched not in putty, but in granite. More than the future of this one state is at stake. California is ranging out ahead of America. To study its people is to turn a view-finder on the national tomorrow. The California syndrome may yet become the American malaise or its regeneration.

ACKNOWLEDGMENTS

Survival is the overriding requisite for completing a book manuscript, and there are days in the lives of most writers when even survival seems chancy. Perhaps that helps to explain the exuberance, once the job is done, with which writers acknowledge those who have seen us through. Whatever else, we have survived.

Entirely aside from our private conversations, I thank my wife Judith, who steadied me when the project might otherwise have foundered, and detected glimmers of hope when all seemed darkest. The final text is better than it would have been without her warmth and brilliance. My daughter Jill gave many hours to clipping and filing the horde of material that must be maintained to stay abreast of California change. My secretary Miriam McIver, who cheerfully endures my periods of madness, never gave any indication that she was dreading the tedious hours of typing and retyping which she did so knowledgeably.

The historian Earl Pomeroy took time away from his own writing to offer critiques of the text, sparing me from a number of errors. If some remain it is no fault of his. Particular encouragement came from Dean Jennings and Clyde Vandeburg. The time for work was made possible through the interest and assistance of James S. Copley and members of his newspaper organization who are my colleagues: Robert Letts Jones, E. Robert Anderson, Alex De Bakcsy, Victor H. Krulak, Rembert James, John Pinkerman, Eugene F. Williams, Gene Gregston, Leo Bowler, Howard Welty and Robert M. Witty.

Portions of the book appeared in the San Diego *Evening Tribune, The San Diego Union, The Saturday Review, Holiday,* and in other newspapers served by the Copley News Service, and appear here through their permission. Acknowledgment is also made to Gayle Williams for her help in proofreading (although she firmly rejects the author's thesis that Southern California should be capitalized and northern California should not).

CHAPTER NOTES

CHAPTER ONE

The Charles Russell epigraph is from a letter in the collection of the Gilcrease Museum at Tulsa, Oklahoma. A synopsis of Raymond Chandler's descriptions of Los Angeles can be found in *Down These Mean Streets a Man Must Go,* by Philip Durham (Chapel Hill, 1963). Clifton Fadiman on Los Angeles is from *Holiday* magazine for October 1965. Comparative economic rankings of California came from the Union Bank, Los Angeles, and Bank of America, San Francisco. Demographic projections for California youth are from the research department of *Sunset* magazine, Menlo Park, Calif. The quotation from Walt Whitman is from *Song of the Redwood-Tree.* The profile of the typical Californian is drawn from *Statistical Abstract of the United States, 1967; California Statistical Abstract, 1967; Sunset Western Market Almanac* 1967–68, The Bourbon Institute, and files of California daily newspapers. The quotation from John S. Hittell is from *The Resources of California* (San Francisco, 1863). Earl Pomeroy is from *The Pacific Slope* (New York, 1965). John Walton Caughey is from *Gold is the Cornerstone* (Berkeley, 1948). Data on California agriculture is from the University of California at Davis. For further reading on the general nature of contemporary California, one of the most valuable volumes is *California: The Great Exception* by Carey McWilliams (New York, 1949). McWilliams served as editor for a more recent collection of essays, *The California Revolution* (New York, 1968). California receives a major share of attention in Neil Morgan's *Westward Tilt: The American West Today* (New York, 1963) and *The Pacific States* by Neil Morgan and the editors of Time-Life Books (New York, 1967).

CHAPTER TWO

The most valuable book on California geography is *California: Land of Contrast* by David W. Lantis, Rodney Steiner, and Arthur E. Karinen (Belmont, Calif., 1963). Delightful essays on the California environment can be found in a volume edited by Roderick Peattie, *The Pacific Coast Ranges* (New York, 1946). A glittering collection of naturalist volumes has been published by the Sierra Club. Helpful reading is found in *California: A Guide to the Golden State*, revised edition (New York, 1967) and in other volumes of the American Guide series devoted to San Francisco, Los Angeles and San Diego. William Bronson's *How to Kill a Golden State* (New York, 1968) is a leading example of the wave of books deploring the debasement of the California landscape. Material relating to the San Francisco earthquake seems endless; for a combination of succinct reportage and dramatic photographs it is difficult to find better than William Bronson's *The Earth Shook, The Sky Burned* (New York, 1959). Files of daily newspapers in Southern California provide rich content in the lore of regional drought and flood. Historic perspective is given in Carey McWilliams' *Southern California Country* (New York, 1946). A comprehensive treatment of Charles Hatfield is in *Gold in the Sun* by Richard F. Pourade (San Diego, 1965).

CHAPTER THREE

The journal *Cry California* is published quarterly by California Tomorrow, 681 Market St., San Francisco. Data on California traffic and freeways is from the State Division of Highways, Sacramento. The most extensive library in California transit affairs is at the University of California Institute of Transportation and Traffic Engineering, Richmond, California. The Pacific Electric Railways Corporation and its significance in the development of Los Angeles is described comprehensively by Robert M. Fogelson in *The Fragmented Metropolis; Los Angeles 1850–1930* (Cambridge, Mass., 1967).

CHAPTER FOUR

No other volumes approach the works of John Muir in conveying the sense of discovery of the Sierra Nevada. See *The Mountains of California* (New York, 1961), *The Yosemite* (New York, 1962). Francis P. Farquhar has combined history and geography pleasantly in *History of the Sierra Nevada* (Berkeley, 1966). The standard work on Yosemite is The Sierra Club's illustrated *Guide to Yosemite* by Virginia and Ansel Adams (San Francisco, 1963). No photographer has equalled Adams in the extensiveness and beauty of his work in the Sierra Nevada, and many volumes of his photographs are available.

CHAPTER FIVE

Remi Nadeau used anecdote, fact and intuition about California in *California: The New Society* (New York, 1963). The quotation from Carle C. Zimmerman is from his *Graphic Regional Sociology,* a monograph privately printed at Cambridge in 1952. Comparative data on mobility has been gathered by the author from records of gas and electric utility companies and water departments and from the records of newspaper circulation departments, whose stop-and-start figures are a precise measurement of residential mobility. An interesting discussion of the reasons for the high rate of bank robberies in Los Angeles appeared in the *Los Angeles Times* on September 16, 1968. The quotation from Eugene Burdick is from *Holiday* magazine, October 1965. Statistics on suicide, alcoholism and divorce are from federal and state data and the files of the Life Insurance Underwriters Association. Quotations from Melvin Brown and Mrs. Nola Stark are from a special section concerning the California woman in *Ladies' Home Journal,* July 1967. A profile by Hunter S. Thompson is called *Hell's Angels: The Strange and Terrible Saga of the Outlaw Motorcycle Gang* (New York, 1967).

CHAPTER SIX

The quotation from Frank Waters is from his book *The Colorado* (New York, 1946), a personal narrative of the river and its adjacent deserts. Quotations from Mary Austin are from *The Land of Little Rain* (New York, 1962). John Wesley Powell's own account of the discovery of the Colorado River is dramatic: *The Exploration of the Colorado River* (Chicago, 1959). An up-to-date view of the Mojave

Desert can be found in Russ Leadabrand's *A Guide Book to the Mojave Desert of California* (Los Angeles, 1956). Standard California histories give detailed accounts of the rampages of the Colorado River in Imperial Valley. Among them is John Walton Caughey's *California* (Englewood Cliffs, 1953). Richard F. Pourade goes into more detail in *Gold in the Sun* (San Diego, 1965). Remi Nadeau's *Ghost Towns and Mining Camps of California* (Los Angeles, 1965) gives lore of the desert. See also his *The Water Seekers* (New York, 1950).

CHAPTER SEVEN

The quotation from Roger Revelle appeared in an untitled brochure of the University of California at San Diego in 1967. The prime history of the early years of the University is William Warren Ferrier's *Origin and Development of the University of California* (Berkeley, 1930). See also his *Ninety Years of Education in California* (Berkeley, 1937). A galaxy of publications in the University of California centennial year, 1968, updated these and other histories. For the casual reader, *A Brief History of the University of California* is available from the Office of University Relations at Berkeley. Much of the material in this chapter, like that elsewhere in the book, was gathered by the author during visits and interviews over a period of years. Some of the material appeared in other form in the author's "The State as a Campus" in *Holiday* magazine, October 1965.

CHAPTER EIGHT

A continually updated source of information about the San Diego area is the *San Diego Facts Book*, available through the Union Tribune Publishing Co., San Diego. Other publications are offered through the San Diego Convention and Visitors Bureau. The definitive history of San Diego is a six-volume work by Richard F. Pourade: *The Explorers, Time of the Bells, The Silver Dons, The Glory Years, Gold in the Sun,* and *The Rising Tide* (San Diego, 1960–67). Standard California histories give close attention to the era of mission settlement. Among the best are Caughey's *California* (Englewood Cliffs, 1953); Walton Bean's *California: An Interpretive History* (New York, 1968); and *California: A History* by Andrew F. Rolle (New York, 1963). *From Wilderness to Empire: A History of California* is by Robert Glass Cleland, edited by Glenn S. Dumke (New York, 1959). The best regional overview is Pomeroy's *The Pacific Slope* (New York, 1965). Extensive bibliographies are readily available covering the eras of California exploration and settlement and the missions.

CHAPTER NINE

The literature of California migration and the Gold Rush is rich. One should reread Bernard DeVoto's spirited *The Course of Empire* (Boston, 1952), *Across the Wide Missouri* (Boston, 1947), and *The Year of Decision: 1846* (Boston, 1942). George R. Stewart's *The California Trail, An Epic With Many Heroes* (New York, 1962) is excellent on the overland routes of migration. On the California Gold Rush, no one has surpassed Rodman W. Paul in *California Gold: The Beginning of Mining in the Far West* (Cambridge, 1947) and *Mining Frontiers of the Far West, 1848–1880* (New York, 1963). Among contemporary descriptions were Mark Twain's *Roughing It* and Eliot Lord's *Comstock Mining and Miners* and Louise Clapp's *Shirley Letters*. Franklin Walker discusses Gold Rush writers in *San Francisco's Literary Frontier* (New York, 1939). A large bibliography of Gold Rush history can be found in John Walton Caughey's *Gold is the Cornerstone*. Lane Books' *Gold Rush Country* (Menlo Park, 1967) is current and accurate.

CHAPTER TEN

General information about contemporary San Francisco is available through the San Francisco Visitors Bureau, Fox Plaza Building, San Francisco. No other American city has so large a list of adulatory books to its credit. Among them are those of the columnist Herb Caen, including his *Herb Caen's San Francisco* (New York, 1965). The quotation from Herbert Gold is from an article in *The New York Times Book Review*, February 19, 1967. Eugene Burdick is from *Holiday* for October 1965. Wallace Stegner is from the author's *Westward Tilt*. Lewis Nichols is from *The New York Times Book Review*, May 26, 1968. Herb Caen is from *San Francisco: City on Golden Hills* with Dong Kingman (New York, 1967). A still outstanding work on immigration to California is that by Mary R. Coolidge, *Chinese Immigration* (New York, 1909). Pomeroy is incisive in *The Pacific Slope*. Bean treats the subject in *California: An Interpretive History*. The quotation from Remi Nadeau is from his book, *California: The New Society*. Material on Joseph Alioto came from the files of the *San Francisco Chronicle*.

CHAPTER ELEVEN

Joseph Wood Krutch wrote the article, "Can We Survive the Fun Explosion?" for *Saturday Review*, January 16, 1965. Some of the statistics on leisure activities and equipment are from *Sunset Western Market Almanac, 1967–68* (Menlo Park, 1968) and from files of *Sunset* magazine research department.

CHAPTER TWELVE

The quotations from Joan Didion are from her admirable article, "Notes From a Native Daughter," in *Holiday*, October 1965. There is a surprising void of any comprehensive sociologic study of the Great Central Valley. The files of the Commonwealth Club of San Francisco and *Sunset* magazine are helpful in diverse ways—especially the March 1960 issue of *Sunset*. Archives of the University of California at Davis and of the State Department of Agriculture at Sacramento are basic to any interpretation of the region, as is a collection edited by Claude B. Hutchison, *California Agriculture* (Berkeley, 1946). Vincent P. Carosso wrote *The California Wine Industry, 1830-1895* (Berkeley, 1951). The best biography of Henry Miller is by E. T. Treadwell, *The Cattle King* (New York, 1931). Emil M. Mrak summarized his views on the collision of California agriculture and land use in *Cry California*, the quarterly of California Tomorrow, under the title *Food and Land: The Coming Shortage*. The career of Cesar Chávez has been closely reported in recent years by the *Los Angeles Times* and in book form by John Gregory Dunne under the title of *Huelga*. An interesting survey of the California table grape industry and its problems appeared in *The Wall Street Journal* for February 15, 1968. Maynard Amerine discussed California wines learnedly in *San Francisco Magazine*, October 1965. The works of Carey McWilliams are invaluable in any discussion of California agriculture. The quotation from Richard G. Lillard is from his essay in *The California Revolution* (New York, 1968).

CHAPTER THIRTEEN

Among the many books about Los Angeles those by Carey McWilliams and Remi Nadeau are particularly incisive: Nadeau's *City-Makers* (New York, 1948); *Los Angeles: From Mission to Modern City* (New York, 1960); and McWilliams' *Southern California Country* (New York, 1946). A basic history is W. W. Robinson, *Los Angeles From the Days of the Pueblo* (Los Angeles, 1959). On labor, see Louis B. and Richard S. Perry, *A History of the Los Angeles Labor Movement, 1911-1941* (Berkeley, 1963). For later works see Neil Morgan's *Westward Tilt* (New York, 1963), Christopher Rand's *California: The Ultimate City* (New York, 1967), and John L. Chapman's *Incredible Los Angeles* (New York, 1967). Franklin D. Walker's *A Literary History of Southern California* (Berkeley and Los Angeles, 1950) is helpful. Files of *Los Angeles* magazine are valauble in any contemporary research of the city. Historic treatment of the Mexican-American in California is sparse, but all standard histories treat the Japanese-American community, particularly the internment of World War II.

One of the best accounts is in Walton Bean's *California: An Interpretive History*. One work that relates particularly to the physical evolution of the city is Robert M. Fogelson's *The Fragmented Metropolis: Los Angeles 1850–1930* (Cambridge, 1967). The quotation from Earl Pomeroy is from *The Pacific Slope* (New York, 1965). General information about present-day Los Angeles is available through the All-Year Club of Southern California, 705 West 7th Street, Los Angeles.

CHAPTER FOURTEEN

An early economic history of California is that by Robert G. Cleland and Osgood Hardy, *March of Industry* (Los Angeles, 1929). Carey McWilliams brings literary insight to California's economy in *California: The Great Exception* (New York, 1949). Economic affairs of more recent years are discussed in the author's *Westward Tilt* (New York, 1963) and *The Pacific States* (New York, 1967). The most extensive economic publications in Southern California today may be those of the economic research department of Security Pacific National Bank. In northern California, those of the Bank of America are accurate, as are files of the California State Chamber of Commerce. Kiplinger publishes a California business letter. A popular account of the development of railroads in California is Oscar Lewis' *The Big Four* (New York, 1938). On labor, Ira B. Cross, *A History of the Labor Movement in California* (Berkeley, 1935). Statistics of the Depression are found in Paul Woolf's *Economic Trends in California, 1929–34* (Sacramento, 1935). *Biography of a Bank* by Marquis James and Bessie Roland James (New York, 1954) is a reliable chronicle of the Bank of America.

CHAPTER FIFTEEN

A handsome edition of *Two Years Before the Mast* by Richard Henry Dana, Jr., was published by Ward-Ritchie Press (Los Angeles, 1964). Valuable popular volumes on the California coast include those from Lane Books of Menlo Park, especially *Beachcombers' Guide to the Pacific Coast* (1967). The best biography of William Randolph Hearst is by W. A. Swanberg, *Citizen Hearst* (New York, 1961). Oscar Lewis wrote *Fabulous San Simeon, A History of the Hearst Castle* (New York, 1958). A wide selection of pamphlets and articles concerning the redwoods is available through the Sierra Club and the Save-the-Redwoods League, San Francisco.

CHAPTER SIXTEEN

Among a rapid succession of recent books about California politics, one is outstanding: Gladwin Hill's *Dancing Bear* (New York, 1968).

The best novel of California politics is Eugene Burdick's *The Ninth Wave* (New York, 1956). The best biography of Earl Warren is by John Weaver, *Warren: The Man, The Court, The Era* (Boston, 1967). The quotation from Richard Nixon is from an interview with the author. *Boss Ruef's San Francisco* (Berkeley, 1952), by Walton Bean, records an era of political scandal. An overview of California politics is found in George E. Mowry's *The California Progressives 1900–1920* (Berkeley, 1951). Earl Pomeroy has brilliant perspective on the subject in *The Pacific Slope* (New York, 1965). A standard handbook is Frank H. Jonas's *Western Politics* (Salt Lake City, 1961).

CHAPTER SEVENTEEN

The quotation from Garrett Eckbo is from *The Cultural Arts: California and the Challenge of Growth, Conference No. 2* (Berkeley, 1964). George W. Mitchell is from *The Metropolitan Future, California and the Challege of Growth, Conference No. 3* (Berkeley, 1965). Roger Revelle is from an interview with the author. The study by Norval D. Glenn and J. L. Simmons appeared in *Public Opinion Quarterly*, Summer 1967. The quotation from Kenneth Rexroth is from the foreword to the author's *The Pacific States* (New York, 1967). T. H. White is from *America At Last: The American Journal of T. H. White* (New York, 1965). The survey by John O. Wilson was published by Midwest Research Institute, Kansas City, Mo., in 1967.

INDEX